WELCOME TO THE DESERT
OF POST-SOCIALISM

WELCOME TO THE DESERT OF POST-SOCIALISM

Radical Politics After Yugoslavia

Edited by

Srećko Horvat and Igor Štiks

VERSO

London • New York

First published by Verso 2015
Introduction and Postscript © Srećko Horvat and Igor Štiks 2015
The collection © Verso 2015
Individual contributions © Verso 2015

The moral rights of the authors have been asserted

1 3 5 7 9 10 8 6 4 2

Verso
UK: 6 Meard Street, London W1F 0EG
US: 20 Jay Street, Suite 1010, Brooklyn, NY 11201
www.versobooks.com

Verso is the imprint of New Left Books

ISBN-13: 978-1-78168-620-1 (PB)
ISBN-13: 978-1-78168-621-8 (HC)
eISBN-13: 978-1-78168-622-5 (US)
eISBN-13: 978-1-78168-737-6 (UK)

British Library Cataloguing in Publication Data
A catalogue record for this book is available from the British Library

Library of Congress Cataloging-in-Publication Data

Welcome to the desert of post-socialism : radical politics after Yugoslavia / edited by
Srecko Horvat, Igor Štiks.
    pages cm
  Includes bibliographical references and index.
    ISBN 978-1-78168-620-1 (pbk.)
1. Former Yugoslav republics – Politics and government. 2. Post-communism
– Former Yugoslav republics. 3. Identity politics – Former Yugoslav republics.
4. Ethnicity – Former Yugoslav republics. 5. Nationalism – Former Yugoslav
republics. 6. Social conflict – Former Yugoslav republics. 7. Former Yugoslav
republics – Social conditions. 8. Balkan Peninsula – Politics and government – 1989–
    I. Horvat, Srecko. II. Štiks, Igor, 1977–
    DR1318.W45 2015
    320.9497 – dc23

                         2014034946

Typeset in Minion by Hewer Text UK Ltd, Edinburgh, Scotland
Printed and bound by CPI Group (UK) Ltd, Croydon, CR0 4YY

Contents

Part III: Two Decades After Yugoslavia: Bitter Fruits of Transition

Part IV: Towards a Balkan Spring? New Political Subjectivities

Acknowledgments

This volume was born out of numerous discussions held at the annual Subversive Festival in Zagreb since 2008. We are particularly indebted to our friend Tariq Ali who encouraged us to prepare a volume providing a fresh critical look at the contemporary Balkans as well as presenting the growing social movements in this region. We are grateful to Verso for accepting our proposal and its editor Sebastian Budgen for his patience and support.

Throughout the process of preparing the volume we were supported by the CITSEE project, based at the Law School of the University of Edinburgh, with which one of us was affiliated. This project dedicated to research on citizenship in the post-Yugoslav region and the wider Balkans provided us both with the time and research resources to complete this volume. Our special thanks go to Jo Shaw, the principal investigator of the CITSEE project, Nick Holdstock, editor of the CITSEE project's web magazine 'Citizenship in Southeast Europe', who provided valuable editorial and linguistic advice to us and our authors, and, finally, to CITSEE's research assistant Gëzim Krasniqi.

The return of radical and emancipatory politics to the post-socialist Balkans is primarily due to the inspiring work of new social and political movements, organisations and engaged individuals. This book is dedicated to them and their struggles.

The editors
July 2013

Radical Politics in the Desert of Transition[1]

Igor Štiks and Srećko Horvat

Over the last couple of years we have regularly witnessed popular protests and uprisings in the post-socialist Balkans. The well-known mobilisations, struggles and street violence in the southern part of the peninsula, in Greece and recently Turkey, have a constant and yet under-reported echo in other Balkan states. These have had a different historical trajectory: after the disappearance of the state socialist regimes, in all of these states, most dramatically across the former Yugoslavia, a period of violence, conflict or general instability and economic misery has been followed by a seemingly endless transition to liberal democracy and neoliberal economy. During this process some countries have joined the European Union (Slovenia, Romania, Bulgaria and Croatia), further marginalising the 'latecomers' and 'laggards' in the long process of 'European integration' (Bosnia-Herzegovina, Montenegro, Serbia, Kosovo, Macedonia and Albania), all of which are now encircled by the EU border.

The usual story about the post-socialist Balkans revolves mostly around the following tropes: oscillation between liberalisation and authoritarianism; the complex relationship between the state, organised crime and the economy; corruption; the achievements and shortcomings of the International Tribunal for the Former Yugoslavia; regional cooperation or disputes, successes and failures in the EU accession process.

---

1   In parts of this introduction we draw upon our article 'Welcome to the Desert of Transition! Post-Socialism, the European Union, and a New Left in the Balkans', *Monthly Review*, vol. 63(10), 2012, 38–48.

This story is constantly repeated not only by local and international media but also by scholarship. Up until recently, only rarely did we hear about the devastating consequences of the 'transition' to capitalism, such as general impoverishment, huge public and private indebtedness facilitated by a flow of foreign credit, widespread deindustrialisation, social degradation, depopulation through diminished life expectancy and emigration, and general unemployment (ranging between 20 and 30 per cent and even reaching 50 per cent in countries like Bosnia and Kosovo, especially amongst younger generations). It was no surprise that protests started erupting, movements began to form, and diverse groups and individuals commenced openly to question the post-socialist transition that led to brutal capitalism and diminished democracy. In their efforts to defend the remnants of the socialist state (primarily in education and health), natural and social resources (water, electricity, internet), and jobs (remaining industries, the public sector), they also began to formulate a profoundly anti-capitalist and radically democratic vision of their societies. This is how radical politics was reborn in the rebel peninsula.

Although many of the contributions in this volume refer to other Balkan countries, its focus is on the post-Yugoslav states. The anti-fascist struggle, the rebellion against Stalin, experiments in economic democracy (i.e. socialist self-management), multinational federal composition, and international influence (the Non-Aligned Movement) secured a special place for Yugoslavia (1945–90), and even a certain prestige, in the general history of socialist movements. Understanding radical politics 'after Yugoslavia' necessarily entails a critical re-evaluation of socialist Yugoslavia, its successes and its failures, as well as of the post-socialist, post-partition and often post-conflict predicament of these societies today.

Apart from occasional reports, often by activists themselves or their sympathisers, and rare attempts to analyse current struggles, the changing situation in the Balkans and the growth of local social movements has been under-researched and is still largely unknown to a global audience. Mainstream Balkan scholarship still focuses on either obsessively explaining the disintegration of Yugoslavia, the wars and their consequences, or on monitoring the EU integration of the region (invariably understood as a natural and unquestionable political and economic process). This volume challenges the existing scholarship and its failure to take into account the disastrous consequences of the introduction of neoliberal capitalism and the deep socio-economic transformation this entailed, resulting in drastic inequalities between a tiny layer of the newly rich, diminishing middle class and the increasingly populous poor strata. In addition, the volume challenges the failure of the social and political sciences to account for the emergence of new movements and political subjectivities outside the established political system and electoral procedures. Another big challenge is directed towards wider international left forces, movements and intellectuals and their frequently, often obstinately, held view that there is nothing much to look at in Eastern Europe in general, and especially in the Balkans. These regions have been seen as a lost cause for progressive forces after 1989 and prone only to right-wing politics and extremism, support of pro-US and pro-NATO policies, and unconditional surrender to neoliberalism. We believe that the contributions in this volume will not only challenge but change these superficial and now largely obsolete views.

We believe that this volume makes four major contributions both to general radical thought and to scholarship on the Balkans. First, it offers a critical examination of the Yugoslav socialist experience, including the experiment in self-management and the political economy. It rejects folkish nostalgia while interrogating activist accounts of the socialist heritage for experiences that can help us develop a political stance towards our present and think about alternatives. Second, it offers a critical deconstruction of the Balkan imaginary, the persistent forms of seeing and understanding the peninsula through the orientalist lenses which perceive the region as a repository of ethnic conflicts, moral, economic and political corruption, and a violence that requires containment and external tutelage. Third, the volume undertakes a critical analysis of post-socialist economic and political transformation and its outcomes, involving unequal societies, neoliberal economies and oligarchic 'democracies'. Finally, it offers an account of contemporary radical politics in the Balkans, after the disappearance of Yugoslavia from the political map.

In the Desert of Transition

None of these changes, events and political subjects can be fully comprehended without an initial examination of the twenty-year-old experiment in political, social and economic engineering known as the transition. Nowhere are its consequences so painfully obvious as in the Balkans. The state of this region, encompassing almost 60 million people, allows us to question the whole teleological narrative of the post-socialist transition and its underlying political and economic ideology. In this huge transformation, with equally colossal social and economic consequences, the leading role was reserved for the European Union. This huge enterprise is in a deep crisis today not only as an institution but within the Balkans as well. To understand these crises and their possible ramifications, one has to take into account the wide range of mechanisms used by the EU to pacify, stabilise and incorporate (without necessarily fully integrating) the Balkans. Nowhere else did the EU experiment so extensively with its 'transformative power', often producing many unwanted results.

In spite of the democratic promise of 1989 and the final arrival of 'the End of History', post-socialist citizens today feel largely excluded from decision-making processes: most elections have turned out to be little more than a reshuffling of the same political oligarchy with no serious differences in political programmes or rhetoric. Many lost their jobs (during the 'privatisation' campaigns) or saw their labour conditions worsen and their pensions evaporate; most of the previously guaranteed social benefits (such as free education and health care) gradually disappeared. In addition, citizens are heavily

in debt, owing money to foreign-owned banks that prolifer-
ated in the Balkans to the point of controlling its whole
financial sector.[2] After the series of devastating wars across
the former Yugoslavia that claimed up to 130,000 lives, the
'democratic promise' was unfulfilled for a second time after
the end of the authoritarian rule of Slobodan Milošević and
Franjo Tuđman in 1999/2000. The last decade brought
another wave of impoverishment, this time managed by
'Euro-compatible' elites ready to implement further neoliberal reforms portrayed as a necessary part of the EU accession
process.

After 1989, the dismantling of the remnants of the socialist
state was legitimised by demands for the rapid reduction of the
omnipresent state apparatus. This process usually entailed the
dismantling of existing social protection as well as privatisation
(which more often than not turned into a pillage of social and
state assets), or the total corruption of what remained of the
apparatus. The EU, along with several international organisations such as the WTO and the IMF, favoured the neoliberal
paradigm of privatisation, deregulation and a free market
within a minimal state. These international authorities served,
in turn, as an external source of legitimisation for local political
elites engaged in the predatory project of extracting the existing
state resources or preying on citizens' wealth in general. When
the transition went hand in hand with war, this extraction of
wealth met with weak resistance. The discourse of nationalism
helped the local elites to channel previously socially owned or
state-owned capital into private hands – their own or their networks' members – thus giving them a huge economic, social
and political advantage at the end of hostilities. When the dust
finally settled, ordinary citizens found themselves not only in a
devastated country, but also with empty pockets and without
the old social safety net.

By questioning the totality of the communist institutional
legacy the 'national question' was also dangerously reopened,

---

2 See Živković in this volume.

as exemplified in the former Yugoslavia and some parts of the former Soviet Union. In practice that meant transforming the institutionalised ethno-national groups into competitors whose predatory elites were eager to grab and control as many resources as possible in order to secure a better position in the 'transitional game'. The story is yet to be written of 'ethnic conflicts' initiated by the incorporation of Eastern Europe into a Western-dominated capitalist economy that activated existing federal ethno-territorial institutional arrangements and encouraged land-grabbing as a type of primitive accumulation by ethno-nationalist elites. So far, we have mostly heard about the consequences without questioning how local political entrepreneurs saw the relationship between their ethnic groups and territory and the economic exploitation from, and exchange with, the West. If ethno-politics became the only credible source of political opportunities and the only possible way of keeping or grabbing power, it is not surprising that in the multi-ethnic environment of the former socialist federations, so-called inter-ethnic conflict, managed by the political elites themselves, was the immediate consequence.

The process of turning the former socialist states into liberal democracies and free-market economies (apparently the inseparable twins of the new era) was famously called 'transition', bringing into public and political discourse quasi-biblical connotations of acceding to the 'land of plenty' after four decades of 'slavery'. Although liberal democratic practices were introduced immediately after 1989 and free market policies started appearing from the early 1990s, transition turned into a never-ending process. Its 'varieties' generated an enormous amount of intellectual work, from journalism to the mountains of scholarly products involving hundreds of PhD theses, newly established departments and chairs, all aimed at observing this colossal transformation. And even today, more than twenty years later, we hear that the transition is incomplete. The wandering in the desert seems to be endless.

In spite of the rhetoric of incompleteness (similar to the

rhetoric of incomplete modernisation for the Third World), we can observe that the free market reigns supreme; post-socialist Eastern Europe is fully incorporated into the capitalist world with a semi-peripheral role. In practice this means the availability of cheap and highly educated labour in proximity to the capitalist core, quasi-total economic dependence on the core and its multinational banks and corporations, and, finally, the accumulation of debt. On the political side, liberal democratic procedures formally seem to be in place. In spite of that, the notion of an incomplete transition still dominates the media and academic discourse, while political elites are using it to justify yet another wave of privatisation. It is as if no one dares to say that the transition as such is long over. There is nothing to 'transit' to anymore. In our view, there are two main factors inherent in the rhetoric of incomplete transition: the avoidance of a full confrontation with the consequences of transition, and the preservation of the discourse and relations of dominance vis-à-vis the former socialist states. One of the underlying assumptions of the eternal transition is therefore the 'need' for tutelage and supervision.

Observers often point to another transitional phenomenon: the appearance of a 'communist nostalgia'. Fervent liberals might point out that it is the 'Egyptian pots of meat' story: 'slaves' are always nostalgic about their tyrants instead of being happy to be 'free', even, as now, when they are within close reach of the 'promised land'. Reading 'nostalgia' as the expressed 'wish' to return by magic to the state socialist regime – as if anyone were offering that alternative – means avoiding the questions that simmer behind these feelings. Why do people feel politically disempowered and economically robbed and enslaved today? Why and when did liberal democracy and the capitalist free-market economy go wrong? Was there any other possibility? And why is it not getting any better? Since 'communist nostalgia' does not generate any political movement or programme, the answer has to be found in a widespread feeling that something is not working in the new system and that it should be changed according to the ideals that lay behind the generous social policies of the former socialist states.[3] Those who cannot or who refuse to acknowledge these feelings are turning a blind eye to the growing discontent and social demands that are putting transition into question, both as a process of reform and as the teleological-ideological construct of dominance.

The European Union in the Balkans

The European Union is the main protagonist of the Eastern European Transition. According to its 1993 Copenhagen policy, it is supposed to educate, discipline and punish while offering EU membership as the prize at the end of the bumpy road of transition (where awaits, so the story goes, the democratic and economic pay-off). The reality, however, has destroyed the fable: even when the goal was finally achieved, the promise was not fully kept: all but three member states from 'old' Europe immediately imposed labour restrictions on free circulation for citizens from 'new' Europe, breaking the promise of equal European citizenship. Moreover, there was even a need for further 'monitoring' of the 'Eastern Balkan' countries.

The EU has been the most powerful political and economic agent in a post-socialist Balkans whose political landscape is more varied than any other place in Europe. Nowhere else on this peninsula is the EU's *mission civilisatrice* so evident. Though it fully integrated Slovenia in 2004, it has been 'monitoring' Romania and Bulgaria, which have been heavily criticised and sanctioned (especially Bulgaria, which lost millions in EU funds) for not being able to 'catch up' since they joined the EU in 2007. Four years after integration, these countries have been hit hard by the economic crisis. The newcomer to the club is Croatia, which joined in July 2013 and was immediately ranked as the third poorest EU member, with a problematic economic record and an enormous debt.[4] The EU not only supervises the

---

3   See Velikonja in this volume.
4   See S. Horvat and I. Štiks, 'Croatia Has Become the Latest Member of the EU Periphery', *Guardian*, 1 July 2013, at www.guardian.co.uk.

'Western Balkan' candidates ('negotiations' being a euphemism for a one-way communication process amounting to little more than the 'translate-paste' operations employed during the adoption of the *acquis communautaire*), but actually maintains two semi-protectorates (Bosnia and Kosovo). The EU has developed varied approaches: disciplining and punishing certain members (Romania, Bulgaria and Croatia), bilaterally negotiating membership by punishing and rewarding (Montenegro, Serbia and Albania), managing (Bosnia), practically governing (Kosovo), and, finally, ignoring (Macedonia blocked in the naming dispute with Greece).

Social gloom reigns today over the so-called Western Balkans, a geopolitical construct forged in Brussels, composed of the former Yugoslav republics that have still not joined the EU, 'plus Albania'. It has been entirely surrounded by the EU members in a sort of 'ghetto' around which the Schengen ring has been slowly deployed, with Slovenia, Hungary and Greece patrolling the fortress, a role for which Romania, Bulgaria and Croatia have also been practising. One could see the Schengen Area's enlargement – instead of the EU enlargement – as a continuation of the containment policies of the 1990s when the main aim was to prevent the war in the former Yugoslavia spilling over its former international borders. In this respect – and save for the 'Western Balkans' approach that hides the fact that Slovenia and Croatia are still deeply involved with their southern brethren and that Albania is primarily close to its kin in Kosovo – 'Yugoslavia' or, as Tim Judah puts it, the 'Yugosphere', has not disappeared as a geopolitical space.

The EU took direct action in the Balkans. It effectively runs Kosovo, via its Law and Order Mission (EULEX), although five EU member states still refuse to recognise the new state even while participating in the mission. This reveals the failure of the US-led and mostly EU-backed Kosovo independence strategy that left the country and its population in the limbo of a partial recognition that prevents it from joining international organisations. Besides Bosnia and Kosovo, the European forces, led by Italy, intervened in Albania in 1997; the EU militaries were also present in Macedonia, and many EU members were involved in the NATO bombings of the then Federal Republic of Yugoslavia. The EU in the Balkans is therefore not only a club that tests its candidates. It is an active player in transforming the region, politically, socially and economically.

'Stabilising' the region is thus a priority, whereas economic integration via neoliberal restructuration is or will be achieved without being necessarily followed, and certainly not with the same speed, by full political integration. The EU insists furthermore on continuous neoliberal reforms – and lately on austerity measures – that are supposed to be undertaken by the very same 'democratically elected', hugely corrupt and deeply undemocratic elites, who will be the only ones to benefit from these reforms. The trouble is that neoliberal reforms are opening up more opportunities for corruption and predatory behaviour by local elites, as the Croatian case amply shows. The privatisation process includes infrastructure such as telecommunications, big industries, natural resources such as water or energy, media outlets and public services, as well as foreign bank investments and devastating credit lines, representing just some of the 'opportunities' arising from neoliberal restructuring, as the first phase of incorporation into the EU sphere. The case of the former Croatian Prime Minister Ivo Sanader, praised by the EU at one time and now serving a long prison sentence for widespread corruption schemes involving many European partners, is a telling example of how the local elites can profit from the 'restructuring' process.

The eventual result is a mutual delegitimisation of the EU and the political elites of the candidate countries or recent member states. EU-backed political elites are delegitimising the EU as a whole by implementing unpopular neoliberal reforms, while the EU, with its pressure to continue these reforms, in turn delegitimises the political elites who happen to be their obvious beneficiaries, along with the whole political structure that keeps them in power. The result is a recent surge in Euro-scepticism in general. This came as a surprise to many observers, political elites and EU functionaries, since for more than two decades EU membership has been the highest goal of almost all political forces in the Balkans. This Euro-scepticism is not, as might be expected, merely a right-wing nationalist reaction to supra-national integrations, or merely a radical leftist critique of how these integrations have been handled and of the EU as a mechanism in general. It has to be understood also as a refusal of the teleological narrative of the transition, with the EU as its sacred end but also as the tutor in this 'coming of age' story.[5]

New Rebels: Mapping the New Movements

Given the multi-faceted situation described above, it is unsurprising that the protest movements are diversified in their struggles, ideological orientations, and type of actions. They are mostly reacting to the deteriorating social and economic situation and the numerous abuses of power by political elites. Nonetheless, they often serve as hubs for new ideas and more proactive projects offering a progressive vision of their societies. Here we sketch a typology of these movements and actions by dividing them into five main blocs: anti-regime protests, mobilisations for the commons, student movements, various workers' struggles and, last but not least, hegemonic cultural and intellectual efforts.

Anti-regime protests erupt regularly across the Balkans. In Croatia in spring 2011, up to 10,000 people marched across Zagreb every evening for a whole month, denouncing the political system and all political parties. In Slovenia in 2012 and 2013 general 'uprisings' mobilised the whole country, contributing to the fall of the right-wing government and a number of corrupt officials. In Bulgaria in spring 2013 huge protests triggered by rising electricity bills brought thousands to the streets, only to be followed after the general elections by even larger protests in the summer. For weeks, the masses

---

5   See Buden in this volume.

protested against corrupt political elites and their ties to powerful mafia and media moguls. In Romania protests have been sporadically erupting since 2010, in response to unbearable social conditions and continuing austerity measures. In June 2013, even divided Bosnia-Herzegovina saw protests that began as a means to put pressure on politicians to resolve the issue of citizens' registration numbers – exploited like many other things in this country by nationalist politicians – before turning into general anti-elite protests across all communities and all sub-state units. Similar types of protests, with differing intensity, have been seen in Serbia, Macedonia, Montenegro and Albania.

All these examples show that for the first time we have more than anti-government rhetoric per se – instead there is a true anti-regime sentiment. Not only the state but the whole apparatus on which the current oligarchy is based is called into question by self-organised citizens (albeit chaotically). And no colour is needed to mark this kind of revolution that obviously cannot hope for any external help and that rarely gets international media coverage. The emergence and nature of these protests invite us to rethink the categories used to explain the social, political and economic situation in the Balkans, and elsewhere in post-socialist Eastern Europe. They also compel us to understand the nature not only of state institutions, in their weakness or failure, but the nature of the post-socialist regime (almost) cemented over the last two decades but susceptible to cracking under the weight of its own contradictions and products, such as, for instance, rampant poverty. Rebelling against these regimes is that much harder because they often have no single face, no dictator, no governing families, and are not characterised by open repression and censorship. These occasional expressions of anger are indeed the seeds of new political and social dynamics. However, they are also characterised by volatility and by random triggers, and are usually followed by confusing and often contradictory political messages.

Among the most developed struggles are those concerning

the commons – the defence of public and common goods such as public spaces (often parks), nature (water, forests, hills, landscape), urban spaces and public utility infrastructure (electricity, railways, etc.). Examples are abundant: 'The Right to the City' movement in 2009/2010 in Croatia mobilised thousands in defence of a square in downtown Zagreb; in Dubrovnik citizens organised to defend a nearby hill from being turned into a golf resort; in Bosnia's second largest city, Banja Luka, citizens tried to defend one of the few public parks; in Belgrade smaller mobilisations were triggered by the cutting down of old trees in one of the main streets so as to obtain more parking space, or by the destruction of a neighbourhood park; in Bulgaria in 2012 people demonstrated against the privatisation of forests, and in Romania in 2012 against the privatisation of emergency services, etc. These single-issue movements, although rarely successful, proved to be channels of general public dissatisfaction and enjoyed support from the vast majority of citizens who see the privatisation of the commons and the neglect of public interest as intolerable practices.

To these we should add the strong student movements that have developed since 2009 in Slovenia, Croatia, Serbia, and to a certain extent in Bosnia-Herzegovina and Montenegro. The trigger is the commercialisation of public education, which many see as the ultimate common and social good. While students mostly protest in classic ways in Bosnia-Herzegovina and Montenegro (by marches and petitions), in Slovenia, Serbia and, especially, Croatia, the student movements extensively experiment with occupations and direct democracy.

It is worth paying special attention to the Croatian case, where an independent student movement articulated a strong resistance to the privatisation and commercialisation of higher education. Their protest against neoliberal reforms in the field of education turned into probably the first strong political opposition not only to the government, but to the general political and social regime. For thirty-five days in spring and two weeks in autumn in 2009 more than twenty universities all over

Croatia were occupied, with students practically running them.[6] In itself, this was nothing new, one might say, but the way they occupied and ran the universities deserves our attention for its originality in a much larger context than that of the Balkans or Eastern Europe. The students set up citizens' plenary assemblies – called 'plenums' – in which not only students but all citizens were invited to debate issues of public importance such as education and, in addition, to decide upon the course of the rebellious actions. The most active plenum at the Faculty of Humanities and Social Sciences in Zagreb gathered up to 1,000 individuals each evening to deliberate on the course of action.[7] This event gave rise to the movement for direct democracy, which was seen as a necessary corrective of electoral democracy and 'partitocracy' and, possibly, as a true alternative to it. The new Croatian left, whose ideas quickly spread around the post-Yugoslav space, sees direct democracy not as limited to referendum practice but rather as a means of political organisation for citizens from local communes to the national level. This horizontal model has been used since then during many collective actions across post-Yugoslav space (from occupy movements to street marches, workers' strikes and farmers' protests).

The recent period has also been marked by reinvigorated workers' struggles.[8] They are not uniform and range from classic strikes, workers influencing companies in majority state ownership and defending them from further privatisations (e.g. the Petrokemija factory in Croatia), examples of workers' successful

---

6   We have written extensively about the student and civic rebellions that involved the occupation of universities and of public spaces in Zagreb in our book *Pravo na pobunu – Uvod u anatomiju građanskog otpora* [The Right to Rebellion – An Introduction to the Anatomy of Civic Resistance], Zagreb: Fraktura, 2010. For a detailed analysis of the student movements in post-Yugoslav states, see Baćević in this volume.

7   For a detailed overview of the student actions in Croatia see *The Occupation Cookbook, or the Model of the Occupation of the Faculty of Humanities and Social Sciences in Zagreb*, New York: Minorcompositions, 2011.

8   For a history of trade unions since socialism and the new workers' struggles, see Grdešić and Kraft in this volume.

and unsuccessful takeovers (e.g. Jadrankamen and TDZ in Croatia), and models of workers' shareholdership (the most famous being Jugoremedija in Serbia). We are also witnessing a new cooperation between different social movements, such as students and workers, in building a common anti-capitalist strategy.

Finally, there is another type of struggle deserving attention: that of hegemonic cultural and intellectual efforts whose aim is to change the general public climate, challenge dominant media discourses, and reintroduce progressive ideas into wider society. Its primary goal is to undermine the (neo)liberal hegemony that since 1989 has successfully delegitimised left traditions and promoted multi-party electoral democracy – although often ending up in autocracies – and the free market as the *only game in town*. In the post-Yugoslav context, this general post-socialist orientation was coupled, not always harmoniously, with nationalist-conservative, right-wing extremist and anti-communist dominance. It clashed, however, with liberal attempts at 'democratising' these societies, which focused mostly on institutional reforms and the EU integration process that problematised only criminal privatisations and practices but not the general neoliberal orientation.

Introducing a progressive agenda and radical thinking into the dominant discourse was an almost impossible task until fairly recently. The 2008 economic and financial shocks followed by the crisis of the EU opened a space for hitherto marginal movements to articulate their critique of the current political and economic regime. These attempts range from public gatherings, forums and festivals (such as the Mayday school in Ljubljana, the Subversive Festival in Zagreb, and Antifest in Sarajevo), summer schools, activist and academic workshops and conferences, to newspapers, reviews and online magazines (from *Zarez* and *Le Monde diplomatique* in Croatia to *CriticAttac* in Romania or *Mladina* in Ljubljana).

Indeed, these Gramscian hegemonic struggles have proved to be as necessary as concrete mobilisations. They pave the way for new rebels and allow them to articulate a clear political

agenda. However, their political strategies remain for now confined to occasional protests and occupations – often marked by
rejection of representative democracy in the name of horizon-
tality – petitions and even referendum initiatives. Although the
model offered by Syriza, a coalition of movements ready to
engage in parliamentary politics, is widely appreciated, we
cannot detect so far any serious attempt at taking these struggles towards institutional politics.[9]

Conclusion

We have shown here that the very concept of transition as an
ideological construct based on the narrative of integration of
the former socialist European countries into the Western core
actually hides a monumental neo-colonial transformation of
this region into a dependent semi-periphery. The adjunct concepts of 'weak state' or 'failed state', for example, conceal the fact
that these are not anomalies of the transition but one of its main
products. The famous corruption problem poses a puzzle for
observers and scholars leading many to conclude that, since the
liberal system as such is beyond questioning, the widespread
corruption must be related to culture- or path-dependent
behaviour in the 'East', or whatever is, in the good orientalist
tradition, understood under the term 'the Balkans'.

However, corruption in reality seems to be a direct consequence of the post-1989 neoliberal scramble for Eastern Europe,
and, furthermore, a behaviour endemic across the EU itself. In
order to understand the post-communist, eternal transitional
predicament, and especially the current political and economic
situation in the Balkans, we suggest that one has to go beyond
the analysis of the state, its failures and weaknesses, and engage
with the concept of regime. The post-socialist regime is a con-
glomerate grouping political elites, attached businesses and

---

9   The only noteworthy exception so far, among a number of small left-
leaning parties, is a political party in Slovenia – the Initiative for Democratic
Socialism – that grew directly from street protests.

their Western partners, media corporations, NGOs promoting the holy couple of electoral democracy and neoliberal economy, organised crime (itself intimately related to political and economic elites), predatory foreign-owned banks and, finally, a corrupt judiciary and controlled unions. Other ideological 'apparatuses of the regime' have their place here, as well as helping to cement the results of the big neoliberal transformation.

However, as this volume shows, this transformation is now being openly challenged by the rise of new social movements and by the return of radical politics in the post-Yugoslav and wider Balkan region. A new generation enters politics via direct democratic actions and the street and not through political channels of electoral democracy and classic party politics. The new left we detect within these movements is dissociated both from the past of state socialism and from traditional social-democratic parties. Sometimes in unlikely places, such as the post-socialist and post-conflict Balkans, we can see a sudden explosion of original radicalism from which many similar movements across the globe could learn a great deal about the forms and methods of subversive and rebellious politics in the twenty-first century.

PART I

From Self-management to Disaster Capitalism

Self-management, Development and Debt: The Rise and Fall of the 'Yugoslav Experiment'

Vladimir Unkovski-Korica

For a long time during the Cold War, Tito's Yugoslavia was a symbol of a 'third way' between the superpower blocs. Worker self-management, or 'market socialism', in which workers played a role in the management of their workplaces, promised to be an alternative to both private property and the state as the dynamo of development. The failure of the 'Yugoslav Experiment' and the ensuing bloody disintegration of the country itself at the end of the Cold War has been trumpeted widely as proof that 'workers running factories' was, to put it euphemistically, a bad idea. This has been accompanied by the claim that there is no alternative to liberal democracy and market capitalism. Nevertheless, the growth of the global anti-capitalist movement and the breakthrough of political parties with an anti-neoliberal agenda, especially in Latin America, slowly put alternatives back on the map. The recent onset of what has come to be termed the 'Great Recession' will only intensify debates about alternatives to capitalism. It is in that context that an investigation of the 'Yugoslav Experiment' takes on significance. There are still enthusiasts who suggest that the model is worth emulating on one level or another. This contribution will emphasise the negative lesson of the 'Yugoslav Experiment': that the top-down institutionalisation of worker participation and its subordination to the market is inimical to the emancipatory project of non-capitalist development. Rather than accepting that the problem in Yugoslavia was lack of market integration, it will show that market integration systematically undermined development and the promise of worker management. Any alternative in the future will need to come from below and emphasise solidarity against competition to avoid repeating the mistakes of the past.

The Origins of the System, 1948–1950: 'Factories to the Workers!'

The 'Yugoslav Road to Socialism' emerged from a mass movement, a peasant-based, anti-fascist resistance led by the Communist Party during the Second World War. The Yugoslav communists hoped to emulate and supersede the Soviet Union's state-led developmental path of the interwar period, and to lead their country out of underdevelopment and end its dependence on the West. Dizzy with their wartime success, they believed they were embarking on this task from a higher stage of development than the Soviets had done several decades previously. They also believed that international relations were more favourable to development than in the interwar period, with socialism on the advance across the globe. Not just in the Soviet Union, Eastern Europe and the Balkans, but in Western Europe, China and Vietnam, communist parties appeared to be on the cusp of power or were already holding important positions in ruling coalitions. With the fraternal help of the USSR, Yugoslavia could hope, perhaps as part of a Balkan federation, to advance towards a diversified and open economy within the space of a single five-year plan. It was not to be. Tito's refusal to submit to Soviet domination in the emerging Cold War resulted in confrontation with Moscow. The Tito–Stalin split of 1948 stunned the world and set back Yugoslav communist ambitions. Facing a blockade and even possible invasion from the nascent Soviet bloc, Tito's Yugoslavia soon leaned westwards for aid and security. But Tito was still convinced that Yugoslavia should remain independent. More than that, he told the Central Committee in 1948 that he wanted Yugoslav development to be 'a big, beautiful contribution to the progressive movement in the world', a symbol for the likes of 'Burma and other countries'.[1]

This was like walking a tightrope. On the one hand, the Yugoslav communists had to soften their image and differentiate themselves from the USSR to gain aid from the West. On the other hand, they wanted to appeal to a radical global audience, especially in the developing world. It was in this context that the idea of self-management emerged. Milovan Djilas, then a member of Tito's inner circle, and later Yugoslavia's most famous dissident, captured the top-down spirit in which the decision was taken, even if his own version of events is overly simplistic. He wrote in his memoirs that the idea of worker management of economic life originated with three top communists who sought Tito's approval to put the idea into practice. Pacing up and down, Tito finally exclaimed, convinced: 'Factories belonging to the workers – something that has never yet been achieved!'[2] The actual process of decision making was, of course, far more complex but the ideological power of worker management in terms of raising Yugoslavia's profile abroad was certainly crucial. Historians claimed for a long time that the Communist Party's Central Committee never mentioned workers' councils in the period 1948 to 1950, when the institution was finally officially promulgated into law, but this is incorrect. The Party's chief ideologue and foreign minister, Edvard Kardelj, in fact delivered a speech on foreign policy issues to the Central Committee at the close of 1949 in which he did mention workers' councils. He argued that 'the strengthening of the democratic relations in our production – with the formation of workers' councils, of which we have spoken, it seems to me, almost a year ago, as well as all the other forums [of popular participation] – is exactly that which we shall be able to present to the world as the difference between us

---

1   V. Dedijer, *Novi prilozi za biografiju Josipa Broza Tita* [New Contributions for a Biography of Josip Broz Tito], vol. 3, Belgrade: Rad, 1984, 385.

2   See M. Djilas, *The Unperfect Society: Beyond the New Class*, London: Methuen, 1969, 222–3.

[Yugoslavia] and them [the East]'.[3] Self-management differentiated Yugoslavia from the USSR not only in the minds of its
creditors, but also in the minds of those who Yugoslavia could
look to as friends and who could prevent political strings being
attached to aid: social democrats in the West.[4]

Thus, while the external environment was the decisive
factor behind the decision to introduce self-management, it was
not the only one. The Yugoslav communists also had to respond
to a specific mood from below. Under threat of foreign invasion,
they relied both on intensified political repression and on
renewed political mobilisation of their wartime base to retain
power and maintain production. The renewal of political mobilisation involved decentralisation. The hope was that this would
strengthen Yugoslav unity by giving the constituent republics
of the federation a greater say, and that bringing government
closer to the people and renewing the Partisan spirit would
legitimise communist rule and Yugoslav patriotism. Indeed,
patriotic appeals to increase industrial production and admin-
istrative measures to recruit new workers from the countryside
did work and helped stave off economic collapse, but they also
proved expensive and disruptive of agricultural production.
Management tried to build up reserves of labour, especially
skilled labour, in order to meet targets. This meant they paid
higher wages than the government envisaged and this money
often served as the basis for the emergence of a black market,
trading with the countryside for food and other consumer
goods. These policies could not be a long-term solution.

It was in this context, in late spring 1949, and in the thick
of the production drive, that self-management as an idea was
born. It was at first part of a number of strategies designed to
empower workers' initiatives against conservative management

---

3   B. Petranović, R. Končar and R. Radonjić, eds, *Sednice Centralnog Komiteta
KPJ (1948–1952)* [Sessions of the Central Committee of the CPY], Belgrade:
Komunist, 1985, 480.

4   V. Unkovski-Korica, 'The Yugoslav Communists' Special Relationship with
the British Labour Party 1950–1956', *Cold War History*, published online, April
2013, in print vol. 14(1), 2014, 23–46.

layers. The government hoped that the councils could use labour and organise production more rationally than the existing system, which was often chaotic. It also believed that this was a way to reverse the trend of ballooning wage demands. For a time, the plan met union resistance, since the draft bill envisaged workers' councils usurping union prerogatives as the transmission belts of industrial policy. By the time the councils were being implemented on an experimental basis in key industrial plants at the turn of 1950, the government had regained the upper hand. In late summer, confirmation came that foreign aid was on its way. Moreover, Yugoslavia's election to the UN Security Council in late 1949 had staved off the threat of war. The government reversed labour mobilisation, allowing many to go home to the rural areas. The government and the unions co-signed the directive instituting experimental worker councils in industry. At that point, councils were given oversight competencies but had no real power over management. The aim was to increase labour participation but tighten financial discipline without the need for state intervention, and to build the unions into the new system of labour management rather than have them oppose it.[5]

The First Phase of Self-management, 1950–1961: Growth of a Subsidised and Protected Market

The new system therefore sought to harness but also channel and limit popular participation, allowing government to retain its policy-making initiative. This was clearly not a genuinely democratic system, but it did create forms of pluralism not seen in the rest of the Soviet bloc. The official claim was that

---

5   See, for instance, S. Woodward, *Socialist Unemployment: The Political Economy of Yugoslavia, 1945–1990*, Princeton, NJ: Princeton University Press, 1995, and S. Zukin, 'The Representation of Working Class Interest in Socialist Society: Yugoslav Labour Unions', *Politics & Society*, vol. 10(3), 1981, 281–316. My own doctorate, dealing with the same issues, will be published as *The Economic Struggle for Power in Tito's Yugoslavia: From World War II to Non-Alignment*, London: I.B. Tauris, forthcoming.

Yugoslavia was building a new system in which the state was withering away, in contrast with the East and West, where its influence was growing. The process of extending self-management from the workplace to the political sphere began in June 1950, with the adoption and broadening of the scope of worker-management across industry, and ended in January 1953, with the enactment of a 'mini-constitution' which introduced 'councils of producers' as legislative chambers at all levels of the state. Self-management had thereby become the building block of a decentralised economic and political system, embedded in a complex multinational and federal setting. The Party itself made a concerted effort to dismantle command structures and even reduced its own professional apparatus in order to force its membership to adapt to the new environment. The Party's new role was no longer to command but to lead by persuasion. The Party even changed its name in 1952 from the Communist Party of Yugoslavia to the League of Communists of Yugoslavia (LCY) to symbolise the change. While this soon led to major disorientation and demobilisation in the League and the mass organisations subordinated to it, the communist leadership appeared set on underlining the country's departure from the Soviet model. This new 'commune state' of mass participation placed itself in the tradition of Lenin's *State and Revolution* against the 'state capitalist despotism' prevailing, according to Yugoslav communist ideologues, in Stalin's USSR.[6]

The gap between theory and practice soon became obvious, but it disappointed intellectuals quicker than workers. Djilas was among the first to criticise the bureaucratic alienation and ostentatious privilege of the communist leadership. Some years after he was purged, Djilas argued that the system had bred a ruling communist 'new class'. In his extensively documented study of Yugoslav elites, the Western sociologist Leonard J. Cohen also found that 'conformity and political

---

6 A.R. Johnson, *The Transformation of Communist Ideology: The Yugoslav Case 1945–1953*, Cambridge, MA: MIT Press, 1972. For a more recent treatment, see D. Jović, *Yugoslavia: A State that Withered Away*, West Lafayette, IN: Purdue University Press, 2009.

careerism replaced the revolutionary outlook or Partisan political culture which had predominated during the war years'.[7] This ruling bureaucracy was secure in power but its primary purpose and characteristic was not in fact to consume surplus extracted from the workforce. It saw itself rather as the moderniser of the backward country it had led to independence. Raising the country's industrial capacity to safeguard independence became its prime motivating concern. Dijana Pleština, in her study of regional development in Yugoslavia, interviewed leading economic policy makers of the time. She quotes Svetozar Vukmanović Tempo, chairman of the Federal Planning Commission, as saying that 'the main issue was the accumulation of capital'.[8] She noted that, among policy makers, 'the feeling predominated that whatever was built, wherever it was built, would be all right, since lacking "everything", "anything" would be useful'.[9]

Yugoslavia was indeed among the fastest-growing economies of the 1950s, possibly second only to Japan, and this growth did not appear to come from a brutal squeeze on living standards. The endeavour to maintain high investment rates through the 1950s was based on transfers of labour and value from the countryside but also on foreign aid and loans. In order to 'drive a wedge' into the Soviet bloc, the US had decided to send funds to 'keep Tito afloat'.[10] For instance, in this 'period of uncertain policy orientation and uncertain performance in agriculture, the Yugoslav authorities had little need to worry about food supplies to the growing towns' because of US food aid.[11] Living standards fluctuated in the 1950s and consumption

7   L.J. Cohen, *The Socialist Pyramid, Elites and Power in Yugoslavia*, Oakville, Ont.: Mosaic Press, 1989, 151.

8   D. Pleština, *Regional Development in Communist Yugoslavia: Success, Failure and Consequences*, Oxford: Westview Press, 1992, 28.

9   Ibid., 35.

10   L.M. Lees, *Keeping Tito Afloat: The United States, Yugoslavia, and the Cold War*, University Park, PA: Pennsylvania State University Press, 1997.

11   D.A. Dyker, *Yugoslavia: Socialism, Development and Debt*, London: Routledge, 1990, 45.

probably did not reach pre-war levels until 1960.[12] Nevertheless, policy makers were adamant that there had been an increase in the social wage in the form of welfare. Their choice of concentrating on communal goods was largely aimed at stopping the fluctuation of the labour force between urban and rural areas.[13] All this appeared to result in growing optimism and participation by workers in the system. Labour productivity rose, as did rates of participation in organs of management. Sociological studies found that areas under discussion by the workers' councils were also increasing. That was despite the continued predominance of issues relating to the rationalisation of production, as opposed to business operation. Finally, even though studies suggested workers did not feel they ran their workplaces, rank-and-file satisfaction with the councils was ever greater in the 1950s.[14]

Beneath the surface, however, dramatic change was under way and it would soon lead to a confrontation that proved crippling for the future of Yugoslavia. Precisely because a growing economy was important for the maintenance of national independence, quick returns on investments became ever more central to the calculations of the Yugoslav communist leadership. Market measures became ever more pervasive. At first, the marriage of self-management with 'socialist commodity production' meant that there was an attempt to provide material incentives for workers through the creation of a finished goods market. The use of market forces was, however, slowly expanded. The centralised determination of wages was abolished after 1955 and a new income-sharing system was introduced in 1958. Workers no longer received a wage from an employer. They now had the right to an income on account of their membership of a work collective which enjoyed usufruct over its workplace.

---

12   L. Sirc, *The Yugoslav Economy under Self-management*, London: Macmillan Press, 1979, 51.

13   See S.V. Tempo, *Revolucija koja teče – Memoari* [The Revolution which Continues – Memoirs], vol. 2, Belgrade: Komunist, 1971.

14   E.T. Comisso, *Workers' Control Under Plan and Market*, London: Yale University Press, 1979, 42–71.

This meant that, since the workplaces were social property, the worker collectives had the right to run and benefit from their workplace, but within certain legal limitations, like paying various taxes according to government regulations, which were often justified by references to the common good or national interest. In the words of Yugoslav economist Rudolf Bićanić, the result was that personal income was 'no longer an independent variable, but a function of the proceeds, business gains and losses of the enterprise'.[15] Distribution was not according to 'work' but according to the 'results of work'. Thus, it was not the quality or quantity of labour performed by an individual worker that determined wages but the success of the workplace on the market. That encouraged competition among workers not only within but also between workplaces. In a country as diverse as Yugoslavia, where market conditions were regionally uneven, this was bound to have wider implications. Struggles over state investment and economic policies were increasingly regionally contested, which meant that workplaces tended to identify their interests with their enterprise management or the regional government of their republics rather than with other workplaces or other republics of the federation. This symbiosis turned out to be a political bomb at the turn of the decade. Its explosion shattered irreparably the unity of the League of Communists.

The background to the explosion involved in essence a struggle over the extent to which the country's worsening balance of trade deficit could be fixed by cutting imports or increasing exports. The country's second five-year plan, for the period 1957–61, envisaged an uneasy compromise on this matter. It also aimed to mollify Slovenia and Serbia, respectively the most developed and the most populous republics of the federation. The plan projected the cutting of the deficit through increased exports, as sought by Slovenia in particular. Slovenia stood to gain from this orientation because of increased external demand for its processing industries and because imported raw

---

15 R. Bićanić, *Economic Policy in Socialist Yugoslavia*, London: Cambridge University Press, 1973, 108.

materials were often cheaper than domestic ones. The latter situation resulted in large part from a politics of prices which had favoured the industrialised areas rather than the resource-rich but industrially less developed regions throughout the 1950s. At the same time, however, the plan did also project some redistribution at the federal level and more investment going towards agriculture. This benefited only one republic, the agricultural hub of Serbia, largely at the expense of resource-rich Bosnia, which lost its status as a less developed region and the coveted subsidies which accompanied that status.[16] To understand why the leadership was prepared to go to such lengths to placate Slovenia and Serbia, it is necessary to underline the importance that the communists accorded to the correct solution to the national question in Yugoslavia. They were wary of making the country appear like the Serb-dominated interwar kingdom, since the country's stability would then come under question and jeopardise independence. At the same time, they were desperate to keep Serbia on board, since it would otherwise be tempted to upset the delicate federal checks and balances.

This had become clear even before the adoption of the 1957–61 plan and increasingly became articulated in the language of self-management. Rumours were rife that a cabinet split had pitched Serbs and Slovenes against each other over the planned transfer of some plant from Serbia to Slovenia in 1955. Tito had apparently sided with the latter, making a speech against centralist hegemonism in Belgrade.[17] Public spats among intellectuals followed in 1956 over the meaning of the policy of 'socialist Yugoslavism' and also involved prominent Slovene and Serb intellectuals. The policy, launched in 1955, was developed in May by the Ideological Commission of the Central Committee, chaired by the Serb, Petar Stambolić. Hilde Katrine Haug points out that the policy involved 'the establishment of

16   J.T. Bombelles, *Economic Development of Communist Yugoslavia, 1947–1964*, Stanford, CA: The Hoover Institution of War, Revolution and Peace, 1968, 148.

17   T. Jakovina, *Socijalizam na američkoj pšenici* [Socialism on American Wheat], Zagreb: Matica Hrvatska, 2002, 426.

all-Yugoslav cultural and scientific institutions with the prefix "Yugoslav", and encouraged greater unity within the fields of linguistics, literature, cinema and art'.[18] A public polemic expressing disquiet among non-Serbs showed there was great suspicion towards the policy. Kardelj's republication of his pre-war classic *The Development of the Slovene National Question* in 1957 appeared to be a response to the situation.[19] In a new introduction, Kardelj posited his own view of what the policy meant and he provided a framework within which compromise could be negotiated. He argued that, on the one hand, the richer republics should help develop all of Yugoslavia, but that, on the other hand, their own progress should not be retarded. Those who stressed the former at the expense of the latter, according to this view, threatened self-management socialism in the name of Soviet-like centralism and, inevitably given Yugoslavia's composition, Serb hegemony. Those who stressed the latter at the expense of the former also represented a danger for self-management socialism. Their localism distorted the system and opened the door to the return of bourgeois nationalism, which could in turn provoke the return of a revanchist centre. On balance, centralism rather than localism remained more dangerous since it rested on the bureaucracy, a force existing within socialism, rather than potential bourgeois elements, who represented the old and defeated order. Moreover, the implicit menace was Soviet intervention in Yugoslav affairs. This view would duly be written into the Programme of the LCY, adopted at the Seventh Congress in 1958.

The balancing act in the leadership nonetheless became ever more difficult between 1958 and 1962. The first labour strike in self-managed Yugoslavia, in an old mine in Slovenia in January 1958, upset the leadership's federal balancing act, seemingly irreparably. The fact that the strike had occurred in an old mine was particularly symbolic. Older industry was for a long time

---

18   H.K. Haug, *Creating a Socialist Yugoslavia: Tito, Communist Leadership and the National Question*, London and New York: I.B. Tauris, 2012, 150.

19   E. Kardelj, *Razvoj slovenačkog nacionalnog pitanja* [The Development of the Slovene National Question], Belgrade: Kultura, 1957.

not renewed but in fact taxed in order to raise new plants, often in the less developed regions. This policy was resented in Slovenia, but remained in force in the second five-year plan. The strike could not be seen as separate from this context by the political actors in the drama. In fact, Bosnian delegates to the Central Committee openly accused the Slovene leadership of instigating the strike in order to protest federal policy. The leadership appeared so badly shaken by the open expression of mutual suspicions that the Central Committee hardly met over following years. High growth rates papered over differences and the five-year plan exceeded expectations, being fulfilled earlier than scheduled, in 1960. The balance of trade deficit, however, increased five times, suggesting that the underlying problems had not been solved. If anything, they were getting worse. If in the period 1947–56, one-third of Yugoslav investment in production had come from foreign funds, largely grants, and the country was still running a balance of trade deficit, then the situation was likely to deteriorate in the period 1957–60, when aid had switched from a grant to a credit basis and older loans were coming to term.

The Second Phase of Self-management: Restructuring on the Open Market, 1961–1976

In response, the leadership took steps to dismantle import substitution and implement an export orientation. Diane Flaherty suggests this phase lasted from 1961 to 1976. Nonetheless, the move was not yet decisive. The five-year plan for the period 1961–5 was once again an uneasy compromise. Greater enterprise autonomy, flat enterprise taxes, legalisation of worker emigration, and a raft of measures like the devaluation of the national currency and abolition of multiple exchange rates suggested the country was opening up. Increases in spending on heavy industry and continuing price controls on 70 per cent of industrial goods suggested the move was still circumscribed. Tensions in the leadership soon flared up again, this time even more spectacularly. The recession of 1961–2 prompted an extended meeting of the Central Committee's Executive Committee. Once again, Slovene representatives warned of a threat to self-management from centralisers. Meanwhile, secret police chief and Serb strongman Aleksandar Ranković warned that it was not centralism that was the main danger but decentralisation, with radicalism in the autonomous province of Vojvodina threatening the integrity of Serbia. Neither side won a decisive victory. Exasperated, Tito even offered to resign several times during the meeting, while the army offered to replace the LCY as the basic institution of rule should Tito choose the option. The radical union position, favouring a market interpretation of the demand 'reward according to work' but without losing sight of the need to strengthen the material basis of self-management through state investment and full employment, met with rebuke. In the end, Tito settled for another round of compromise in which economic reform was to continue but with political and social actors playing an increasingly coordinated role in the federation.

The forces of cohesion were, however, losing out to the centrifugal pull of the external market. The principle of integrated development of the country as a whole was finally abandoned in 1963 with the abolition of the Federal Investment Fund. Its funds were transferred mostly to various banks, and the role of the federation was reduced to a redistributive function. Unable to win at the federal level, the two major factions had retreated into the safety of their republics. By 1964, the developed north-western republics of Slovenia and Croatia were seeking a decentralised federalism, while Serbia's attempt to rally the underdeveloped republics was undermined by blatant hypocrisy, for example the retention instead of the dispersion of the assets of three defederalised banks situated in Belgrade. Indeed, Belgrade's resistance to reform increasingly resembled the actions of an embittered hegemon, and Tito finally ousted Ranković in 1966. Tito's action followed the victory of reform forces at the Eighth LCY Congress in 1964 and the passing of a major market reform package in 1965. The apparent triumph of the market reform coalition did not halt the fracturing of Yugoslav federalism, however, but, in fact, intensified it. Disparities rose across the board. Income inequalities rose in different skills categories, different enterprises and industries, regions and republics. The national question came into public view for the first time in Tito's Yugoslavia. Underdeveloped Bosnia complained about its Development Fund allocation and Albanians in Kosovo and Macedonia protested long years of neglect and oppression in 1968. Soon thereafter, the more developed north-western republics, Slovenia and Croatia, challenged federal authorities over allocation of foreign development funds and distribution of tourism receipts, respectively, in 1968–9 and 1971–2. The latter even witnessed a major popular mobilisation around national issues. Experimentation with freer local elections also witnessed a rise in popularity for candidates who appealed to nationalist sentiments. Tito's response amounted to a combination of repression and concession, culminating in a new decentralising constitution in 1974.

Yet many of the problems that would be blamed on that constitution were already present and were far advanced following the reforms of 1965. Indeed, and crucially, the country's failure to leap from extensive to intensive modes of growth and the long-term origins of the debt trap that later choked the country can be traced to the effects of the reformers' blind faith in the market. For it was the 1965 reform that reinforced a fatal dependency on foreign technological supply. Liberalisation of the conditions for the transfer of technology turned Yugoslavia from a world leader in innovation before 1965 to the country with the lowest number of patents realised in relation to the number of citizens by the early 1980s. Imports of technology from foreign partners gave birth to restrictive clauses in more than 90 per cent of contracts: by 1983, more than three-fifths of contracts forbade export of products produced with purchased technology; more than two-fifths obliged the buyer to inform the seller of innovations; and more than a quarter obliged Yugoslav importers of technology to use it in combination with imported materials and spare parts from sources stipulated by the seller.[20] As part of the decentralising reform, 'Yugoslav scientific associations were forced – despite protests from their members – to become fragmented republic-based associations.'[21] The departure from economies of scale, functional differentiation and integration was accompanied by the establishment of new barriers, with implications for not only domestic efficiency but also international cooperation. During this period, investment rates continued to be high, but were accompanied by falling growth and productivity rates.[22] While disaster was highly predictable, it appears not to have been predicted at the time. This must be explained in part by the fact that economic growth still continued in the decade following 1965. Nevertheless, this growth was lagging behind by international standards: while Yugoslavia had almost caught up in terms of gross national product per head with the average in southern Europe in the period 1952–64, it fell back to second from bottom of the table in the years 1964–81.[23]

The pressures of the world market not only exacerbated horizontal pulls on the federation, preparing the way for the country's debt trap, but also put pressure on the shop-floor. Two thousand strikes took place over the period 1958–69. The tendency was for workers' representation in the LCY and the organs of self-management to fall over the same period. With the gap between theory and practice turning into a gulf, the door opened for a radical critique of the system from the standpoint of making the practice fit the theory. Increasing worker intransigence even witnessed attempts to elect a non-Party leadership in the union, just before a student revolt took place in Belgrade in 1968. Articulating their demands in the language of humanist Marxism, much influenced by both the

20   C.U. Schierup, *Migration, Socialism and the International Division of Labour: The Yugoslavian Experience*, Aldershot: Avebury, 1990, 217.

21   Ibid., 223.

22   Dyker, *Yugoslavia*, 92.

23   B. Horvat, *Jugoslovensko društvo u krizi* [Yugoslav Society in Crisis], Zagreb: Globus, 1985, 8.

international New Left and the domestic Praxis school of philosophy, the students denounced the rise of technocracy and
nationalism as aberrations from true self-management and the
fault of the 'Red Bourgeoisie'. Prominent sociologist Nebojša
Popov details the steps taken by the authorities to prevent communication between the two groups during 1968.[24] Tito's
television appearance supporting the students was a part of a
complex mix of the usual give and take employed by the LCY
to defuse tensions. Purges of radicals in the union and at the
university followed as part of the same strategy, which worked
in the short term. Strikes petered out, to return only by the late
1970s.[25] In the meantime, the LCY rammed through a regressive reform of the self-management system in 1969, aiming to
restore hierarchies in the workplace. The director could now
appoint a Business Board in the place of an elected Management
Board. In the words of Pat Devine, 'the market placed a pre-
mium on financial and marketing skills at the expense of
production'.[26] Inflation and wasteful investments duly increased.
To make up for their lack of size and get ahead in the market,
often in collusion with local political bosses keen on building
business empires, enterprises took out massive loans from
banks, flush with money following the abolition of the Federal
Investment Fund. They were then faced with major debt-
servicing obligations, which workers did not want to be
burdened with. Increasingly removed from decision making,
workers made use of self-management institutions to redress
traditional union concerns: wages, welfare and grievances.[27]
Sharon Zukin recorded widespread apathy towards the official
ideology during her research in Yugoslavia in the early 1970s

---

24   See, broadly, N. Popov, *Društveni sukobi i izazov sociologiji, 'Beogradski
jun' 1968* [Social Conflicts and the Challenge to Sociology, 'The Belgrade June'
1968], Belgrade: Službeni glasnik, 2008, Chapters 3 and 4.
25   Zukin, 'The Representation of Working Class Interest in Socialist
Society', 306–7.
26   P. Devine, *Democracy and Economic Planning*, Cambridge: Polity Press,
1988, 97.
27   Dyker, *Yugoslavia*, 63.

and believed the leadership was more afraid of national than worker explosions.[28]

The horizontal and vertical challenges to the LCY apex at the turn of the 1970s resulted in yet another contradictory compromise. On the one hand, Tito rose above the fray and re-established LCY authority on the basis of his unique charisma and through the use of the army. On the other hand, the LCY pushed through a further self-management reform designed both to placate national sentiments and to break up the power of local political-technocratic monopolies from below. This was symbolised by the passing of the 1974 constitution and the 1976 law on associated labour, which created a new institution: 'basic organisations of associated labour' (BAOLS), 'the smallest units whose product or service could be expressed in terms of market value', as Goran Musić pithily puts it.[29] The idea was for the BAOLS to participate in a 'bottom-to-top-down-again iterative process' of self-management agreements which would ultimately become the federal five-year social plan.[30] This necessarily involved close cooperation with the local LCY and mass organisations, agreement across branches of industry, and negotiation at all the various levels of the federation. The LCY leadership went to great lengths to show it was still committed to its idea of 'the withering away of the state'. It launched an all-out offensive against the technocracy by decentralising fiscal and monetary policy further than ever. It banned directors from seeking more than one term of office and tried to force internal reorganisation so as to smash up existing clientelist networks in enterprises. Kardelj also famously argued for the need to recognise 'the pluralism of self-managing interests'. Seeking a way to break from consensus decision making and essentialist identity politics, he argued for an institutional setting whereby changing

---

28 S. Zukin, *Beyond Marx and Tito: Theory and Practice in Yugoslav Socialism*, New York: Cambridge University Press, 1975.

29 G. Musić, 'Yugoslavia: Workers' Self-Management as State Paradigm', in Immanuel Ness and Dario Azzelini, eds, *Ours to Master and Own: Workers' Control from the Commune to the Present*, Chicago: Haymarket Books, 2011, 186.

30 Devine, *Democracy and Economic Planning*, 97.

majorities of multiple and irreducible interests could pursue 'cross-cutting cleavages' issue by issue. The LCY was still to retain a vital role in this scheme as an initiator and dynamo of the negotiation process.[31]

The Third Phase of Self-management: From Debt Crisis to State Collapse, 1976–1991

It was this extraordinarily complex process of reform initiated by the 1974 constitution and the 1976 law on associated labour that mediated the system's interaction with global economic trends and pressures. In effect, the new wave of reform reproduced many of the worst results of the 1965 reform but introduced additional layers of problems. Though the new system attempted to close itself off from the world market and depend once again on import substitution, this proved impossible. The Yugoslav economy had come to rely on emigrant remittances to run balance of trade deficits caused by imports of key capital goods and raw material inputs from the West. Part of the 1961 reform moving the country towards greater openness had been the legalisation of emigration. This move had been an attempt to find an outlet for increasing domestic unemployment. Remittances from the just under one million workers temporarily employed abroad in the West thereafter represented a major contribution to mitigating the worst effects of the balance of payments deficits until the early 1970s. The first oil shock in 1973 stopped remittances and erected trade barriers to Western Europe. This reversed the system's temporary success in westward exports, based in large part on an apparently decisive shift in labour productivity. The latter accounted for 100 per cent of industrial increment in the years 1966–70.[32] Another good year in 1976 masked the underlying trend of ever-greater dependency on credits to make up for loss of

---

31   S.L. Burg, *Conflict and Cohesion in Socialist Yugoslavia, Political Decision-Making since 1966*, Princeton, NJ: Princeton University Press, 1983, 306–7.

32   Dyker, *Yugoslavia*, 90–5.

remittances. Yugoslav foreign debt rocketed through the 1970s, from US$3,437.7 million to 20,645.6 million, roughly tripling in the period 1976–81, after the introduction of the new system. Between two-thirds and three-quarters of the debt were incurred annually by the 'private' or self-managed sector at the turn of the 1980s, the exact reversal of the situation at the turn of the 1970s. The intensification of decentralisation and market competition combined with external factors to bring Yugoslavia to the brink of bankruptcy. The country turned to the International Monetary Fund for assistance and received the Fund's largest ever loan hitherto at the start of 1981.[33]

By the end of the same decade, however, self-management and Yugoslavia were nearing their end. At the behest of foreign creditors, successive governments implemented two waves of austerity. These had predictable consequences on the social fabric and political cohesion of the multinational state. Once again, government policy ruptured relations with the working class. With real incomes falling by half between 1980 and 1985, and unemployment reaching a million, strikes escalated from a low in 1980 with 13,507 going on strike to a high of 386,123 in 1988.[34] Popular support for the LCY plummeted from three-quarters of those polled in 1974 to a third by 1983.[35] Newspaper reports quoted workers complaining of bureaucratic behaviour by management and their own powerlessness.[36] Sociologists, meanwhile, showed that bureaucratic patronage continued to rule at the local level, with management figures and municipal politicians distributing favours among each other. In one 'peculiar case . . . an individual who had been formally removed simply remained working in his position, while all colleagues, including the lawyer of the firm, continued

---

33   Ibid., 120–2.

34   D. Marinković, *Štrajkovi i društvena kriza* [Strikes and the Social Crisis], Belgrade: Institut za političke studije, 1995, 83.

35   Devine, *Democracy and Economic Planning*, 99.

36   D. Bilandžić, *Historija Socijalističke Federativne Republike Jugoslavije, Glavni procesi 1918–1985* [The History of the Socialist Federal Republic of Yugoslavia: Main Processes 1918–1985], Zagreb: Školska knjiga, 1985, 541.

to accept his signature on official documents'.[37] Workers no longer believed in working through official channels and engaged in the informal economy, making between a third and a half of their livelihood through such activities as handicrafts and repair. They expected management to leave them to these activities as part of the deal for keeping quiet. As this arrangement began to unravel in the 1980s, family, neighbourhood and friendship networks began to replace workplace loyalties. Urban–rural fluctuation or symbiosis returned where possible, and open conflict on the shop-floor where there was no other option.[38] Strikes became more frequent and intense but were short, atomised, and ever more unsuccessful. This latter tendency in particular was in contrast with the preceding period, when demands were met as part of the official claim that the LCY represented the working class. Minor tendencies towards solidarity across workplaces occurred and usually remained regionally trapped. The overall tendency was for workers to shift their hopes towards the political sphere as the organs of self-management and the unions colluded with the police to break strikes.[39]

Politicians increasingly played the nationalist card, as in the famous episode when, in front of the Federal Assembly, Serb communist leader Slobodan Milošević addressed strikers from a Belgrade district, 'who gathered as workers, and left as Serbs'.[40] The unevenness of the crisis in Yugoslavia was stark and therefore explosive. At one extreme was Slovenia. By the 1980s, Slovenia was increasingly trading on the world market rather

---

37   J.S. Sorensen, *State Collapse and Reconstruction in the Periphery: Political Economy, Ethnicity and Development in Yugoslavia, Serbia and Kosovo*, New York: Berghahn Books, 2009, 132.

38   Schierup, *Migration, Socialism and the International Division of Labour*, 245–69.

39   N.G. Novaković, *Propadanje radničke klase, Materijalni i društveni položaj radničke klase Jugoslavije od 1960. do 1990. godine* [The Decline of the Working Class: The Material and Social Condition of the Working Class of Yugoslavia from the Year 1960 to the Year 1990], Belgrade: Rad, 2007, 123–7.

40   Quoted in D. Đurić, 'Social Dialogue in South-east European Countries', *South-East Europe Review for Labour and Social Affairs*, vol. 5(3), 2002, 35.

than with the rest of Yugoslavia and flouting federal wage ceil-ings to entice back skilled Slovene labour from abroad. At the other extreme was Serbia. By the 1980s, the League of Communists (LC) of Serbia faced a restive population, rising unemployment, and an explosive situation in Kosovo. The latter had even undergone massive repression and a state of emer-gency in 1981.[41] The IMF demanded recentralisation of the federation and the socialisation of debt, since $8 billion of the $19 billion owed in 1988 could no longer be attributed to a specific debtor.[42]

By 1987, both republic leaderships were under pressure to shift to more extreme positions to keep up with popular demands. It was in this context that Milošević rose to promi-nence, diverting social discontent and channelling nationalist mobilisations relating to Kosovo towards a recentralisation of Serbia. This shift represented an open break with the Titoist heritage, and Serbia's apparent desire to press its newfound momentum to recentralise all of Yugoslavia led to Slovenia pro-posing confederalisation as a stepping stone to self-determination within a European setting. Meanwhile, the federal government attempted to resist both tendencies, and to provide a liberal solution. By 1989, a new law on enterprises and foreign invest-ment effectively dismantled the monopoly of self-management on ownership structures in the Yugoslav economy. This did not represent a shock and was only the logical conclusion of the acceptance of the programme proposed by the IMF. With the collapse of the Berlin Wall, few were at this stage prepared to defend the heritage of a system in apparent free fall, not just in Yugoslavia but all over East Europe. The federal government itself, lacking its own mechanisms of rule, was soon under-mined by the republic leaderships, none of which had an interest in its success. The following year, the LCY too broke up,

---

41   S. Woodward, *Balkan Tragedy: Chaos and Dissolution after the Cold War*, Washington, DC: The Brookings Institution, 1995, 65.

42   M.J. Calic, D. Neutatz and J. Obertreis, *The Crisis of Socialist Modernity: The Soviet Union and Yugoslavia in the 1970s*, Göttingen: Vandenhoeck & Ruprecht, 2011, 80.

as the Slovene delegation to the LCY Congress refused to accept the Serb-led drive for recentralisation. Soon after, the country that had put self-management on the global map was unravelling.

Conclusion

The rise and fall of the Yugoslav model does not prove the unfeasibility of socialism. Rather the reverse, it shows that any system hoping to provide an alternative to capitalism needs to begin from the premise of the progressive elimination of the market. Self-management in Yugoslavia was linked to the market from its inception. As such, it was devoid of emancipatory potential from the beginning. Rather than worker participation increasing across its successive phases of implementation, the opposite was the case. In the first phase, from 1950 to 1961, self-management did unlock creative energies from below, but it also channelled them towards feeding an economic system designed to protect national independence. Key to the enterprise was access to US aid. Quick returns on investment became a priority, and the marriage of worker collectives and market incentives stressed the competitive nature of the enterprise. In a diverse country like Yugoslavia, this inevitably fuelled regional struggles, easily translatable into inter-ethnic rivalries. Yugoslavia's rapid development could not be sustained by resources internal to the economy, since its competitors were bigger and had greater access to world trade.

The second phase, from 1961 to 1976, therefore saw Yugoslavia attempt to open up, diversify its economic production and consumption, and develop niche export sectors. Entering the world division of labour was risky enough but Yugoslavia entered it itself divided. The stresses of competition ruptured forces working for federal cohesion and severed relations with the working class on the shop-floor. This atomisation led to technological regression and the reversal of integration processes across the economy. Nonetheless, increasing exposure to the world market demanded major investments, and decisions were devolved to the financial sector rather than the state sector. Increasing speculation and unproductive investment were the result, based on unregulated import of foreign capital and technology, which could not be financed except through running an increasing balance of trade deficit. When remittances from workers sent abroad to solve the problem of unemployment began to dry up, the only way to continue to finance growth was through debt.

The third phase of the debt crisis, from 1976 to 1991, saw Yugoslavia decimated by IMF-imposed and communist-executed austerity. Worker rights, already diminishing, came under heavy attack and unemployment rose to intolerable levels. The elites were no longer sure how to govern, and the subaltern classes were no longer prepared to continue in the old way. The ruling bureaucrats in the more developed regions seemed to want to cut their losses and run, while those in the less developed regions often preferred reintegration, even under IMF auspices, though ultimately only Montenegro went along with Serbia. The result was the end and reversal of the glorious national liberation tradition that had reunited Yugoslavia in the Second World War. The subsequent advent of liberal capitalism has not reversed the region's pervasive poverty and underdevelopment. Instead, it has deepened dependency on foreign capital, imposed limited sovereignty, and limited democracy across the region. Reversing the situation will not be easy but it must involve learning from the past, understanding the *longue durée* of today's debt crisis,[43] and standing in the tradition of the great worker and student struggles that pointed to what self-management socialism could be if it came from below.

---

43   A. Živković, 'Povratak u budućnost: Tranzicija na Balkanu' [Back to the Future: Transition in the Balkans], in M. Jadžić, D. Maljković and A. Veselinović, eds, *Kriza, Odgovori, Levica: Prilozi za jedan kritički diskurs* [Crisis, Responses, the Left: Contributions Towards a Critical Discourse], Belgrade: Rosa Luxemburg Stiftung Southeast Europe, 2012, 188–219.

CHAPTER 2

From the Market . . . to the Market: The Debt Economy After Yugoslavia

Andreja Živković

Transition or Repetition?

The transition to the market economy in the post-Yugoslav states is usually held to have been derailed first by war and subsequently by a failure to open up sufficiently to foreign capital. Indeed, the International Monetary Fund (IMF) now blames the present crisis in this part of the Balkans on an incomplete transition to the market, an 'unsustainable pre-crisis growth model', 'unrealistic memories of past high consumption standards', and an 'oversized public sector focused on consuming rather than investing', and prescribes the standard neoliberal remedy of further privatisation and liberalisation.[1]

Underlying the concept of a 'transition' is the transformation of command into market economies, economic liberalisation where market forces rather than central planning bodies set prices, macroeconomic stabilisation to control inflation and impose hard budget constraints on firms, the creation of a financial sector to channel savings into investment and the privatisation of state enterprises to foster market competition. But, even by this neo-classical definition, it is clear that a market economy had long existed in the Socialist Federal Republic of

---

1   IMF Country Report, 'Republic of Serbia', cited in A. Živković, 'Povratak u budućnost: Tranzicija na Balkanu' [Back to the Future: The Transition in the Balkans], in M. Jadžic, D. Maljković and A. Veselinović, eds, *Kriza, Odgovori, Levica: prilozi za jedan kritički diskurs* [Crisis, Responses, the Left: Contributions Towards a Critical Discourse], Belgrade: Rosa Luxemburg Stiftung Southeast Europe, 2012, 189.

Yugoslavia. As Jože Mencinger, Finance Minister in the first post-Yugoslav Slovenian government, recalls:

> A number of parameters of the market economy existed before 1989: firms had their autonomy, the basic institutions of the market were in place and the government had at its disposal many standard macroeconomic instruments. Indeed, the coordination of the economy was decentralized for many years; since the 1980s, the impact of inadequate demand prevailed over any eventual shortage of supply, and the very concept of 'excess liquidity' was unknown.[2]

We will argue here that the present debt crisis in Croatia, Serbia and Slovenia is not due to the lack of market mechanisms, but is precisely a crisis of the market, the expression of the contradictions of half a century of integration into the world market. The concept of the transition implies regional separation both from the dynamics of the world economy in general before 1989 and from the crisis of profitability faced by all advanced economies from the 1970s in particular, a crisis that led all states to seek growth through liberalisation, financial integration and restructuring of labour markets and the public sector. It thereby mystifies the real processes at work: growing economic dependency and peripheralisation, taking the form of successive debt crises since the 1970s. Each debt crisis has been the pretext for a new wave of integration, of opening to foreign capital to repay debt, and each has ended in an even greater debt crisis and economic destruction. The debt crisis today is both a regional expression of the global crisis of financialised capitalism and a regional crisis of *European integration before formal European integration*, mirroring that of Greece and peripheral Europe. The solution, I claim, lies not in any further opening to foreign capital, but in regional alternatives to *integration into the crisis*

---

2   J. Mencinger, 'Les Slovènes du tolar à l'euro, à . . ', *Outre-Terre*, vol. 2(32), 2012, 295.

of European integration. But before arguing for that claim I will trace the history of the Yugoslav debt economy.

From the Market to . . . the Market: The Rise of the Yugoslav Debt Economy

In 1949, faced with economic blockade and the threat of invasion by the USSR, Tito's Yugoslavia made the fateful decision to turn to Western aid, trade and credits. Henceforth it found itself obliged to seek greater 'integration into the world division of labour' to finance the technological imports that would lay the economic basis for geopolitical survival. The strategy of export-led growth was soon brought into question by the division of Europe into three competing superpower-sponsored trade blocs: the Council for Mutual Economic Assistance (Comecon), the European Economic Community (EEC) and the European Free Trade Association. Yugoslav agricultural exports were faced with the prospect of increasing tariff discrimination as the common external tariffs of each bloc were gradually harmonised and internal tariffs abolished, especially with the establishment of a Common Agricultural Policy by the EEC in 1962. Since Yugoslavia ran a structural trade deficit with the EEC – a deficit that continued to the very end – it was forced onto the path of deeper market integration with the Community in order to import finance and technology. To pay for these it had to sell its mainly agricultural exports to the EEC, and thus open its market to EEC trade.[3]

Integration reflected a pattern of dependent, financialised development, which can still be seen in the region today. Yugoslavia's export orientation in fact meant the adjustment of its production to European markets that financed the necessary capital investment. Although Yugoslavia was rapidly becoming an industrial nation, its trade with the EU remained

---

3 See A. Živković, 'Bankrot Evropske Unije: ili kako izaći iz Evrodezintegracije' [The Bankruptcy of the European Union: Or How to Exit Euro-disintegration], *Zarez*, vol. 13(322), 2011, 28–30.

characteristic of that of a less developed country – importing
capital and intermediate goods in exchange for raw materials,
agricultural products and subcontracted processed goods.
Western export of capital goods took the form of the leasing of
patents and licensing agreements – for example, the Zastava
licensing agreement with Fiat – to maintain technological
dependency, representing a transfer of value to EEC capitals.
Unable to compete in the technological race, Yugoslavia saved
on labour costs.[4] To cover its growing trade deficit and foreign
debt it became a major exporter of unskilled labour to the boom
economies of Western Europe, a pattern of dependency that
continues to this day.

The 1970 and 1980 trade agreements, which liberalised
trade with the EEC, accelerated dependency on capital and hard
currency imports to finance export growth. Since these exports
struggled to find Western buyers and had to be sold on soft
currency Comecon markets, the result was a worsening of the
balance of trade deficit, increasing inflation, and a ballooning
of the foreign debt to $20 billion by 1980. These problems were
in turn the product of a debt economy where the overvaluation
of the Yugoslav dinar made the financing and repayment of
foreign credit and capital imports easier, but at the same time
made exports uncompetitive and tended to lead to high rates of
inflation, thus requiring further borrowing to maintain investment growth, a pattern repeated in Croatia and Serbia in the
2000s. Another problem that would later reappear was that
trade liberalisation with the EEC was a one-way street. While
import dependency implied a remarkably open trade regime on
the part of the Yugoslavs, after the global recession of 1974–5
the EEC raised trade barriers in precisely those areas where
Yugoslavia enjoyed competitive advantage (steel, textiles,
tobacco, beef and veal). In order to cover the yawning trade

---

4   Contrary to the neoliberal myth that the system of 'self-management'
enabled workers to increase wages at the expense of investment, it was, as Susan
Woodward has demonstrated, designed from the very beginning to minimise
labour costs and increase productivity. See S.L. Woodward, *Socialist Unemployment:
The Political Economy of Yugoslavia*, Princeton, NJ: Princeton University Press, 1995.

deficit, Yugoslavia borrowed heavily on international financial markets and fell into a terminal debt trap.

The Yugoslav financial crisis of the 1970s was an integral part of the global transition to a financialised capitalism and a neoliberal policy regime. During the crisis of the 1970s, flows of money capital, primarily petrodollars and Eurodollars, seeking profitable sources of investment, became recycled as international loans, as banks began to lend on a much larger scale to countries like Mexico, Argentina, Yugoslavia, Poland and Hungary – the 'emerging economies' of their day – to enable them to promote exports. All defaulted on their loans in the course of the global recession of 1980-2. A new neoliberal ideology took advantage of these debt crises and the economic shocks of 1974-5, 1980-2 and 1991-2 to open up national markets to international flows of capital, goods and services.

Raging economic crises in the 1980s in Yugoslavia led to the imposition by international financial institutions of one of the first structural adjustment programmes in the world (from 1982-5 and again in 1989-90). The IMF and EEC demanded the recentralisation of the Yugoslav federation to drive through macroeconomic stabilisation and financial discipline, and thereby ensure the repayment of the Yugoslav debt. Market integration had tended to splinter the national economy into a set of regional economies competing with one another for state credits, foreign currency and resources, and widen inequalities in regional development – the hothouse of nationalism in Yugoslavia from the 1960s onwards. Recentralisation meant stripping the republics of control over companies, banks and finance and eventually overturning the 1974 Constitution which had transformed Yugoslavia into a confederation of semi-independent states. Two opposed programmes emerged, both of which linked nationalist ambitions with neoliberal reform and greater European integration. For Serbia's politicians, federal recentralisation meant revoking the autonomy of Serbia's provinces so as to provide weaker Serbian industry with a domestic market. For the politicians of the rich northern republics (Slovenia and Croatia), less, not more, of the state was the answer. They wanted less spending on the poorer republics and possibly less of the Federation, since they thought these to be a barrier to their competitiveness on the European market. By demanding the republics be stripped of their powers, by imposing destructive but ineffective shock therapy and by ending the redistribution of wealth from richer to poorer republics, the IMF and European Community at that time fuelled the nationalist collapse of Yugoslavia. In this way, the EEC was not only the agent of the economic disintegration of Yugoslavia, but through promises of future political integration accelerated its political disintegration.

From the Yugoslav Debt Economy . . . to the European Debt Economy: Serbia and Croatia

After the Yugoslav wars, the second phase of the debt economy in Croatia and Serbia was unveiled under the new transition ideology which proclaimed that only the opening of markets to Foreign Direct Investment (FDI) and the removal of 'supply-side rigidities', through privatisation of state assets and the deregulation of labour markets, could deliver investment, technological innovation, productivity and thereby growth and prosperity. In fact what was at stake was a new round of forced opening to foreign capital and finance in order to repay the outstanding ex-Yugoslav debt. Far from improving the competitiveness of the export sector or creating real demand as expressed in investment in fixed capital, financialisation institutionalised the credit and import-led model of economic growth of the past. Foreign flows of investment and credit, as in Hungary, the rest of the Balkans, and the Baltic states, spawned a speculative consumer bubble, based on ballooning private debt and trade deficits, which powered high rates of growth in the 2000s, collapsing when the tap ran dry with the bankruptcy of Lehman Brothers in September 2008.

Total Croatian external debt quintupled, from 20.3 per cent to 101.6 per cent of GDP in the period 1995–2012. In Serbia, where significant post-Milošević debt write-offs sweetened the bitter pill of yet another IMF structural adjustment (shock therapy) programme, total external debt fell dramatically from 140 per cent of GDP in 2000 to 54.1 per cent in 2004, before embarking on an unstoppable ascent, reaching 85.6 per cent of GDP in 2012, and still rising. The states of the former Yugoslavia now have a combined debt five times greater than Yugoslavia in 1990. The debt crises of the 1970s and 1980s have returned with a vengeance, accompanied by the same unsustainable trade deficits (in Croatia -22.6 per cent and in Serbia -22.3 per cent of GDP in 2008). At the end of 2012 the Croatian foreign debt amounted to $64.25 billion, while its total stock of FDI came to an estimated $31.6 billion. The respective totals for Serbia for the end of 2012 were $33.7 billion and an estimated $23.2 billion. Thus the opening to foreign capital (FDI and financial flows) in reality represented a transfer of value to EU capitals, the very sign of dependent development, taking the concrete form of the combination of a debt trap and external recession (i.e. the collapse of external financial flows).

The present regional economic crisis is bound up with the long-term decline in profit rates in the advanced capitalist countries. Neoliberalism represented a series of measures geared to the intensification of the rate of exploitation. But this only partially restored profitability and left the problem of unsold goods as wage earners faced falling living standards. According to David Harvey, the origins of neoliberalism lie in the attempt to resolve this contradiction by inducing households and consumers to increase levels of borrowing and spending.[5] This was made possible by the greater autonomy of the financial system: the proliferation of new financial institutions (fusion of commercial and investment banking, rise of mutual funds and the shadow banking sector of hedge funds, private equity firms and structured investment vehicles) and instruments (e.g. credit derivatives), and the integration of these and other economic actors, including households and

---

5   D. Harvey, *A Brief History of Neoliberalism*, Oxford: Oxford University Press, 2005.

non-financial companies, into the financial markets. Surplus capital that could not find outlets for productive investment was captured by the financial markets, resulting in international speculative and asset booms in mergers and acquisitions, real estate, consumer lending, currency markets and credit derivatives, which in turn provided markets for export economies like Germany, Japan and China. Financialisation orchestrated a global system of imbalances between creditor economies with large trade surpluses and high rates of saving (China, Japan and Germany) and economies with large trade deficits and high rates of borrowing (principally the US, but also the backward economies of Southern, Central and Eastern Europe, and the Balkans).

Notwithstanding the transition mantra of export-led growth, Croatia and Serbia were assigned the part of peripheral debtor economies in the global system of financialisation, obliged to open up to the rapine of excess financial liquidity generated by the cheap money policies of the Eurozone centre, thereby becoming completely dependent on external sources of growth. Let us now examine the key dimensions of regional financialisation and the resulting patterns of capitalist development.

Firstly, and most importantly, there is the financialisation of the exchange rate regime. In line with the 'Washington Consensus' propounded by the international financial institutions, and institutionalised in Yugoslavia since the 1980s, macroeconomic policy has sought to control the money supply and target inflation with the aim of 'price stability'. The mechanism to achieve this is the 'monetary anchor', a type of fixed exchange rate; in the case of the Croatian kuna, indexed to the euro. The anchor can only work if a tight monetary policy based on high interest rates is pursued. The real function of monetary policy is not price stability but to 'anchor' the debt economy; that is, to prevent the depreciation of national currencies and so maintain the flow of debt repayment and keep down the cost of imports. High interest rates and 'strong' currencies were designed to attract foreign credits, enabling the borrowing needed to pay for imports. In this way foreign credits subsidised the import and credit boom of the 2000s. The same monetary regime that attracted foreign credits and privatisation receipts was also responsible for destroying industry. Expensive money acted as a disincentive to investment in the real economy, while overvalued currencies made exports uncompetitive.

In the 1990s, industrial output declined dramatically, initially due to IMF-imposed liberalisation and shock therapy in 1989–90, which was anchored by a fixed exchange rate regime, followed by the disintegration of the all-Yugoslav market, and then international sanctions and wars. The main driver thereafter of deindustrialisation and loss of export competitiveness was expensive money and overvalued currencies. In Serbia industrial production in 2010 was barely 50 per cent of 1990 levels, while in Croatia it was still only slightly above 90 per cent. Croatian exports shrivelled from 40 per cent of GDP in 1987 to 19.5 per cent in 2010, and from 39.2 per cent to 24.7 per cent of GDP in Serbia over the same period. The lack of competitiveness of exports intensified two related Yugoslav era trends: technological dependency as expressed in low-wage, labour-intensive economies; and structural unemployment reflected in the export of migrant labour to the EU.[6] Deindustrialisation went hand in hand with structural budget and trade deficits, which could only be covered by increased borrowing, foreign worker remittances, and privatisation receipts, resulting in the debt crisis we see today.

A system of fixed exchange rates presupposes the (at least partial) coverage and the convertibility of domestic money into foreign currency reserves. Hence in such a regime the state no longer controls the money supply (as in the Eurozone). Any

---

6   Croatia's unemployment rate was 8 per cent in 1989 (around 5 per cent from the mid 1960s, but increasing under neoliberal shock therapy in the 1980s) and 18 per cent at the end of 2012. Serbia's unemployment rate grew from less than 15 per cent to over 20 per cent over the same period. Worker remittance share of GDP in Croatia was on average 3.1 per cent for the period 1997–2005, but fell to an estimated 2.2 per cent by 2012. In the years preceding the present economic crisis, Serbian remittances represented as much as 17.75 per cent of GDP, before crashing down to an estimated 7.3 per cent by 2012.

deficit in the current account (balance of trade and capital flows) directly uses up currency reserves and thus contracts the quantity of money in the national economy, which has a negative knock-on effect on economic activity. Hence the goal of monetary policy is to build up fiscal surpluses, which must be invested in the purchase of foreign currencies in order to cover the issue of domestic money. As the primary goal is price stability, appreciative pressures on national currencies accompanying capital account liberalisation are countered by the purchase of foreign currencies on exchange markets. But this merely increases the money supply, necessitating further such purchases to rein in inflation. In Croatia and Serbia foreign currencies are purchased from foreign banks by the issuing of government bonds denominated in both national currencies and euros at lucrative rates of interest. The outcome is an outflow of capital to the foreign banks as expressed in a permanent current account deficit. Fiscal policy is geared to improving state finances through privatisation and FDI receipts, thereby integrating government spending with the financial flows that underpin the debt economy. The financing of state budgets is itself financialised.

The exchange rate regime found its inseparable twin in the liberalisation of the banking system, the second major dimension of regional financialisation. FDI receipts from the sale of the regional banking sector to foreign banks provided much needed foreign currency reserves to preserve fixed exchange rates, repay public debt and cover current account deficits.[7] To

---

7   Dependence on foreign currency flows to anchor monetary policy virtually predetermined the sale of the state banking sector to foreign banks (which own 80 per cent of the Serbian and 90 per cent of the Croatian sectors), especially given high levels of debt and illiquidity in the sector. In Serbia the state had been obliged to take on the debt to the Western banks of the banking sector dating from the Yugoslav period as part of its debt restructuring agreement with the Paris Club and London Club of international creditors. In Croatia, the cost to the state of restructuring the bad debts of the newly privatised banking system amounted to 31 per cent of GDP in 1999 values. At the beginning of the 1990s, the banks participated in the privatisation process by exploiting the conversion of foreign savings into public debt to engage in risky lending, forcing the state to step in to write off the debt of the privatised companies. Later in the decade, seizing on strong capital inflows encouraged by the fixed exchange rate regime, private banks engaged in

encourage market entry, minimum equity investment require-ments were set at ludicrously low levels (e.g. €5 million in Serbia), thereby institutionalising 'fractional banking', where currency reserves placed in central banks only partially cover deposits, and the growth of bank assets is highly leveraged. Under the system of partial reserves central banks offered sur-plus liquidity on the money market to highly leveraged banks, so providing institutional support for the debt pyramid.

The introduction of the euro and the downward convergence of interest rates across the Eurozone signalled a more aggressive entry by the European banks into the region. More generally, the extra profits accruing from the difference between Eurozone and domestic market interest rates stimulated the rapacious growth of private sector credit, especially in mortgage lending, inflating real estate prices and a construction bubble. Consumer bor-rowing exacerbated current account problems as it typically financed the purchase of imported goods. The Euroisation of private credit, whereby the majority of loans are denominated in or indexed to European currencies, was both an outcome of the fixed exchange rate regime and a further sign of the loss of inde-pendence of monetary policy. Euroisation allowed the banks to transfer exchange rate risks to domestic borrowers. For the latter, the attractiveness of foreign currency credit rested on lower interest rates (than domestic currency loans) and expectations that exchange rates would continue to appreciate, or remain fixed to the euro. In the context of the financial crisis, the appreciation of the Swiss franc, and in Serbia the depreciation of the Serbian dinar, have transferred a share of foreign bank losses and risk to, respectively, Croatian and Serbian households and businesses. Here we see another dimension of financialisation – the future wealth of households is made dependent on financial market fluctuations over which they have no control.

Privatisation represented a third major dimension of

---

another wave of lending, leading to numerous bank failures in 1998–9 when mon-etary policy tightened in response to a worsening of the external account and loans could not be repaid.

financialisation. FDI was concentrated in the wholesale and retail trade, transport and communications, financial services and banking. However, these 'non-tradable' sectors do not contribute to exports. In fact they sucked in imports, widening trade deficits. FDI rarely took the form of 'greenfield' or industrial investment. Capital flows were dominated by bank loans to the private sector and households. State monopolies became private monopolies and profits were repatriated. Contrary to neoliberal dogma, FDI has not served to open regional economies to competition or investment. Its real function was quite different; namely, as a component of financial flows. In general privatisation was simply a link in the chain of the debt economy, allowing the insider class of state and firm managers to secure property rights, or criminals to launder illegal earnings, at the expense of the destruction of industry. Property titles allowed owners to strip assets, resell company plant, equipment and land, or take out loans against these, using the money to speculate in real estate transactions, the import trade and government securities, which in turn provided surety against new borrowing.[8] Interest rate differentials both set privatisation capital flows in motion and completed the debt circle as superprofits were repatriated by the foreign banks. The economics of fictitious growth (in financial claims on future values) by means of the plunder and destruction of the real economy was conditioned by the contradictions of the fixed exchange rate regime, which both drew in a plentiful supply of money capital and acted as a disincentive to investment in the real economy.

The debt economy was in fact an engine of wealth transfer from the poor to the rich. Rising inequality found its

---

8   Workers were left without salaries for months, even years on end, their work serving only as a virtual link in a chain of borrowing, speculation and money laundering, until such time as the firm could be declared bankrupt, while new owners walked away from any debt. In Serbia, 30 per cent of privatisations have been annulled because new owners stopped production, stripped assets and failed to pay workers – by the very same Agency for Privatisation that awarded tender agreements to them! Few have faced prosecution.

concentrated expression in the rise of a class of monopoly capitalists, known locally as 'tycoons'.[9] The reverse side of this concentration of wealth was mass unemployment, falling living standards due to permanent inflationary pressures, and hence forced borrowing from the banks to supplement inadequate wages. This was the class significance of financial-isation.

The inescapable conclusion is that the three major regional processes of financialisation – the fixed exchange rate regime, financial liberalisation, and privatisation – have been respon-sible for a catastrophic integration into the Eurozone debt economy, amounting to European integration before the actual European integration of these countries. Monetary convergence and Euroisation destroyed industry and flung the region into debt slavery at the hands of the European banks. In Croatia today, the defence of kuna parity against the euro in order to prevent an uncontrolled default only deepens the crisis. The situation is identical to that of peripheral countries like Greece in the fixed exchange rate system of the Eurozone. Indexing prevents external adjustment through devaluation and imposes what is called an 'internal devaluation', that is, debt repayment by means of prolonged austerity and wage compression, which depress demand and thus the means to repay debt.[10] Further integration will merely intensify these trends, as can be seen from the Slovenian experience.

---

9 The capital value of the top ten tycoons was approximately 30 per cent of GDP in Serbia in 2009. This was just below the Russian level and similar to the majority of Central and East European countries, while in the US, Japan and other advanced economies the comparable figure is between 5 per cent and 7 per cent of GDP.

10 In Serbia, macroeconomic stabilisation under yet another IMF structural adjustment programme has seen the maintenance of high interest rates and inter-vention to the tune of billions of euros on the foreign exchange market in a vain attempt to hold up the value of the dinar (which has depreciated by 40 per cent since 2008). This is hardly surprising since, as we have seen, the very same policies strangle domestic sources of growth and decrease foreign demand for domestic currency.

The Slovene Exception?

Slovenia is not normally thought of as a 'transition economy'. Indeed it is often held up by Keynesians and Marxists[11] as a model of an export economy that has achieved high living standards and levels of investment in the real economy by avoiding the horrors of liberalisation. Appearances are, as they say, deceptive, and I will argue that its present banking and debt crisis reflects a crisis of integration in the EU, which also led Slovenia to become dependent on cheap foreign credits for growth. This crisis calls into question the long-term viability of the Slovene model and offers a negative lesson in the likely impact of EU integration for Serbia and Croatia.

The European single currency spelt the end of national macroeconomic policy as national governments lost the right either to issue money or to alter exchange rates, and could only vary interest rates and public borrowing within very narrow limits. Monetary union reflected the interests of the most technologically advanced capitals, led by Germany, whose exchange rate policy was determined by the need to prevent inflation from increasing the international prices of their exports. Weaker capitals, which had often employed devaluation to make their exports more competitive, and the resulting inflation to redistribute value away from the working class, could no longer employ these tools.

In exchange, they obtained two apparent advantages.[12] Firstly, the loss of the power to issue money or vary interest rates, combined with the tight monetary regime of the ECB,

---

11   See, for example, Mencinger, 'Les Slovènes du tolar à l'euro, à . . .'; H. Hofbauer, *Osterweiterung. Vom Drang nach Osten zur peripheren EU-Integration*, Vienna: Promedia, 2003; C. Samary, 'Enjeux sociaux de la Grande Transformation capitaliste à l'Est', *Revista Theomai*, vol. 17, 2008, 109–38; and M. Žitko, 'Tranzicija financijskog sektora u Hrvatskoj i Sloveniji' [The Transition of the Financial Sector in Slovenia and Croatia], in A. Veselinović, P. Atanacković and Ž. Klarić, eds, *Izgubljeno u tranziciji* [Lost in Transition], Belgrade: Rosa Luxemburg Stiftung Southeast Europe, 2012.

12   See G. Carchedi, *For Another Europe: A Class Analysis of European Integration*, London: Verso, 2001.

forced all capitals to increase labour productivity. Secondly, for the more peripheral members of the EU like Greece, the adoption of the euro narrowed the spread between the interest rates on their bonds and on those of the strongest European economy, Germany, enabling them to borrow more cheaply.

However, while all capitals were able to force down labour unit costs, Germany achieved the greatest savings, resulting in increasing imbalances across the Eurozone as German exports opened up big trade deficits with the more backward countries of the Eurozone periphery.[13] The latter took advantage of cheaper interest rates to borrow money from the banks of the core in order to cover these deficits, laying the basis for unsustainable debt-financed growth and thus the financial crisis of the Eurozone.

The Slovenian export model – supplying the manufacturing industry of Germany, Italy and Austria – was predicated on the rejection of the neoliberal regime of shock therapy, fixed exchange rates and opening to foreign capital. A floating exchange rate was managed so as to prevent currency appreciation from cutting into export competitiveness. Monetary convergence with the euro from 2004 marked the end of an independent exchange rate policy. At the same time Slovenia was unable to hold down unit labour costs as much as its German, Austrian and French competitors, resulting in a growing trade deficit.[14] Monetary convergence cut into the competitiveness of its exports, revealing a relative decline in labour productivity.[15] As a labour-intensive producer, Slovenia increasingly lost out to more technologically advanced producers like Germany.[16] Hence it began to fall into the same

---

13   In this paragraph we follow the pioneering analysis of Costas Lapavitsas: see C. Lapavitsas et al., 'Eurozone Crisis: Beggar Thyself and Thy Neighbour', *Research on Money and Finance Occasional Report*, March 2010.

14   The fact that the deficit rose from -3.7 per cent in 2006 to -7.1 per cent of GDP in 2008 at precisely the point at which Slovenia joined the Eurozone (2007) is telling.

15   See Živković, 'Bankrot Evropske Unije', 212.

16   Thus, *pace* Lapavitsas et al., 'Eurozone Crisis: Beggar Thyself and Thy Neighbour', the loss in competitiveness to Germany in the Eurozone was not purely

pattern of financing its trade deficit with consumer borrowing as the peripheral economies of the Eurozone.

From 2004, an orgy of borrowing was unleashed, centred on the construction, mortgage and retail industries, and on financial services. Enticed by lower interest rates in the Eurozone, Slovene banks borrowed heavily abroad and became dependent on short-term Eurozone finance. Private sector debt shot up from 50.8 per cent of GDP in 2006 to 82.7 per cent in 2008. Record borrowing financed a wave of highly leveraged management buyouts – i.e. the debt contracted to pay for privatisation was loaded onto companies – which turned sour when stock markets tumbled during the crisis, the real estate bubble burst and construction companies went bust. Problems were exacerbated by a system of cross-shareholdings that had a knock-on effect on other companies which banks were forced to seize as collateral, increasing the weight of bad debt on their books and provoking a banking crisis, and, with the bailout of the banks, a full-blown public debt crisis (public debt tripled from 23 per cent of GDP in 2008 to just under 70 per cent in 2013).

Thus the Slovenian financial crisis is a crisis of European integration. It reveals that Slovenia has not escaped the regional crisis of dependency on external markets and finance. It is European capital that determines what, how and for which markets it will produce. From this perspective rising living standards are a barrier to further accumulation. FDI outflows in the 2000s are a sign that Slovenian capital is increasingly compelled to outsource production to the low-wage ex-Yugoslav region. The ambition to use outward investment to undermine domestic wages and welfare spending reveals that a Slovene exception to regional neoliberalism is an illusion.

---

a question of higher labour costs, but also reflected lower levels of technological innovation and capital investment (Marx's technical composition of capital). This criticism of the Lapavitsas's thesis, which we first put forward in Živković, 'Bankrot Evropske Unije', has subsequently been empirically confirmed by Guglielmo Carchedi. See G. Carchedi, 'From the Crisis of Surplus Value to the Crisis of the Euro', *Marx 2010*, 15 August 2012, at marx2010.weebly.com.

Regional Alternatives to EU Regionalism

The lessons of the Slovenian experience are clear. EU integration will further undermine the competitiveness of the Croatian and Serbian export sectors, resulting in a continuing transfer of value to the European banks, via the structural trade deficit and external debt. Once again debt will serve as the lever for another round of opening to foreign capital. So far foreign capital has been reluctant to invest in the real economy, outside limited branches, since it faces a series of small consumer markets that are weakly integrated and do not promise expanding sales. To create the kind of internal market that would be attractive to foreign investors, the EU imposed the Central European Free Trade Agreement (est. 2006) on the Western Balkans (including Serbia, Croatia, Bosnia, Macedonia, Montenegro, Albania, Kosovo and Moldova).[17]

CEFTA aims to create a free market (limited to tariff and quota reductions), not a customs or currency union: in other words, the aim is to prepare the region for integration with the EU, not to promote a regional integration that would conflict with EU integration. Integration takes the form of a 'hub and spokes' model in which trade and investment in each of these countries is diverted towards the EU. The EU has become the main trading partner of all countries, accounting in 2008 for 55 to 80 per cent of the imports and exports of the Western Balkans. Therefore, given the structural weakness of regional exports under the system of fixed exchange rates, CEFTA in fact represents a free trade zone for EU exports. Furthermore, as in the case of the trade agreements between the Socialist Federal Republic of Yugoslavia and the EEC, and of the first CEFTA

---

17   We draw in this section on A. Živković, 'Evropska integracija pre evropske integracije: o poreklu sadašnjih dužničkih kriza u bivšoj Jugoslaviji' [European Integration Before European Integration: On the Origins of the Present Debt Crises in the Former Yugoslavia], in S. Ćurković and M. Kostanić, eds, *Kriza eurointegracija – lijeve perspektive s periferije* [The Crisis of Euro-integration – Left Perspectives from the Periphery], Zagreb: Centar za radničke studije, forthcoming.

(established in 1991 between Poland, Hungary and the Czech Republic), access to the EU market is restricted precisely in areas of regional comparative advantage. Therefore the second CEFTA, just like the first, will mean the restructuring of the regional economy to serve the needs of the European multinationals and yet more deindustrialisation.[18] The present structural adjustment programmes in Slovenia and Croatia, under which the public sector, health provision and pensions are being opened to foreign capital in order to repay external debt, are the sign of things to come.

Due to the need to balance external deficits with the EU there has been a limited trend towards the revival of intraregional trade, facilitated but not caused by the liberalisation of tariff barriers under CEFTA. In many ways this is a return to the 1970s when difficulties in EEC markets forced Yugoslavia to reorient exports to Comecon markets. The problem here is that each ex-Yugoslav state tries to run a trade surplus with the others to compensate for deficits with the EU, thereby blocking the further development of intra-regional trade.[19] It is partly to address this difficulty that Slovenia has begun to extend import credits and outsource production to the region.[20]

The case of Slovenia, as the most advanced regional economy, shows the limits of intra-regional integration. It is both impelled by external dependency on EU finance and structurally limited by it. The EU model of Balkan integration spurs

---

18   By restricting East European exports in steel, textiles, agriculture and retail food the first CEFTA handed competitive advantage to EU capitals facing overcapacity and over-competition in EU markets. The outcome was a significant deindustrialisation of Eastern Europe. See P. Gowan, *The Global Gamble: Washington's Faustian Bid for World Dominance*, London: Verso, 1999.

19   The average share of regional trade bounced back to 16.2 per cent of overall trade. However, regional exports in 2000 represented 24.3 per cent of total exports, but imports only 12.4 per cent of total imports.

20   By 2010, total stock of Slovenian FDI into ex-Yugoslavia amounted to $5.25 billion, representing 69 per cent of total Slovenian stock of outward FDI. At present 1,400 Slovenian companies operate in Serbia and employ around 25,000 people. One-third of outstanding Slovenian bank loans to foreign non-banking sectors at the end of 2008 consisted of loans to Croatia (EUR 976 million), and a little more than a quarter (EUR 686 million) was to Serbia.

deindustrialisation and erects a fragile consumer economy built on a pyramid of debt. As we see in the current regional double-dip recession, without external finance there is no economic growth. Regional integration is caught between the Scylla of EU dependency and the Charybdis of the narrowness of the national market. The whole of the former Yugoslavia is locked into a process of peripheralisation.

EU regional policy for the Balkans is also part and parcel of the imperialist fragmentation of the region into a set of competing statelets and neo-colonial protectorates (Bosnia, Macedonia and Kosovo). Under the doctrine of 'regional cooperation' the EU has sought to police the new geopolitical order and prepare the region for EU integration, following on the heels of NATO expansion. A moveable set of iron curtains has been erected, dividing regional 'winners' and 'losers' in the race to European integration. In the 1990s the EU raised undeclared sanctions against Croatia when President Tudjman rejected regional cooperation outright, while Milošević was rewarded for guaranteeing the Dayton Agreement of 1995 with an EU trade agreement. Today, one of the main reasons for the advancement of Croatian EU accession is that the Serbian–Albanian struggle over Kosovo has become a proxy for struggles between the EU-US and Russia for hegemony in the post-Soviet East. EU regionalism thus creates a new arena for the nationalist struggles in the post-Yugoslav states.[21]

The EU model of regional financial integration is both iniquitous and unviable. Regional nation-states have not been able to withstand external economic and military pressures, and have tended to respond by competing with each other for external sponsorship in the vain and disastrous pursuit of regional hegemony. The alternative, I believe, lies in a Balkan

---

21   For example, an additional protocol on agriculture to CEFTA was blocked due to Serbian opposition to Kosovo's independence. Or take the July 2012 customs war between Serbia and Kosovo. Or even the fact that Greek opposition to the EU accession of Macedonia under its present name has now been redefined in terms of the EU's regional approach as an issue of 'regional cooperation', and as such has become official EU policy towards Macedonia!

federation,[22] that is, a form of cooperation uniting the peoples of the region in a common purpose: to liberate the region from external dependency and internal strife, maximise the welfare of its peoples and make them the subjects of their own destiny. The experience of the Socialist Federal Republic of Yugoslavia is proof that the logic of market competition itself produces uneven development, and can only exacerbate existing inequalities between regions, fanning nationalist resentments. Hence the first step towards a new regional order is a break with the political economy of financialisation, and its defence of the value of money (debt) at the expense of the destruction of commodities, in favour of a political economy that promotes the welfare of labour by redistributing resources towards employment, welfare provision and living standards. The nationalisation of the banks and industry would provide the instruments for regional coordination of investment to tackle inequalities in development; for the establishment of mechanisms of regional solidarity and cooperation; and for a participatory economics in which sovereignty resides in the direct producers and local communities. It is time to make a transition from the transition.

22   For the history of socialist discussion about the Balkan federation see A. Živković and D. Plavšić, eds, 'The Balkan Socialist Tradition: Balkan Socialism and the Balkan Federation, 1871–1915', *Revolutionary History Journal*, vol. 8(3), 2003.

CHAPTER 3

Workers and Unions After Yugoslavia

Marko Grdešić

The working class has undergone huge transformations since the break-up of Yugoslavia. In the 1980s, workers were still living in a society where they constituted more than a third of the adult population and employment was secure. Official ideology saw blue-collar workers as the most vital part of the society, as 'self-managers' and producers who worked with their hands; official unions tried hard to demobilise discontent while organising small-scale social policy. If we switch to the present, the picture is one in which workers are much less numerous, with more of them unemployed, retired or working in precarious employment positions, while unions are smaller, independent and often irrelevant. The prevailing ideology no longer celebrates the creativity and simple honesty of an idealised worker but chooses instead to celebrate the entrepreneur, who is often on the other side of the class divide.

During this time, unions in the former Yugoslavia, as the organisational representatives of workers, have made the transition from sleeping giant to niche actors in a divided labour market. In the old regime, unions were present in every workplace, but their activity was restricted to paperwork and petty services to their members, most famously distribution of apples, pork chops, holiday gifts for children, and, for the lucky ones, holidays on the Adriatic Sea. From a membership rate of close to 100 per cent, unions have, in most of the former Yugoslavia, fallen to roughly a third of the employed workforce. They cluster in the public sector, utilities and large companies. They remain very weak in the new private sector, which they have been unable to enter and unionise, often due to employer resistance.

The story of self-management and its transformation in the former Yugoslavia has several unique twists. In some aspects, self-management improved the picture for labour, compared to the rest of post-communist Eastern Europe. For example, workers' councils and social ownership of the economy gave workers a sense of empowerment and entitlement. These institutional innovations could have provided a basis for a transition to a corporatist or social-democratic model of economy. This was the case with Slovenia, where the old regime was transformed in an organic way in the early and mid 1990s. By the end of the decade, Slovenia began to look more and more like a corporatist economy, similar to Austria and Germany with respect to its industrial relations. Yet the last decade has seen a shift in Slovenia's trajectory. Although it is often held up as a model for leftist policy, this may soon no longer hold true. Even if people in other parts of the former Yugoslavia are often envious of Slovenia, its living standards and social achievements, it appears that it is converging with the industrial relations model that has established itself in the rest of the former Yugoslavia, as the northernmost former republic dismantles its corporatist institutions.

More than two decades since the start of the transition to liberal democracy, it now matters very little that the socialist regime was based on the ideas of self-management and not on the more statist socialism present in the other countries of Eastern Europe. Yet, despite the fact that self-management is receding into history, it remains something of a conundrum even today. During the socialist period, the picture of self-management was heavily ideological, obfuscating its real potential in mobilising workers for conflict. Since the regime preferred to view Yugoslav society as organic and harmonious, it steered self-management practices into convoluted procedures with a conservative bias. When the transition to liberal democracy began, the picture of self-management began to change but remained just as ideological. For neoliberals, self-management is seen, in a simplified way, as a highly inefficient economic system that stymied economic dynamism and initiative, a humorous delusion of a failed regime. Both images have made it very difficult to begin a public reassessment of self-management that would make it possible to learn from the past. Instead, the self-management experience is swept under the carpet.

Despite several deeply detrimental trends, such as deindustrialisation, corrupt privatisation, impoverishment and war, workers have on occasion shown not only a capacity to collectively organise, but even a capacity for militancy. In several cases they have organised campaigns to save their companies from bankruptcy and suspicious privatisation, sometimes through factory occupations. Yet labour movements in most of the former Yugoslavia, with the partial exception of Slovenia, remain internally heterogeneous. Pockets of militancy and several very capable and motivated unions and unionists cannot compensate for the overall lack of organisational capacity and policy vision that the unions demonstrate on the aggregate level. Such hampered labour movements are also functioning in the context of weak states, weak civil societies and economic structures typical of the European periphery. Slovenia is a partial exception to this description, yet it has, since adopting the euro, begun to show some of the same symptoms that have hampered other countries in the region.

In order to break out of the equilibrium which is asserting itself across the former Yugoslavia, more than the current practices and ideas will be required. In particular, the ideological hegemony of neoliberalism has evolved to the point where neoliberal ideas and policies require no justification but are accepted as common sense. Workers and unions are ill-equipped to attack this development unless they can form a broader societal coalition of forces.

Industrial Relations

The industrial relations systems that emerged after the break-up of Yugoslavia have roughly the same contours in most of the former Yugoslav republics. Union membership is at around a third of the workforce. According to data from EIRO,[1] the union membership rate is 44 per cent in Slovenia, 35 per cent in Croatia, 30 per cent in Bosnia-Herzegovina, 35 per cent in Serbia, 26 per cent in Montenegro, 28 per cent in Macedonia (for Kosovo the only reported figure is 90 per cent in the public sector). Union membership figures are much higher in the public sector than in the private sector. Employers are organised at roughly the same levels as unions. The membership of employer organisations is 25 to 30 per cent in Croatia, 30 per cent in Serbia, 6 per cent in Bosnia-Herzegovina, 24 per cent in Macedonia, 16 per cent in Kosovo, 65 per cent in Montenegro (the latter is a self-reported and probably highly inflated number). The one exception is Slovenia where the figure stands between 80 to 90 per cent. This is due to the fact that Slovenia relied on the chamber of commerce as the employers' representative in collective bargaining. However, recent legislative changes may lead to less organisation on the employers' side. In particular, the chamber's policy of obligatory membership for all companies has been changed in favour of voluntary membership.

There are few differences in collective bargaining in most of the former Yugoslavia. Collective agreements are signed predominantly at the company level. Sectoral bargaining exists but is weak. Several countries have nation-wide collective agreements but the full implementation of these agreements has proven difficult. As a consequence of such general collective agreements, several countries in the region have almost complete collective bargaining coverage, i.e. the percentage of employees covered by a collective agreement is close to 100: 96 per cent in Slovenia, 100 per cent in Bosnia-Herzegovina, Montenegro and Macedonia. Elsewhere, the collective bargaining coverage stands at around 60 per cent in Croatia and 55 per cent in Serbia. Since the economic crisis began, austerity measures have begun to chip away at the collectively bargained

---

1   EIRO (European Industrial Relations Observatory), at http://eurofound.europa.eu/eiro.

security that employees, especially in the public sector, managed to secure. As a consequence, the collective bargaining coverage may drop further still. Minimum wage and working week regulation exists in all of these countries with the minimum wage set at between 30 and 40 per cent of the average wage (all data from EIRO).

Labour movements in the region continue to rely on the old trade union apparatuses inherited from the socialist period. Where the transition to liberal democracy was more successful, most obviously in Slovenia, transformations of the old union confederations were quicker. In Slovenia, but also in Croatia in the early 1990s, the old trade unions quickly became politically autonomous and began to forcefully push for collective bargaining. In other countries, for example Serbia, the old trade union confederation continued to align itself with the government, often to the detriment of the living standards of a large membership base.[2] Since the early 1990s, only in Slovenia has the main trade union confederation proved to be a consistently capable and strong actor. New trade union confederations have been formed in all countries in the region, mostly as splinter factions, but have much fewer members. Therefore, the large trade union confederations inherited from the socialist period remain important, even if they are often inert, bureaucratic and distant from their rank and file members.

Union fragmentation is an especially chronic problem. Ideological rivalries between unions are rare, but distrust and personal rivalries between union leaders are rampant. Unions have been side-tracked by struggles over union property inherited from the socialist period, as well as struggles over the exact

---

2   M. Arandarenko, 'Waiting for the Workers: Explaining Labor Quiescence in Serbia', in S. Crowley and D. Ost, eds, *Workers After Workers' States: Labor and Politics in Postcommunist Eastern Europe*, Lanham, MD: Rowman and Littlefield, 2001, 159–79; M. Grdešić, 'Mapping the Paths of the Yugoslav Model: Labour Strength and Weakness in Slovenia, Croatia and Serbia', *European Journal of Industrial Relations*, vol. 14, 2008, 133–151; T. Meszmann, 'The Role of Trade Unions in Economic and Political Reforms after 1988: Serbia and Slovenia Compared', paper presented at the *Tenth Annual Kokkalis Graduate Student Workshop on Southeastern Europe*, Harvard University, Cambridge, MA, 2008.

number of members and their legitimacy to bargain collectively as defined in representativeness laws. However, the most obvious problem for unions is their clustering in the public sector. New medium and small companies in the private sector are virtually union-free. Instead, unions have adopted the approach of lobbying for national legislation or national collective agreements to provide some protection to employees in the private sector. Yet implementation is patchy and oversight by state officials and inspectors is weak. Furthermore, even this amount of protection may be rolled back relatively quickly, as the economic crisis has shown. Unions do not have the organisational strength to mount large drives in the private sector and when they have attempted to reach new members they have often met with employer resistance which the state has done little to curtail.

The clustering of unions and collective agreements in the public sector has led to a segmented labour market of insiders and outsiders. Labour codes in most of the former Yugoslavia offer substantial protection to those with indeterminate contracts, which has led to a drive, on behalf of employers, to remove labour market 'rigidities'. Quantitative scores for employment protection legislation are slightly higher in the region than the OECD average.[3] Given the comparatively generous severance packages and notice periods stipulated in labour codes, most employers have avoided creating new jobs with indefinite contracts and have embraced fixed-term contracts instead. This division between insiders and outsiders corresponds, in its broad contours, to a division between old and young workers, the public and the private sector. Those outside the protected 'core' workforce can more easily be hired and fired. Slovenia is not exempt from this trend. In fact, the percentage of workers with fixed-term contracts is higher in Slovenia than elsewhere. According to Eurostat, in Slovenia around 19 per cent of all employees have fixed-term contracts, while in Croatia the figure stands at 13 per cent, in Macedonia

---

3   OECD EPL index, at www.oecd.org.

at 14 per cent, and the EU average is around 14 per cent.[4] The segmentation of the labour market has led to an increase in anti–public sector rhetoric. Workers in the public sector are demonised as parasitic and lazy. Unions have proved timid in their reaction to this offensive and have not positioned themselves as defenders of all employees, whether they work in the public or the private sector.

Strikes and Protests

Workers and unions have at times shown that collective mobilisation is not only possible but is an effective way to influence politics. For some countries in the region, the 1990s were a period of political instability in which the transition to liberal democracy was incomplete and imperfect. In Croatia and Serbia, unions were among the most important social actors in the democratisation process. For example, in Serbia, the trade union confederation Nezavisnost not only pushed for collective bargaining but also adopted a resolute anti-war stance. In the immediate lead-up to the fall of Serbia's leader Slobodan Milošević in 2000, it was a worker protest, specifically in the national electrical utility, that was crucial.[5] In Croatia, a large protest in the centre of Zagreb, organised in 1998 by unions, was a key event that led to the downfall of the nationalist government. Given the weakness of political parties and the practical impotence of parliaments, it was often unions that became the most consistently pro-democratic social forces. This contribution to democratisation is yet to be fully acknowledged.

After the relative consolidation of liberal democracy in the region, worker protests did not disappear although they changed in form. Given the more permissive political context of the 2000s and, just as importantly, given accelerating privatisation

---

4   Eurostat, at www.epp.eurostat.ec.europa.eu.

5   D. Marinković, 'Strike at Kolubara – A Case Study', *South-East Europe Review for Labour and Social Affairs*, vol. 6, 2003, 41–72.

and industrial restructuring, workers in the region engaged in a wave of company-level activism. Reacting in particular to non-transparent and frequently corrupt privatisation, workers turned to protests, marches, even factory occupations. In the most well-known cases, workers organised 'headquarters' (*stožeri* or *štabovi*) to defend their companies from outside speculators, to secure ongoing production or even to take over the everyday functioning of firms.[6] Sometimes this approach managed to attract enough media attention to enable workers to defend their interests.

Often, these measures were acts of desperation. For example, workers in a bauxite mine in Nikšić, Montenegro, closed themselves in the mine, placed explosives at the entrance and threatened to kill themselves. Hunger strikes have been common in Serbia. In one especially gory incident, a worker in a textile company in Novi Pazar, Serbia, cut off his finger to attract media attention. Where workers had more resources and a capable union, they managed to achieve more success. A more favourable outcome could also be expected in towns where much of the population either works in the same company or has a family member that does. Such 'company towns' are, for example, Kutina in Croatia and Kragujevac in Serbia. The fertiliser company Petrokemija in Kutina is an example of a successful campaign in which workers opposed shady privatisation and secured the continuation of production. Zastava Namenska in Kragujevac is another example of a militant union that managed to defend its interests. Union militancy is further augmented by the fact that, when workers in an arms company organise a factory occupation, they will most probably have access to weapons.

The most famous example of workers taking over the everyday functioning of a company is Jugoremedija, a pharmaceutical company in Zrenjanin, Serbia. Yet the fate of such

---

6   M. Grdešić, 'Uspon i pad stožera za obranu kompanija u Hrvatskoj' [The Rise and Fall of Headquarters for the Defense of Companies in Croatia], *Revija za sociologiju*, vol. 38, 2007, 55–67.

companies now depends not only on a volatile political and legal context in which they have few allies, but also on their ability to find business partners to whom they can sell their products. The wave of factory occupations and company-level activism in the former Yugoslavia bears some similarity to the Latin American movement of 'recovered factories' (*fábricas recuperadas*), but workers in the former Yugoslavia have not attempted to establish parallel economic structures. The highly uncertain future of such worker-run companies is exemplified by Jedinstvo, a metalworks company in Zagreb, where only two workers became managers and owners and have to conduct business with conventional companies.

The exact volume of strikes is difficult to gauge. Data collection is poor in all of the former Yugoslavia, including Slovenia. In 2009, when the economic crisis hit the region, the number of strikes increased, most notably in Serbia, but also in Bosnia-Herzegovina. According to the little data available, strike levels appear to be relatively high. For example, in Serbia in the summer of 2009, a total of forty-five companies with 30,000 workers went on strike.[7] In Croatia, data on the mandatory mediation of collective disputes show that industrial conflict is far from absent (data from EIRO). There were fifty-two cases of mediation in 2008 (twenty-five were settled), eighty-eight in 2009 (twenty-nine were settled) and 122 in 2010 (sixty-five were settled). Strikes in manufacturing are often motivated by late payment or non-payment of wages, often for as long as six months, while strikes in the public sector are motivated by a push for higher wages. The education sector has been especially lively. Most countries in the region have adopted strike laws that require complicated procedures if the strike is to be legal at all. This makes striking unattractive to workers. Furthermore, strikes lose much of their power in a setting in which owners and managers may not be at all interested in continuing production. Instead, many workers have turned to street protests and attempts to attract media attention.

---

7   Figures from OECD and SSSS, at www.sindikat.rs.

Although strike and protest levels appear to be moderately high, it should be mentioned that they occur in a public climate and political environment that show little interest in worker struggles. The partial exception to this is Slovenia, which will be discussed shortly. The bar for successful campaigns is set very high, so that only workers with sufficient resources or community support can achieve the required levels of activism. Furthermore, all of these protests have been defensive in nature. Workers have either demanded that their back wages be paid, that corrupt privatisation be stopped, or that their rights in collective agreements not be cut further. Very rarely have workers gone on the offensive and attempted to expand their rights and influence.

The Slovenian Exception

Slovenia presents an exception to much of the trend described above. Yet it is also important to emphasise that it is a partial exception.[8] In the early 1990s a moderate political elite attempted to build a corporatist or social-democratic economy akin to the economic models of Germany and Austria. They initiated a process of top-level tripartite bargaining and signed a series of social pacts that regulated wage policy as well as other policy areas. This process was not free of union pressure or of employer resistance, but overall, the governments of the 1990s proved receptive to labour's demands.[9] In a period when the independent Slovenian state was just being built, when the Yugoslav market disappeared and the uncertain accession process to the European Union began, an atmosphere emerged that made broad consensus viable and facilitated collective bargaining and concertation. The government was at the time

---

8   S. Crowley and M. Stanojević, 'Varieties of Capitalism, Power Resources and Historical Legacies: Explaining the Slovenian Exception', *Politics and Society*, vol. 39, 269–95.

9   M. Stanojević, 'Workers' Power in Transition Economies: The Cases of Serbia and Slovenia', *European Journal of Industrial Relations*, vol. 9, 2011, 283–301.

headed by Janez Drnovšek, a politician whose patience with and acceptance of union demands has been unmatched since.

The Slovenian economic model relied on gradual reforms of the welfare state, tripartite bargaining with the chamber of commerce as the employers' representative, and modest privatisation which, in the manufacturing sector especially, favoured insider coalitions of workers and managers.[10] All segments of this approach have been attacked in recent years. In particular, mandatory membership in the chamber of commerce was suspended in 2006. If more and more companies opt out of the chamber system, the required level of membership for collective agreement extension (for sectoral agreements) may be in jeopardy. Should this occur, collective bargaining may quickly become decentralised until it is restricted to company-level bargaining. In the public sector, on the other hand, collective bargaining has remained centralised. In short, the direction in which Slovenia is heading is the industrial relations system as it exists elsewhere in the region.

The peculiarity of the initial transitional years seems difficult to replicate. Once economic growth not only returned but transformed Slovenia into a de facto developed country, and once membership in the EU was secure, the atmosphere of crisis that facilitated the initial episode of corporatist policy making disappeared and the conditions for the Slovenian alternative path unravelled. 'Gradualism', the Slovenian model of transition that was opposed to shock therapy, was criticised and openly attacked by economists and politicians on the right. Membership of the European Monetary Union has worsened the position of Slovenian exporters, the industrial backbone that was crucial for the growth of the 1990s.

Unions have attempted to stop or soften the new neoliberal push. In this they have had a fair bit of success. Large union protests in Ljubljana in 2005 and 2007 defeated some proposals,

---

10   J. Mencinger, 'Transition to a National and Market Economy: A Gradualist Approach', in M. Mrak, M. Rojec and C. Silva-Jauregui, eds, *Slovenia: From Yugoslavia to the European Union*, Washington, DC: World Bank, 2004.

such as the flat tax (which exists in Bosnia, Montenegro, Serbia, Kosovo and Macedonia, but not in Croatia). Unions have also been able to stop certain measures through referendums. They have successfully organised several one-day general warning strikes (in the public sector) in order to combat cuts in benefits and wages, most recently in April 2012 and January 2013. Popular discontent exploded in the winter of 2012 with large protests motivated by a variety of grievances in several Slovenian towns. The diffuse character of this discontent has made the protests, though impressive in size and not without a palpable sense of drama, mostly without real consequences. Unions participated as one strand in this protest movement but were unable to offer a proactive agenda. The general thrust of the demands has been one of opposition to corruption and cronyism. Politicians and political parties are attacked *tout court*: all politicians are the same, and all are corrupt. There is also a dose of nostalgia for the early 1990s when Slovenia won an independent state and began to establish the rule of law. The popular cry is that Slovenians must return to the year 1991 and rebuild the system, which the elites have usurped.

A progressive leftist agenda may be compatible with such vague but widely disseminated popular opinions. However, such an agenda has not yet emerged. Though Slovenian unions are livelier and more capable than unions elsewhere in the region, even they have not been able to come up with an appropriate response. Yet, given the fact that right-wing elites and employers are dismantling the system that the unions tried very hard to build in the 1990s, the unions will be faced with a choice of sitting future battles out or turning towards more militant solutions.

Self-management Then and Now

There has been a massive ideological shift since the break-up of Yugoslavia. This shift does not matter quite as much when it comes to the relevance of markets, since Yugoslavia had already experimented with markets in the 1960s. Instead, the crucial change is the place that blue-collar workers occupy in the hegemonic discourses of each regime. The ideology of socialist self-management celebrated the worker as the foundation of communist society: as a producer who uses his hands and manual labour to create tangible products and commodities. All other groups in society lived off the back of manual labour, as its superstructure or its appendage. Furthermore, each worker was, at least on paper, a 'self-manager', i.e. a citizen of the economic democracy that the regime wanted to build. The reality, of course, was different, since the Party's distaste for, and desire to control, autonomous organisation trumped the ideological goals of industrial democracy. Even so, the regime's institutional changes, such as workers' councils and social ownership of the economy, not only moved the country away from the Soviet model of socialism but also gave workers a real sense of empowerment, entitlement and, when reality did not correspond to their expectations, a powerful sense of frustration.

Current regimes in the countries that have emerged in the former Yugoslavia have no ideology which could be called formal or official. Even so, neoliberal ideas have become so pervasive that they occupy the same place that socialist self-management used to. According to this worldview, workers are remnants of a bygone era. They are no longer simple but noble producers but, at best, part of an anonymous mass of citizens each with the same vote every four years. The creative segment of society is located elsewhere, in the class of entrepreneurs who turn ideas into economic ventures. Workers depend on the good will of the new creative class. As workers, they are superfluous to the regime, where they once used to be the cornerstone. This Copernican revolution in ruling discourse has completely altered the rules of the game for workers and unions. They have thus far proved unable to find an alternative source of legitimation for themselves as workers that would give them more clout when they enter into conflict or negotiation with economic and political elites. There have been several attempts to find a new discursive grounding for workers: as workers who are also war veterans (Petrokemija in Croatia) or as workers who are also shareholders (Jugoremedija in Serbia). None of these framings has proved sufficiently resonant.

Discussions of workers or of self-management have a hard time gathering momentum in the public sphere. Even when they protest, workers do not refer to self-management in any way. Some discussion has started within the more militant unions, but has not penetrated the core of the union movement. If elites bring up the topic of self-management at all, it is usually dismissed as an amusing quirk of the old system. To ask whether self-management achieved any worthwhile goals is taboo. Learning from the past is thus closed off. For neoliberals, self-management was hopelessly delusional in its ambition to blend economic democracy with economic efficiency. Nothing beyond a quick dismissive or satirical remark can be expected when public discussion turns to the subject.

The old regime is partly to blame for this since it never allowed open discussion of the realities of self-management but preferred to present a glossy ideological version. Additionally, the regime's tendency to over-regulate self-management made most of its practices convoluted and, because of this complexity, rather conservative. What it nevertheless did achieve was to give workers a sense of empowerment, relevance and, more concretely, an institutional platform that could be used in each workplace.[11] Those are precisely the things that are missing in the current situation.

---

11   For an introductory list of the most informative readings on Yugoslav self-management see: V. Arzenšek, *Struktura i pokret* [Structure and Movement], Belgrade: Institut društvenih nauka, 1984; E. Comisso, *Workers' Control Under Plan and Market: Implications of Yugoslav Self-Management*, New Haven, CT, and London: Yale University Press, 1979; IDE (Industrial Democracy in Europe Research Group), *Industrial Democracy in Europe Revisited*, Oxford and New York: Oxford University Press, 1993; G. Musić, 'Yugoslavia: Workers' Self-Management as State Paradigm', in I. Ness and D. Azzellini, eds, *Ours to Master and to Own: Workers' Control from Commune to the Present*, Chicago: Haymarket Books, 2011, 172–190; V. Rus and F. Adam, *Moć i nemoć samoupravljanja* [The Power and Powerlessness of Self-Management], Zagreb: Globus, 1989; D. Rusinow, *The Yugoslav Experiment, 1948–1974*, Berkeley: University of California Press, 1977; S. Woodward, *Socialist Unemployment: The Political Economy of Yugoslavia 1945–1990*, Princeton, NJ: Princeton University Press, 1995.

For a new generation of leftist activists, industrial democracy is a very attractive goal, especially its component of direct democracy and decentralised and autonomous decision making.[12] Yet finding a place for direct democracy within the contours of the rather firmly established liberal democratic regimes based on representative democracy and a privately owned economy has proved elusive. Furthermore, this new emphasis on direct democracy is disconnected from the legacy of self-management. It is, as yet, too early to say if this new leftist agenda, forged mostly among students, civil society and the youth, can find an organic link to the Yugoslav past.

Outlook: Can Workers and Unions Forge a New Agenda?

Formulating a labour-friendly response to neoliberal hegemony is complicated by several structural factors. In particular, state weakness is a chronic problem in the region, with the usual gradation from the better organised north-west to the more chaotic south-east. Some states, such as those in Montenegro or Kosovo, are so weak that they are completely captured by particular interests and show a very weak capacity to organise public services, collect taxes and enforce legislation. The picture is much better in Croatia and Slovenia in particular but, even here, labour inspectorates are underfunded and understaffed. Therefore, even the basic implementation of labour codes or collective agreements cannot be taken for granted. Furthermore, the capacity of the state to pursue creative developmental solutions outside the neoliberal paradigm is hindered by weak state capacity.

For workers and union activists, mobilisation has often been problematic because of a lack of allies in civil society. Not only does state weakness mean that sometimes a solution will not be implemented even if all agree to it, but the weakness of

---

12   S. Horvat and I. Štiks, *Pravo na pobunu: Uvod u anatomiju građanskog otpora* [The Right to Rebellion: Introduction to the Anatomy of Civic Resistance], Zagreb: Faktura, 2010.

civil society means that more militant worker activists have a hard time finding partners and support. This problem has been less acute in small towns where the community is easier to organise or where the local population is directly tied to the fate of a single company. Building a progressive leftist agenda will therefore have to be connected to building horizontal links and strengthening potential allies in society. Communication between such groups as, for example, blue-collar unions, farmer associations and university students is weak to non-existent, although each group has frequently mobilised by itself. There have been some tentative attempts to forge such links across social sectors, for example during the student occupations at the University of Zagreb in 2009, or in the 'Workers' and Punks' University' in Ljubljana.

And finally, the economic outlook for most of the countries in the region is not bright. The current economic crisis has additionally limited the scope of what is perceived as a viable policy. Most of these countries are located on Europe's periphery and therefore cannot be incorporated into the European economy on favourable terms. Slovenia is the partial exception once again, since its light manufacturing sector has managed to insert itself into Western European commodity and production chains. Yet the loss of monetary sovereignty has hurt the export sector in Slovenia and since the mid 2000s it has, like most of its neighbours to the south-east, relied on domestic consumption, speculative construction booms and financialisation. Paradoxically, those countries that have more state capacity to pursue a heterodox developmental policy, such as Slovenia and Croatia, are also more constrained by the euro or the EU's *acquis communautaire*. European integration laggards have, at least in principle, more room to pursue such policies but do not have the state capacity to do so.

If workers and unions are going to achieve any measure of success in the upcoming struggles with neoliberal doctrine they will have to reach out to other groups in society. Unions need first to reach out to each other, overcoming internal strife, then to workers with fixed-term contracts, and then to workers in the non-unionised sectors. After that, a progressive coalition of unions, farmers and the academic community should be considered. Should such a horizontal alliance be forged, whether with or without the support of a political party, all elites would surely pay attention. Without an effort to engage other actors, the unions will be doomed to a fate of defending an ever-shrinking set of rights.

PART II

Re-imagining the Post-Socialist Balkans

CHAPTER 4

Re-imagining the Balkans[1]

Maria Todorova

Since the publication of *Imagining the Balkans* almost fifteen years ago, political events in Europe have eloquently illustrated the law of unintended consequences. After 1989, Central Europe's emancipatory ideology, over which much scholarly ink was spilled, became a device entitling its participants to a share of privileges, most importantly accession to NATO and a place at the front of the queue for the European Union. While the final historical verdict may legitimate this strategy, an unintended consequence has been the death of 'Central Europe' as an idea. Extending a protective arm around the old centres of the Habsburg Empire, the West, motivated in part by sentiment, neatly followed the new trench lines of Samuel Huntington's clash of civilisations. Tony Judt wrote in 1997 that this would create 'a sort of depressed Eurosuburb beyond which "Byzantine Europe" would be made to fend for itself, too close to Russia for the West to make an aggressive show of absorption and engagement'.[2]

Things changed almost overnight with the beginning of NATO expansion in 1997. Since 1989, the question of the alliance's mission has never ceased to be high on both the European and the US agenda. With the disbanding of the Warsaw Pact in 1991 and the disintegration of the Soviet Union in 1992, NATO's

---

1   This text is a version of a lecture given in Paris on 27 June 2011, which is based on the afterword to the new edition of M. Todorova, *Imagining the Balkans*, New York and Oxford: Oxford University Press, 2009, and the introduction to M. Todorova and Z. Gille, eds, *Postcommunist Nostalgia*, New York: Berghahn, 2010.

2   T. Judt, 'A Grand Illusion? An Essay on Europe', quoted in *New York Times*, 24 January 1997, A2.

main adversaries and targets ceased to exist, and with them its *raison d'être*. There were serious plans in Europe to disband NATO and build alternative security systems confined to the continent. Yet NATO remained the only truly transatlantic institution in which the United States continued to play the role of a European great power, and it was reluctant to lose this position. The United States was and continues to be the chief advocate for further NATO expansion, despite a 1990 pledge that NATO would not expand beyond German borders, while Europe's proximity to and dependence on Russian natural resources make it more circumspect. In 1997 three former Warsaw Pact countries – Poland, Hungary and the Czech Republic – were invited to join the alliance, and became members in 1999. The invitation was extended to Lithuania, Latvia, Estonia, Slovenia, Slovakia, Bulgaria and Romania in 2002, all of which joined in 2004. In 2008 another two Balkan countries – Croatia and Albania – were invited and Macedonia is bound to follow soon. This trajectory of NATO's evolution, alongside the development of events that led to the disintegration of Yugoslavia, brought about the unexpected intersection of two processes. Until 1999, the international community confined its pressure on and involvement in Yugoslavia almost exclusively to the United Nations. There were a few minor UN-sanctioned NATO operations after the Srebrenica massacre and before the Dayton Accord, including the maritime enforcement of the arms embargo and the brief bombing of Republika Srpska in Bosnia in 1995. However, this intervention, as well as contemporaneous events in Somalia and even the First Gulf War, were aimed at restoring or preserving the status quo. Even the ethnic cleansing of Krajina, the secessionist Serb enclave in Croatia, where hundreds of thousands of Serbs were swept away by the Croatian army in 1995, was done with the active approval and tacit participation of the United States.

The three-month-long NATO bombing of Yugoslavia in 1999, for all intents and purposes carried out by the United States, marked a new precedent. It effectively underwrote the secessionist claims of a minority population and set the stage for Kosovo's full independence some nine years later – another precedent, whose ominous repercussions play out in the Caucasus and northern Africa today. 'Even at the time of the NATO air strikes, it was difficult to distinguish an intervention to prevent genocide, from one intended to support the long-term political aims of a guerrilla army.'[3] This became a fundamental departure from the treatment of similar conflicts (between Palestinians and Jews in Israel/Palestine, Kurds and Turks in Turkey, Kurds and Arabs in the First Gulf War, and others) where sovereignty and territorial integrity had been the dominant principle since the end of the Second World War. In another respect the Kosovo war saw what one observer has called 'the rise of humanitarian hawks' and became a dress rehearsal for the American unilateralism that culminated in the Second Gulf War. In this respect, the Balkans once again became a laboratory for experimentation with new approaches and solutions. There were a host of political and moral considerations for the 1999 intervention, not least among them the desire to revive the last European organisation in which the United States played a leading role. Whatever the motivations, the bombing had unintended consequences. Before the Kosovo war, the dominant paradigm applied to the Balkans translated into the practical ghettoisation of the region. The pre-Kosovo European Union visa regime absolved Central Europe but not the rest of Eastern Europe and the Balkans, where restrictions were placed on the movement of populations. This was *balkanism* in action. The rhetorical legitimisation of the 1999 intervention – as defence of universal human rights – effectively brought the Balkans back into the sphere of Western politics. Both the bombing and its aftermath bound Europeans and Americans much more closely – even inextricably – to the Balkans. Through KFOR, the NATO-led force under UN mandate, both Americans and Europeans began running two official protectorates (Kosovo and Bosnia-Herzegovina). There

---

3   C. King, 'The Kosovo Precedent', *NewsNet: The Newsletter of the AAASS*, vol. 48(3), May 2008, 1.

emerged, for the first time, a significant lobby among Eurocrats who believed that it would be in Europe's best interests to bring the Balkans into the European sphere, rather than ghettoise them. Although a general EU expansion fatigue has set in, Croatia, one of the five official Balkan candidates alongside Macedonia and Turkey and, more recently, Montenegro and Serbia, was admitted in 2013. Albania and the other remaining Yugoslav splinters have all been recognised as potential candidates. All of this has been accompanied by the curious but predictable subsiding of the balkanist rhetoric, though it is still encountered abundantly in journalism and fiction, as well as scholarship. Even the vocal and often spiteful objections to Turkey's accession focus on Islam, Middle Eastern culture, women's or human rights, but are not clad in the balkanist rhetoric.

Now journalists too are becoming careful of how they articulate opinions about the Balkans. We even have a new politically correct designation: the Western Balkans. During the Cold War, Yugoslavia was neatly exempt from any connection to the Balkans, while its civil war in the 1990s was generalised as a Balkan war, although none of the other Balkan countries – Greece, Bulgaria, Romania, Turkey, even Albania – were in danger of entering it. With the changed political conjuncture, the Western Balkans is a problematic zone, and the rest are exempt from the designation. Thus, while the balkanist rhetoric is still with us, conveniently submerged but readily at hand, it no longer serves power politics. *Balkanism* has not disappeared, but has shifted, for the time being, from the centre stage of politics.

This may allow us to reflect more calmly on the scholarly project of making sense of the Balkans. I argued that a specific discourse, *balkanism*, moulds attitudes and actions towards the Balkans and could be treated as the most persistent form or 'mental map' in which information about the Balkans is placed, most notably in journalistic, political and literary output. By introducing the category *balkanism*, I was directly inspired by – and at the same time invited critical comparison to – Said's *orientalism*. While, understandably, most readers' attention was dedicated to the six chapters of *Imagining the Balkans* that described, exposed and critiqued the balkanist discourse, the seventh chapter, dealing with the *realia* of the Balkans, remained overshadowed, and the book was perceived by some solely as a deconstructivist exercise. Others, conversely, felt that this final chapter, in which I introduced the concept of historical legacy, deviated from a modernist approach back to a realist and empirical one. Here I will try to address the topic relevant to this discussion: the general relevance of the notion of historical legacy. When I started writing this book, whose working title was 'Balkanism', I found to my surprise and delight that *balkanism* was an uninhabited category, something exceptionally rare in the humanities. This circumstance allowed me to use *balkanism* as both a mirror and a foil of *orientalism*. To put it succinctly, *balkanism* expresses the idea that explanatory approaches to phenomena in the Balkans often rest upon a discourse or a stable system of stereotypes that place the Balkans in a cognitive straitjacket. I argued for the historicity of *balkanism*, which was shaped as a discourse in the early decades of the twentieth century, but whose genealogy can be traced to patterns of representation from the sixteenth century onward. I thus insisted on the historical grounding of *balkanism* in the Ottoman period, when the designation *Balkan* first entered the peninsula. Arguably, some aspects of the *balkanist* discourse grew out of the earlier schism between the churches of Rome and Constantinople, but the most salient aspects emerged from the Ottoman period.

The *Balkans* have a number of different incarnations, which can be roughly grouped into four categories. At its simplest, 'Balkan' is a name: initially, the name of a mountain, used increasingly since the fifteenth century when it first appeared, until the nineteenth century, when it was applied to the peninsula and region as a whole. 'Balkan' is also used as a metaphor. By the beginning of the twentieth century, it became a pejorative, triggered by the events accompanying the disintegration of the Ottoman Empire and the creation of small, weak, economically backward and dependent nation-states, striving to modernise. The difficulties of this modernisation process and the accompanying excesses of nationalism created a situation in which the Balkans began to serve as a symbol for the aggressive, intolerant, barbarian, semi-developed, semi-civilised and semi-oriental. It is this use and its present utilisation in the real world of politics – *balkanism* – that shapes attitudes and actions towards the Balkans. Unlike the Orient, however, the Balkans can be addressed as a scholarly category of analysis – a concrete geographic region – and in this capacity it is currently most often used as a synonym for south-eastern Europe. Finally, the Balkans can be approached and interpreted through the notion of historical legacy, which is intimately intertwined with the character of the Balkans as a region and, thus, linked to its concreteness.

How do we study historical regions? Regions have attracted much scholarly attention in recent years and are now studied with all the seriousness once conferred primarily on national identities. Where regional allegiances were once seen simply as leftovers of provincial mentalities, today they are often seen as places of resistance to centralised authority and harbingers of reform. They can also be seen as a more adequate structural base to accommodate ethnic or economic differences. Today, the category is utilised for territorial expanses of different sizes, and regions are studied as both sub-national entities and supra-national formations. In today's increasingly interdependent world certain regions may supersede the nation-state, or at least attempt to do so. Such is the ongoing experiment with the European Union, primarily an economic unit but with growing political and cultural ambitions, which symbolically appropriated the name of the larger geographic region: Europe. Some scholars, in an effort to move beyond the territorial tautology, point out that in order to be marked off from the outside world, regions have to possess some internal similarities, cohesion and affinity. Europe can be approached as the component of different intersecting regional formations, of which geography is but one aspect: the region of Western Christianity; of contact and complex historical interplay between the three monotheistic world religions; of nations; the core region of world colonisation and industrialisation. Numerous other definitions might be applied within the framework of different disciplines or approaches. Historians in particular are caught between two poles: one is Marc Bloch's notion that French history does not exist: there is only European history; against which there is well-argued scepticism that European history could ever be approached holistically in any methodologically convincing way. Though it often is, Eastern Europe should not simply be identified as a territorial sub-region of Europe – and neither should south-eastern Europe or the Balkans be treated as sub-regions of the sub-region. As territorial sub-regions, they are locked in a hierarchical matrix where they become, to utilise some Jakobsonian terminology, *marked* categories. At American and European universities, if a general position in European history is advertised, it is usually specified as British, German, French, Italian, Spanish, Russian, even Irish history, while Polish, Czech, Hungarian, Romanian, Bulgarian, Serb, Croatian, Macedonian, Latvian, Estonian, Albanian and other national histories are subsumed under the umbrella of East European history. 'Eastern Europe', then, is a *marked* category as a subfield of European history. The rest of Europe, however, is not represented by commensurate categories of 'North-eastern Europe', 'West Central Europe', or even 'Western Europe'. These are, then, *unmarked* categories. Marked categories become different while unmarked categories retain the power as the standard against which the rest must be positioned.

It is against this background that I introduce the notion of historical legacy, which focuses on the element of time. Historical legacy retains the valuable features of spatiality while simultaneously refining the vector of time, making it more historically specific. Any region can be approached as the complex result of the interplay of numerous historical periods, traditions and legacies, and of these categories, historical periods are the most straightforward. Tradition and legacy are less so. Yet, while tradition involves a conscious selection of elements bequeathed from the past, legacy encompasses everything – chosen or not

– that is handed down from the past. In this sense, it neither betrays the past nor surrenders it to active meddling. Legacy as an abstract signifier is neutral. For purely cognitive purposes I distinguish between legacy as continuity and legacy as perception. Legacy as continuity is the survival (and gradual decline) of some of the characteristics of the entity immediately before its collapse. Legacy as perception, on the other hand, is the articulation and re-articulation of how the entity is thought about at different times by different individuals or groups. These should not be interpreted as 'real' versus 'imagined' characteristics: the characteristics of continuity are themselves often perceptual, and perceptions are no less a matter of continuous real social facts. In both cases, the categories designate social facts, which are at different removes from experience, but in the instance of perception, the social fact is removed yet a further step from immediate reality.

Let me provide two concrete examples from the Balkans and Eastern Europe to illustrate each type of legacy. If we look at the numerous historical periods, traditions and legacies that have shaped south-eastern Europe, some overlap and others are completely segregated; some play themselves out in the same geographic space while others involve different macro-regions. These periods and legacies can be classified according to their influence in different spheres of social life. In the religious sphere, one can single out the Christian, Muslim and Judaic traditions, along with their numerous sects and branches; in the sphere of art and culture, the legacies of the pre-Greeks, the Greeks, and numerous ethnic groups that settled the peninsula; in social and demographic terms the legacies of large and incessant migrations, ethnic diversity, semi-nomadism, a large egalitarian agricultural sphere, and late urbanisation alongside a constant continuity of urban life. Of the political legacies that have shaped the south-east European peninsula, two can be singled out as crucial before the nineteenth century. One is the Byzantine millennium, with its profound political, institutional, legal, religious and cultural impact. The other is the half millennium of Ottoman rule that gave the peninsula its name and established its longest period of political unity. The Ottoman elements – or those perceived as such – have contributed to the most current Balkan stereotypes. In the narrow sense of the word, then, one can argue that the Balkans are, in fact, the Ottoman legacy. This legacy is different from the Ottoman polity or the Ottoman period; it is a process that began after the Ottoman Empire ceased to exist, and is the aggregate of characteristics handed down chiefly from the eighteenth and nineteenth centuries. After the First World War, the Ottoman legacy as perception is not a reconstruction, but rather a construction of the past in works of historiography, fiction, journalism and everyday discourse. The legacy as perception is one of the most important pillars in the discourse of Balkan nationalism and displays striking similarities in all Balkan countries. It is at the centre of securing present social arrangements, above all legitimising the state, and is bound to be reproduced for some time to come. The countries defined as Balkan have been moving steadily away from their Ottoman legacy, and with this also from their 'balkanness'. I want to strongly emphasise here that this statement is devoid of any evaluative element. I argue that what we are witnessing today in the geographic Balkans – namely, the eradication of the final vestiges of a historical legacy of ethnic multiplicity and coexistence, and its replacement by institutionalised ethnically homogeneous bodies – may well be an advanced stage of the final Europeanisation of the region, and the end of the historic Balkans and the Ottoman legacy.

Let us now take the larger concept of Eastern Europe to illustrate the concept of historical legacy. Geographically, Eastern Europe encompasses the Balkans, yet in a politico-historical sense it actually divided the region during the Cold War period. If we look at the historical periods, traditions and legacies that shape what is Eastern Europe today, we see that some of these periods and legacies have overlapped, while others were completely segregated; some encompassed the whole region, while others involved only some of the area's constituent parts. Eastern Europe's most recent and shortest legacy, communism, is usually neglected, most often by those who insist on the permanence of the previous imperial legacies. It is preposterous to look for a socialist legacy *in* Eastern Europe: as a political space today, it *is* the socialist legacy. After the Second World War, its nineteenth-century role as an intermediary space balancing between two centres of political and economic expansion (Western Europe and Russia), which in the interwar period had given way to the function of a *cordon sanitaire* against Bolshevism, dramatically changed. Pre-1989 Eastern Europe as an intermediary space made sense only as a political synonym for Warsaw Pact Europe. The moment the socialist period ended, around 1989, it turned into a legacy. Under the rubric of legacy as continuity, the socialist heritage in the political, economic and social spheres is strikingly similar in all post-communist countries. Most 'transitologists' prefer Eastern Europe as a logical sphere of reference. The socialist legacy as continuity displays different degrees of perseverance in separate spheres and countries but, like any legacy, it is bound to subside, after which it will be relegated to the realm of perception. As a long-term process, Eastern Europe is gradually fading away. Integration within the European institutional framework may occur over the next few decades, but in the realm of perception, we are speaking of the discrete experience of two or three generations. Eastern Europe will soon disappear as a category, though attitudes will be more difficult and slow to change. The state socialist legacy is the latest in a sequence of legacies and became one only after the end of the socialist period in the early 1990s. Unlike the Ottoman legacy, which bears only the characteristics of the last two centuries of the Ottoman era, the socialist legacy, because of its relative brevity, reflects the characteristics of the whole period. But the socialist period is itself a subcategory of a larger phenomenon. I am referring to what came in the wake of the Ottoman period, which, depending on the preferred paradigm or terminology, has been defined as the capitalist world economy, the capitalist mode of production, the 'iron cage' of capitalist modernity, the age of industrialism, urbanism, modernisation or globalisation. For Zygmunt Bauman, capitalism and socialism are 'married forever in their attachment to modernity'.[4]

There is, in this sense, a new phenomenon which is not as persistent as *balkanism*, nor does it have the same pedigree, and arguably will go away, but it has a strong pejorative motion. Twice in the last twenty years, I have used the Marxist dictum, once for *balkanism*, this time for something else: 'A spectre is haunting the world of academia: the study of post-communist nostalgia.' It may not be too bold to state that there is a broad consensus on the fact that the phenomenon exists. While practically all studies of nostalgia start with brief accounts of its history and etymology, it is clear that as a concept it long ago traversed the boundaries of the medical profession and entered the terrain of writers and poets. It has been linked to memory, history, affect; attached to political allegiances and models of consumerism. More importantly, nostalgia is no longer treated as the programmatic equivalent of bad memory, as a social disease, the abdication of memory.

But how about the specific case of post-communist nostalgia? Is it so different from 'normal' free-world nostalgia? Media coverage would let us believe this is the case. It consistently treats the phenomenon as a malady. In the conceptual apparatus of journalism and NGO discourse the comparative notions are communism and fascism, or communism and Nazism, not capitalism and communism, or liberalism (including neoliberalism) and communism. In such circumstances post-communist nostalgia can be subsumed only (and appropriately) under the Marxist notion of false consciousness. To this day there is a pervasive prescriptive or normative quality to much of the research on Eastern Europe: the obsession over *Vergangenheitsbewältigung*. Indeed, Timothy Garton Ash posits the existence of a new norm of integrity, a DIN standard (i.e.

---

4 Z. Bauman, *Intimations of Postmodernity*, New York and Abingdon: Routledge, 1992, 222.

Deutsche Industrienorm) in history writing.[5] To counter the moralising and mildly patronising motif, it is not only the East Europeans who are not following this road. It took a whole generation in post-Franco Spain after 1975 to reach the climactic moment of opening mass graves in 2000 and putting the issue on the table. And it is enough to evoke the lag of a generation and over two decades for the Germans to begin to come to terms with their legacy, a process which is still not complete. Besides, it is not entirely true. Practically all capital cities in Eastern Europe have a monument to the victims of communism, and most have museums, not commemorating but condemning communist rule: from the House of Terror in Budapest to the Occupation Museum in Riga and the Museum of Genocide Victims in Lithuania, the Stasi headquarters in Berlin, and so on. The point here is not to explain (or excuse) why *Vergangenheitsbewältigung* is not a household phenomenon in Eastern Europe, but to question the mandatory character of this approach. First and foremost, it is premised on drawing a straight line between Nazism and the comparatively long East European experience, which went through different stages, and displayed amazing geographical varieties. Scholars who do on-the-ground research tend to refrain from big moralising lectures (although their research contains big moral lessons). A lot of precious studies have already been accumulated although not quite yet coordinated. What they have come up with is a serious symptomatology. Here is a kaleidoscopic and impressionistic overview:

A study, carried out by two Polish sociologists in 2003, discovered strong symptoms of nostalgia among middle-class, middle-aged Poles, 'the social group which is commonly thought to have been the chief beneficiary of the process of market transition'. All opinion surveys report vast majorities of respondents with positive attitudes towards socialism. The study concludes that the main source of nostalgic attitudes is

---

5   T. Garton Ash, 'Mesomnesie', *Transit. Europäische Revue*, vol. 22, 2001–2, 32–48.

the merging of economic and social status after the transition: 'The ongoing fusion of social and economic status gives those less financially successful a feeling of being deprived of both social position and of economic well being.'[6] Another study on Poland points out that

> what people remember about socialism is a pride in production and in their labour, and also a sense of being part of a project that was *modern* and directed towards the general good. When people speak angrily about Poland being turned into a 'Third World' country, their anger is both about economic decline, about what they see as a two-sided coin of dependency and exploitation, and about being transformed not into the (even more modern) capitalist future but back into a pre-socialist past.

This 'trauma of deindustrialisation' has brought about alcoholism, drug abuse, homelessness and the feminisation of poverty. But

> rather than a case of collective amnesia or even nostalgia, this should be taken partly as an invocation of a past in order to contrast it with, and thereby criticise, the present. Social memory is selective and contextual. When people evoked the 'good' socialist past, they were not denying the corruption, the shortages, the queues and the endless intrusions and infringements of the state; rather, they were choosing to emphasise other aspects: economic security, full employment, universal healthcare and education.[7]

------

6   B. Wieliczko and M. Zuk, 'Post-Communist Nostalgia Among the Middle-Aged Middle-Class Poles', paper presented at the annual meeting of the American Sociological Association, Atlanta Hilton Hotel, Atlanta, GA, 16 August 2003.

7   F. Pine, 'Retreat to the Household? Gendered Domains in Post-socialist Poland', in C. M. Hann, ed., *Postsocialism: Ideals, Ideologies and Practices in Eurasia*, London: Routledge, 2002, 111.

I purposely started out with Poland because of its paradigmatic status as the A-grade transitioning country.

In Bulgaria, the traditional response both before and after the fall of communism has been jokes. A popular one is about a woman who sits bolt upright in the middle of the night in a panic. She jumps out of bed and rushes to the bathroom to look in the medicine cabinet. Then, she runs into the kitchen and opens the refrigerator. Finally, she dashes to the window and looks out into the street. Relieved, she returns to the bedroom. Her husband asks, 'What's wrong with you?' 'I had a terrible nightmare', she says. 'I dreamt we could still afford to buy medicine, the refrigerator was absolutely full, and the streets were safe and clean.' 'How is that a nightmare?' the husband asks. The woman shakes her head, 'I thought the communists were back in power.' The joke captures nicely the ambivalence of attitudes towards the communist past. It is asserted that the nostalgic discourse is binary by definition, with the past always depicted as better. But this is not the case in Eastern Europe. And it is not only the longing for security, stability and prosperity. There is also the feeling of loss of a very specific form of sociability, and of the popularisation of cultural life. Above all, there is a desire, among those who have lived through communism, even when they have opposed it or were indifferent to its ideology, to invest their lives with meaning and dignity, not to be thought of, remembered, or bemoaned as losers or 'slaves'. Lastly, there is a new phenomenon: the tentative but growing curiosity among the younger generation.

In Yugoslavia, a recent study on self-organised choirs who sing partisan and labour songs insists on the rejection of nostalgia: 'We are not nostalgic, we merely believe in values such as solidarity, faithfulness to one's beliefs, bravery and valour.' This rejection of nostalgia is a response to the dominant discourses in which any positive attitude towards the social or cultural life of socialist Yugoslavia is given the label of Yugo-nostalgia, and is delegitimised as irrational, unpatriotic, reactionary and immoral. It is doubly buttressed through a European discourse, insisting on the post-socialist inability to practise 'Europeanness'. Although the values on which they insist – such as anti-fascism, solidarity, workers' and human rights – are essentially European and universal, this double delegitimisation makes it impossible to make an equation between socialist (Yugoslav) and universal (European) values.

Another unlikely, because unexpected, carrier of the affliction is Romania. David Kideckel, in his study on the unmaking of the Romanian working class, describes the alienation of workers who decry politicians of all stripes and 'see the whole process as designed to keep workers down' through unemployment, low salaries, deindustrialisation, and education in business, foreign languages, etc., rather than engineering and other skills needed for the industrial workplace:

> Reacting against the increased class divisions and insecurities of neo-capitalism, many workers long for a return to the security and predictability of socialism. Like miners and workers elsewhere in Russia and East-Central Europe, from the best case of the Czech Republic, through wartorn Serbia, to Russia and Ukraine, declining economic circumstances encourage a turn to socialist nostalgia, nationalist cant or frustrated inaction.[8]

But let us ask a few analytical questions. 1) Who is speaking or performing nostalgia? After all, none of the subjects of nostalgia, the ones who are producing its artifacts and who are identified as its agents, define it as nostalgia. Nostalgia or 'post-communist' nostalgia is an ascriptive term, and when it is used, mostly in journalistic accounts, it had a strong tinge of censure. It continues to be avoided as a self-description. 2) What does nostalgia express? What is its content? It was already pointed out that there are the elements of disappointment, social exhaustion, economic re-categorisation, generational

---

8   D.A. Kideckel, 'The Unmaking of an East-Central European Working Class', in C.M. Hann, ed., *Postsocialism: Ideals, Ideologies and Practices in Eurasia*, London: Routledge, 2002, 124.

fatigue, quest for dignity, but also an activist critique of the present using both the past as a mirror and irony, all of which elements run alongside a purely consumerist aesthetics not much different from the one that we see in the West. Can we offer a typology of post-communist nostalgia, one that is also sufficiently discriminating between regional and national differences? After all, the communist experience was diverse enough to produce different post-communist responses despite the systemic similarities. There is the post-communist nostalgia with a certain tinge of imperial or colonial nostalgia (the case of the USSR and even Yugoslavia). Svetlana Boym introduces a distinction between restorative nostalgia, which is about truth and tradition, and reflective nostalgia, ironic and ambivalent, which calls absolute truth into doubt.[9] One could also distinguish between restorationist (in the sense of the desire to restore the past) and curative nostalgia. 3) What are the spheres of life and particular genres in which nostalgia is expressed? How much is it censured and self-censured? Here we have everything in the oral domain from casual conversations to scholarly interviews, formal genres from song and literature to film, monumentalisation and celebrations. How do we document nostalgia, how do we analyse and represent it – with what kinds of analytical tools and within what kinds of narrative or other genres? And most importantly, do we consider this a phenomenon solely East European? As Dominic Boyer recently warned us, the 'post-1989 Western European obsession with Eastern Europe's obsession with the past must be understood as an anxious lateral signal that the pastness of Eastern Europe can no longer be taken for granted'.[10]

I have tried to elaborate here on the heuristic qualities of the concept of historical legacies for general historical analysis. Thinking in terms of historical legacies – characterised by simultaneous, overlapping and gradually waning effects – allows

---

9   S. Boym, *The Future of Nostalgia*, New York: Basic Books, 2001, viii, 41–56.

10   D. Boyer, 'From Algos to Autonomous: Nostalgic Eastern Europe as Postimperial Mania', in Todorova and Gille, eds, *Postcommunist Nostalgia*, 23.

us to emphasise the complexity and plasticity of the historical process. In the case of the Balkans and Eastern Europe, it allows us to rescue the region from a debilitating diachronic and spatial ghettoisation, and insert it into multifarious cognitive frameworks over space and time. Europe, in this vision, emerges as a complex palimpsest of differently shaped entities, which not only exposes the porosity of internal frontiers, but also questions the absolute stability of external ones. In this respect, the task for balkanists and East Europeanists consists not so much of 'provincialising' Europe as of 'de-provincialising' Western Europe, which has heretofore expropriated the category of Europe with concrete political and moral consequences. If this project is successful, we will actually succeed in 'provincialising' Europe effectively for the rest of the world, in so far as the European paradigm will have broadened to include not only a cleansed abstract ideal and version of power, but also one of dependency, subordination and messy struggles.

CHAPTER 5

On the Way to Europe: EU Metaphors and Political Imagination of the Western Balkans[1]

Tanja Petrović

The political discourse of the European Union is expressly met-aphorical. Andreas Musolff studied the dominant metaphors in debates about the EU using a comprehensive corpus of political discourses in Great Britain and Germany. The metaphors pin-pointed by Musolff are also present in discourses about the Western Balkan countries' accession to the EU.[2] The most fre-quently used are the metaphor of family and those from the conceptual domains of journey/road and edifice/building.[3] However, in discourses about the EU itself, the role of these metaphors within political categorisation and argumentation, and the relations they suggest, are completely different from the roles and relations suggested by the same metaphors when they are used in discourses about the Western Balkans.

These metaphors and their discursive uses deserve par-ticular attention for at least two reasons. First, through their usage a symbolic map of Europe is being formed and the place

---

1   An earlier version of this text was published as part of my book, *A Long Way Home: Representations of the Western Balkans in Media and Political Discourses*, Ljubljana: Peace Institute, 2009.

2   The term *Western Balkans*, widely used in political discourse, especially referring to the EU enlargement processes, designates Balkan countries that are still not members of the European Union and are at different stages of accession to the EU. Very often, the term is used as a euphemism for the post-Yugoslav societies. Hence the interchange of the two in this text.

3   A. Musolff, *Metaphor and Political Discourse: Analogical Reasoning in Debates About Europe*, Houndmills and New York: Palgrave Macmillan, 2004.

of the post-Yugoslav states on that map is being defined. Second, the adoption of these metaphors and their reiterative use in various spheres of social life in the post-Yugoslav societies not only leads to routinisation and the consequent deadening of political awareness[4] – with the reduction of all references to Europe to empty political phrases – it also forecloses any possibility of articulation of a different image of Europe.

Images and notions formed through the use of metaphor are much more than discursive means. They provide a basis for the legitimation of political and economic relations in contemporary Europe and significantly determine the possibilities of those who are being placed *outside* Europe through this metaphorical labour: 'at Europe's doors' or 'doorstep', 'on the way to Europe'. After all, one should keep in mind the warning of Ernesto Laclau and Chantal Mouffe that 'a discursive structure is not a merely "cognitive" or "contemplative" entity; it is an articulatory practice which constitutes and organizes social relations'.[5]

Europe Is a Building

The metaphor of Europe as a building became very popular in the mid 1980s, after Mikhail Gorbachev used the phrase 'common European home' to emphasise the 'political vision of a collaborative way of living together for the European nations'.[6] The (common) European home/house metaphor emphasising the unity of Europe in the geopolitical sense has a long history.[7] Nevertheless, in contemporary European political discourses, the 'European house' almost exclusively denotes the EU.

---

4   M. Billig and K. Macmillan, 'Metaphor, Idiom and Ideology', *Discourse and Society*, vol. 16(4), 2005, 459–80, 459.

5   E. Laclau and Ch. Mouffe, *Hegemony and Socialist Strategy: Towards a Radical Democratic Politics*, 2nd edition, London and New York: Verso, 2001, 96.

6   Musolff, *Metaphor and Political Discourse*, 127.

7   As Young writes, it was first used in 1950 by Churchill in a speech in which he argued for the idea of a common European army which would be a message to the world from the *common European house*. H. Young, *This Blessed Plot: Britain and Europe from Churchill to Blair*, London: Macmillan, 1998, quoted in Musolff, *Metaphor and Political Discourse*, 122.

In discourses about the accession of the Western Balkan countries, the EU is represented as an edifice that may be either a house or a fortress, depending on the protagonist. EU politicians and officials frequently refer to it as a house – in the words of Olli Rehn, 'Candidate countries are not at our doorstep. There is a long path ahead of them before they can enter our common house.'[8]

The metaphor of the EU as a fortress is not new. It was even used by the philosopher Komensky in the early seventeenth century, at a time when European awareness had only just been formed.[9] Today, this metaphor is commonly used by those who are 'outside the fortress' or by advocates for their rights. It is often used in the criticism of EU migration policy, as in the famous song 'Fortress Europe' by the Asian Dub Foundation. It is also denounced in the region which 'keeps banging on the wall of fortress Europe': in 2001 the Serbian film director Želimir Žilnik made a movie entitled *Fortress Europe*, and in 2008 the Serbian author Igor Marojević's play *Tvrđava Evropa* [*Fortress Europe*] was staged for the Belgrade summer festival. The fortress metaphor also appears in the context of EU border security, to which migration policy is closely related. The Serbian politician Goran Svilanović stated that 'the Schengen wall is today stronger than the Berlin wall once was' and that 'it has been turning Europe into a fortress'.[10] Slovenian MEP Mihael Brejc used the comparison between the EU and the Berlin Wall in connection with the regulation on local border traffic across the EU external borders, pointing out that 'if the EU implemented the regulation on local border traffic at its external land borders . . . it could mean a new Berlin Wall'.[11]

Understandably, the fortress metaphor is not present in the

---

8   *Delo*, 7 June 2006.

9   T. Mastnak, *Naša Evropa* [Our Europe], in A. Drolc and M. Pajnik, eds, *Obrazi naše Evrope* [Faces of our Europe], Ljubljana: Peace Institute, 2001, 9–22, 16.

10   *Danas*, 19 May 2006.

11   www.24ur.com, 16 September 2005.

discourses of EU officials and politicians of its member states, except in response to or denials of such criticism as mentioned above. In a broadcast by Voice of America, Bertin Martens of the European Commission stated that the EU wants 'to prevent creating of new borders. We do not want the EU to become a fortress and to exclude the rest of the world. We want an osmosis with our neighbours.'[12]

However, such explicit articulations of the metaphor of the EU as an edifice are relatively rare in political discourse. The image of the EU as an edifice is more forcefully impressed by two other frequently used metaphors referring to the particular parts of a building that separate its interior from the outer world and enable passage between the two: These are the 'door' and the 'doorstep'. The metaphor 'of being at the EU's door' or 'at Europe's doorstep' defines the position of those who are outside the building and strive to enter it, referring to those countries that are undergoing the accession process or are preparing for it. These metaphors are ambiguous, and their meaning depends on which country is at the door or doorstep. In some cases, being at the EU's doorstep carries positive connotations and means that a country is just about to join the EU. For example, Slovenian journalist Igor Mekina used the metaphor in a positive context when writing about Slovenia's successful economic transition.[13] Turkey's being on the EU's doorstep[14] also indicates that its achievements are positively assessed. By contrast, Slovenian MEP Jelko Kacin used this metaphor in a completely different sense when he argued that 'the Balkans are not at Europe's doorstep nor are they Europe's courtyard. The Balkans are part of Europe and they deserve to be part of the enlarged European Union' (European Parliament, 30 December 2006). In line with the ambiguous meanings of these metaphors, the EU door is open for some and closed for others. The latter are also at risk of being left in front of the door forever. The Serbian

---

12   Voice of America, 25 January 2006.
13   I. Mekina: 'Pred vratima EU' [On the EU's Doorstep], *AIM*, 2001, aimpress.ch.
14   *Delo*, 29 June 2005.

journalist Slobodan Reljić, writing for the weekly *NIN*, stated that 'the position of the government in Kosovo has been ruined, the verbal support for reforms is increasingly rare, and messages about a plan to leave Serbia outside Europe's doors have begun to come in';[15] the leader of the Civic Alliance of Serbia (GSS), Nataša Mićić, emphasised at the convention of opposition parties in Belgrade, on 26 May 2006, that 'Serbia got stuck in the past and was stopped at Europe's door'.

The concept of a 'shared European house', from which the Balkan countries are excluded metaphorically by being placed at the door or in Europe's backyard, has a rather long history in Western discourses on the Balkans. Vesna Goldsworthy provides several illustrative examples of such discourses. Harold Spender, in his book *The Cauldron of Europe* (1925), stated that 'the Balkans remain an open question at the back door of Europe'. The same metaphor was frequently used during the 1990s by Western historians who referred to the war in the territories of the former Yugoslavia as 'a war in our own backyard'. In 1992, the *New York Times* wrote that 'the blood of the Balkans is seeping under the European door'.[16] A diachronic look at the conceptualisation of Europe as a house contrasted to the Balkan countries therefore shows that this metaphor is not a novelty in political discourse. It has been more often used as a 'tool' to exclude this part of Europe than it has been used to include it in the shared European space.

Europe Is a Family

In contemporary Western European political discourses, the metaphor of the family is most frequently used to describe the relations between EU member states. The accession of new member states in 2004 and 2007 was represented as a 'coming home' of 'lost children' into the 'fold of the family'.[17]

---

15   *NIN* 2724, 13 March 2003.
16   V. Goldsworthy, *Inventing Ruritania: The Imperialism of the Imagination*, New Haven, CT, and London: Yale University Press, 1998, 8–9.
17   Musolff, *Metaphor and Political Discourse*, 14, 17.

The metaphor of the family makes possible, among other things, the hierarchisation of European states and the paternalism of certain states in relation to others, and on several levels. In the case of the accession of new members in 2004 and 2007, as Mitja Velikonja shows in his study of the new Eurocentrism, Europe's paternalism towards newcomers was obvious in the symbolic representations of accession/entry. For example,

> in the cover picture of the brochure *The EU is Here! A Guide for New EU Citizens*, the then president of the European Commission, dressed in a classic suit and wearing a tie with a European pattern, awaits, with his hands wide open, the approaching young woman and man clad in traditional Slovenian costumes and carrying the Slovenian flag. They are surrounded by camera-men and by an audience who approvingly observe this event. This stereotypical duality, i.e. the 'almost Europeans', 'Ruritanians' in peasant or traditional folk costumes approaching the classically dressed 'old European', was present in all ten accession countries.[18]

Such a depiction of new members, their 'folklorisation' and representation as 'authentic', is also related to the creation of the image of the Other. It is precisely through such representations that the hierarchy within 'the European family' is being established, the one between the 'old' modern Europeans and the 'new' ones, presented 'as new settlers (usually wearing traditional costumes), who have to climb to reach the elite club'.[19]

In the case of the Western Balkan countries, the paternalistic attitude is also conspicuous, but to become members of the European family they still have to 'qualify' for membership, or prove their maturity. This kind of representation is connected

---

18   M. Velikonja, *Eurosis – A Critique of the New Eurocentrism*, Ljubljana: Peace Institute, 2005, 79.

19   Ibid., 81.

with the very nature of the accession process, which is imagined as the road to Europe/the EU, along which the Western Balkan countries should be transformed from non-European to European countries. They are expected to become mature while travelling down this road, turning from irresponsible, immature children into responsible, adult persons. That is how the task of the Western Balkan nations and their chances of early accession to the EU was formulated by Miroslav Lajčák, the Minister of Foreign Affairs of Slovakia and the former High Representative of the international community in Bosnia-Herzegovina: 'They are still not mature enough for that, but they must know that we are serious and that the perspective will open for them as soon as they are mature enough.'[20]

The child metaphor was also used by Slovenian politician Dimitrij Rupel, speaking about the responsibility of Slovenia and the EU towards the youngest post-Yugoslav state, Kosovo: 'We recognized Kosovo and now we have certain duties. Once we send a child to school, we have to buy school supplies.'[21] Discourse on countries undergoing the accession negotiations frequently 'borrows' from the field of education. The Western Balkan countries are represented as students who have to fulfil their tasks, who receive marks for their work and the like. 'Serbia will certainly become an EU member, but the date of accession depends on Serbia itself', said the Austrian Foreign Minister Ursula Plassnik, adding that 'Serbia must complete its homework to become an EU member';[22] the European Commission's report on the progress of candidate countries made it clear that Serbia was a difficult student.[23]

The image of the Western Balkan countries as children reproduces and legitimises the EU's paternalistic attitude: children cannot be fully responsible for their own behaviour; they are irrational and urgently need assistance, supervision and education. This recognisable image of Eastern Europeans in

20   www.b92.net, 10 February 2009.
21   www.24ur.com, 14 February 2008.
22   www.b92.net, 16 July 2008.
23   *Vreme*, 6 November 2008, p. 16.

post-socialism is noted by Boris Buden, who stresses that the expression 'children of communism' is not a metaphor, but a symptom of the imagination in which the transition to democracy as a radical reconstruction starts from scratch: 'Eastern Europe after 1989 resembles a landscape of historical ruins that is inhabited only by children, immature people unable to organise their lives democratically without guidance from another.'[24]

Accession to the EU Is a Journey

Examples of the path or journey metaphor can be found in political and public discourses in EU member states. These countries travel towards their goals at different speeds and using various means of transport, with some deciding not to embark on the journey at all ('the European train leaving the station without Britain' was a popular metaphor in 1992, when Britain's signing of the Maastricht Treaty ran into difficulties).[25]

Similarly, the political process of the accession of the Western Balkan countries is frequently described using the journey metaphor. In this context, the metaphor stands in contrast to the static image of the EU as an edifice implying security and protection. To reach the goal – accession to the EU – candidate countries may use different means of transport, such as a train or a ship. When interviewing the Slovenian Foreign Minister Dimitrij Rupel, a journalist for the weekly *Mladina* stated that, at the EU summit in Zagreb, 'Croatia has jumped onto literally the last wagon that will move it closer to Europe.'[26] A train as a means of transport may also imply the hierarchical order of countries-carriages – the most successful candidates are at the front, while those farthest away from the EU trail behind. 'Croatia is at the head of the train. It is not difficult to detect the EU's interests in its integration, as it serves as an

---

24   B. Buden, *Zone des Übergangs: vom Ende des Postkommunismus* (trans.), Berlin: Suhrkamp, 2009. See also Buden's contribution to this volume.
25   Musolff, *Metaphor and Political Discourse*, 30.
26   *Mladina*, 11 December 2000.

exemplary model for all the others in the region', wrote a journalist for *Dnevnik's* supplement 'European Cities 2008', published during Slovenia's presidency of the EU on the occasion of a visit by the mayors of Europe's capital cities.

The journey metaphor includes still another aspect that should not be overlooked. The aspiring EU members, starting the journey as 'non-European' countries, must learn, transform themselves and mature along the way, eventually reaching their target destination as fully revamped European countries. Every adaptation to the pattern of 'Europeanness', which is usually effected through fulfilling the EU-defined conditions, brings candidate countries one step closer to the EU: 'The Agreement is a new step in the journey of this Western Balkan country [Macedonia] towards EU membership.'[27] For candidate countries, the journey to the EU is long, difficult, and full of obstacles: 'A difficult journey awaits Croatia which today obtained the status of an EU Associate Member . . . For the Račan government, a much more difficult obstacle on the journey to the EU will be relations with Italy.'[28] One peculiar feature of the road/ journey metaphor applied in discourses on the Western Balkan countries' accession to the EU is that the completion of the journey does not necessarily imply the attainment of the goal set beforehand: the entry into the common European house at the end of this journey/process is not guaranteed, but the very Europeanness with which the candidate countries become impregnated along the way should be enough to ensure their sense of fulfilment. Commenting on the preconditions-based strategy, which imposes reforms on candidate countries in exchange for 'the European perspective', Olli Rehn said that 'the journey is at least as important as the goal.'[29] The journey may therefore turn out to be not merely long, but even endless.

Furthermore, the new members' entry into the European house does not necessarily mean that the journey has been

---

27   www.24ur.com, 1 April 2004.
28   www.24ur.com, 29 October 2001.
29   *Delo*, 10 February 2006.

completed, nor is it unequivocal proof of their Europeanness, particularly in the case of countries that belong to the 'other', post-socialist Europe. This shows that the old patterns of otherness in Europe reproduced through orientalist and balkanist discourses have not disappeared with the arrival of new patterns introduced by the ideology of EUropeanism. This fact is frequently echoed in the statements of political representatives of the Balkan and East European countries. When the European Commission recommended that Bulgaria and Romania should join the EU on 1 January 2007, the Bulgarian Foreign Minister Ivajlo Kalfin stated that Bulgaria 'had succeeded in realising what it has strived to achieve for seventeen years', adding that 'Sofia will now have to convince other European countries that it is worthy of EU membership'.[30] On the same occasion, the Romanian President Traian Băsescu stated that 'Romania has ahead of it a long journey from the accession to the EU to its real integration into the large family'.[31]

At the Walls of Europe

In the words of Maria Todorova,

> before America became the new *antemurale Christianitatis* in the wake of 9/11, this was one of the most important European mental maps which in different periods shifted from one to another European region or nation: Spain, France, Italy, Hungary, Austria, Germany, Poland, Romania, Croatia, Greece, Serbia, Bulgaria, Russia, the Balkans, Slavdom, Central Europe, etc. have all been saving Europe. And this was not something confined to journalistic or purely political rhetoric but has been very much part of the scholarly discourse as well.[32]

---

30   *Delo*, 26 September 2006.
31   Ibid.
32   M. Todorova, 'Spacing Europe: What Is a Historical Region?', *East Central Europe/ECE*, vol. 32(1–2), 2005, 59–78, 76.

The *antemurale Christianitatis* discourse has a long tradition in the Balkans. The countries in the European periphery use it as a tool to emphasise that they are European, moreover, that they protect Europe and its culture from the Turks or Islam. The image of the bulwark protecting Europe, as Ivo Žanić has established in the case of Croatia, is both complementary to and entwined with the related images of the crossroads and the bridge between civilisations often used by the Balkan countries to present themselves.[33] The bulwark supposedly protects civilised Europe from barbaric Turks, while at the same time constituting the border between civilisation and wilderness, between Europe and non-Europe. The *antemurale Christianitatis* discourse in the Balkan context thus becomes a means of producing the 'nesting orientalisms' described by Milica Bakić-Hayden: each country sees itself as a part of Europe and its protector, regarding its border (ordinarily, it is the southeastern border) as a demarcation line between Europe and the land of barbaric, uncivilised and oriental peoples.[34] Slavoj Žižek points out that in the former Yugoslavia 'every actor . . . endeavors to legitimize its place "inside" [Europe] by presenting itself as the last bastion of European civilization . . . in the face of oriental barbarism'.[35] This type of discourse can be found in practically all post-Yugoslav societies.

The Slovenian variant of the *antemurale* discourse is related to myths of defence against 'Turkish' incursions during the Middle Ages in the territories of what is today Slovenia. These were created through the works of 'various intellectuals, primarily historians and literary writers'.[36] During the 1980s, which

---

33   I. Žanić, 'The Symbolic Identity of Croatia in the Triangle Crossroads–Bulwark–Bridge', in P. Kolstø, ed., *Myths and Boundaries in South-Eastern Europe*, London: Hurst & Co., 2005, 35–76, 36.

34   M. Bakić-Hayden, 'Nesting Orientalisms: The Case of Former Yugoslavia', *Slavic Review*, vol. 54(4), 1995, 917–31.

35   S. Žižek, 'Caught in Another's Dream in Bosnia', in R. Ali and L. Lifschultz, eds, *Why Bosnia?*, Stony Creek, CN: Pamphleteers Press, 1993, 233–40, 236.

36   Š. Kalčić, '*Nisem jaz barbika': Oblačilne prakse, islam in identitetni procesi med Bošnjaki v Sloveniji*' [I am not a Barbie Doll: Dressing Practices, Islam and

was the time of Slovenia's intense *Europeanisation*, the image of a bulwark protecting Europe from the undefined barbaric Balkans and a much better-defined non-European communism became even more widespread. Slovenia (much like all newly formed nation-states in the territory of the former Yugoslavia) legitimised its right to EU membership using the argument of its historical defence of Europe against 'the Turks': it not only deserved membership by virtue of its merits from medieval times, but EU membership is its natural right because of its 'thousand-year-old belonging to Europe' (briefly interrupted in the twentieth century).[37] Accordingly, by joining the EU, Slovenia returned to where it always belonged.

The *antemurale* myth has also been one of the constant traits in Croatia's shaping of national identity following the gaining of independence, and its ideological role is similar to the one it played in Slovenia. As Duška Knežević-Hočevar has shown, the *antemurale* myth has become naturalised on the present-day Slovenia–Croatia border, too: the chairman of the Žumberak cultural and art association based in Novo Mesto (Slovenia) stated that 'nearly all the Association's members, approximately 150, were of Uskok descent because "even at that time they [the ancestors] had already defended the entirety of Europe against the Turks". Now, they – their descendants – would continue the tradition of their forefathers by defending the European Union along the forthcoming external EU border.'[38]

The Serbian variant of the *antemurale* discourse was forcefully revived by Slobodan Milošević. In his notorious speech at Gazimestan, on 28 June 1989, he said:

Identity Processes among Bosniaks in Slovenia], Ljubljana: Oddelek za etnologijo in kulturno antropologijo, Filozofska fakulteta, 2007, 82.

37   N. Lindstrom, 'Between Europe and the Balkans: Mapping Slovenia and Croatia's Return to Europe in 1990s', *Dialectal Anthropology*, vol. 27, 2003, 313–29.

38   D. Knežević Hočevar, 'Ideologies of "Fortress Europe" in Two Slovenian-Croatian Borderlands: Case Studies from Žumberak and Bela Krajina', in W. Amstrong and J. Anderson, eds, *Geopolitics of European Union Enlargement: The Fortress Empire*, London and New York: Routledge, 2007, 206–22, 215.

Six centuries ago, Serbia heroically defended itself here, in Kosovo Polje. However, at the same time, it also defended Europe. At that time, Serbia was a bulwark of Europe and it protected its culture, religion and European society as a whole. Therefore, today it seems not only unjust but also unhistorical and completely absurd to question Serbia's belonging to Europe. Serbia has been continually in Europe, now and in the past. In its own way, of course.

The occasion on which Milošević referred to this fourteenth-century defence of Europe against the Ottomans was the 600th anniversary of the battle of Kosovo Polje. The same metaphor would be used and the same role of the Serbs emphasised later, during the 1990s, except that this time the enemies at the walls would be different. The journal *Duga* published an article stating that

the truth about Kosovo and Metohia has not changed much over time, so that even today Muslim fundamentalism, persistently knocking at the door of Kosovo and Metohia, is trying to reach Europe. It is hard to believe that Europe is not aware of this. Even those in Europe who do not hold Serbia close to their hearts know very well that this old Balkan state represents the last barrier to the ongoing onslaught and aggression of Islam.[39]

Dragoš Kalajić, a Serbian poet and painter, wrote in 1994: 'The fact of an Islamic onslaught on Western Europe by peaceful means, the means of mass immigrations, threatening to turn European nations into national minorities within their own states, only accentuates the importance of the Serbian struggle for the overall defence of Europe, European culture and civilisation.'[40]

---

39   P. Šarić, 'Alternativa nasilju' [An Alternative to Violence], *Duga*, 18 August 1990, 67–9, quoted in Bakić-Hayden, 'Nesting Orientalisms', 926.
40   *Borba*, 6–7 August 1994, xvii–xix, quoted in Bakić-Hayden, 'Nesting Orientalisms', 925.

The same picture is conjured up when such discourse is used in the context of EU enlargement to the Western Balkans, except that in this case the protection of Europe from the Turks/ Muslims is replaced (or supplemented) by concerns about security, crime, drug smuggling, human trafficking, illegal migration, terrorism, etc. A very illustrative example of how such an image is created by combining discourses on European otherness, Islam, terrorism, crime and illegal migration is the following passage, whose author is Lucio Caracciolo, the editor of *Limes*, an Italian journal of geopolitics:

Italy's borders continue to be exposed to pressure, with internal pressure exerted from the east and maritime pressure from the far south-east. Various criminal networks destabilise the region by, among other things, collaborating with various cells of Islamic terrorism, primarily pan-Balkan and Bosnian ones. This creates waves of balkanisation. Pressure from the east is exerted by Russia and the countries bordering it (Ukraine, Transnistria, Moldova, the Black Sea, Caucasus), and it extends towards the heart of the Balkans (Bulgaria, Romania, inner Macedonia, Serbia and Bosnia), reaching our side of the Adriatic across former Yugoslavia and Albania. The south-eastern flow originates in Northern Africa and the Middle East and merges with Turkish criminal movements . . . Migration by people of African origin targets primarily our islands, whence it is easier to cross over to the European continent. When these migration flows move through the black holes of the Balkans, they expand and turn into a destabilisation factor which also includes terrorism . . . The merging of migration flows and terrorism strengthens the danger of infiltration by Al-Qaeda and its embryos in Bosnia and Albania into Italy. Similarly, Muslim terrorists nonchalantly use banks in the Balkans to cover their financial operations. Owing to these factors and the proximity of Western Europe, the

Balkans form an ideal logistical base for Osama and his brothers.[41]

Europe's feeling of threat (it is usually individual EU member states that feel threatened) became particularly intense in the 1990s when (Western) Europe became fearful of 'hungry masses' on its southern and eastern gates.[42] 'If Italy were in Schengen the Albanians who have been landing in Brindisi in recent weeks would have an open road to Munich or Hamburg', said one German politician.[43]

In discourses used within the context of candidate countries' accession to the EU, the Western Balkans has been equated with, or rather relocated to, the area south of the European continent, meaning the 'third world'. This has produced a situation in which the region called the Western Balkans, although geographically situated in the south-east of Europe, is increasingly being pushed by the shapers of EU discourses, for ideological reasons, towards the south, outside the symbolic borders of Europe.

In addition to this ambiguous status within the symbolic geography of contemporary Europe, the regional designation of the Western Balkans that dominates today's political discourses makes it even more difficult for post-Yugoslav societies to legitimate their position within the continent. The Western Balkans as a geographical term is difficult both to identify with positively and to take as a stable basis for self-identification. The question of what the Western Balkans is can be answered only if we invert it and ask instead what the Western Balkans *is not*. The answer is then self-evident: the EU. Once a post-Yugoslav state joins the EU, it ceases to be part of the Western Balkans. With Croatia's accession on 1 July 2013, the 'region' has shrunk and changed its geographical shape.[44]

41   L. Caracciolo, 'Ex oriente nox', *Limes Plus*, vol. 2, 2004, 19–27, 24.

42   Goldsworthy, *Inventing Ruritania*, 13.

43   *Independent*, 19 April 1997.

44   In 2006, Lonely Planet published the *Western Balkans Travel Guide* that covers Slovenia, Croatia, Bosnia-Herzegovina, Serbia and Montenegro, Macedonia

Europe Is the Future

Unlike the metaphors discussed so far, which mainly facilitate the spatial conceptualisation of representations concerning the accession of the Western Balkan countries to the EU, this metaphor involves the concept of time. Time is divided into the past and the future in relation to a certain point that belongs to the present. The linear image of time flowing from the past towards the future, supported by accompanying metaphorical processes, calls to mind the idea of progress: whatever belongs to the past is reactionary, backward and undeveloped, while notions of development and progress are associated with the future. Such a perception made possible statements within political and media discourses in which the Western Balkan countries' accession to the EU is portrayed as their 'opting for the future' (and as the 'final break with the reactionary past'); this type of discourse is supported by the spatial metaphor of progress along the road to Europe. EU officials continually repeat that the 'Western Balkan countries should be offered the European perspective or the European future', and talk about these countries 'taking the European course', 'choosing the European course' and the like. Accession to the EU is here presented as the only option for the Western Balkan countries to rid themselves of the burden of the past and destructive nationalisms, and turn to the future. The notions linked with the EU in this discourse are the future, progress, stability and health, and conversely, non-inclusion in the EU is related to the past, instability, chaos, nationalism and disease, meaning the traits that in discourses of balkanism are traditionally associated with the countries of the Balkan peninsula. The EU is therefore both a precondition for normality and the prescriber of normative requirements for

---

and Albania. Although the authors themselves admitted that a more appropriate title would have been *Former Yugoslavia and Albania*, they opted for a widely known and extensively used political term. In the 2009 edition, however, Slovenia was no longer included. It will not be a surprise if Croatia, as a fresh EU member, is excluded from the next edition of the guide.

qualifying as normal. On 28 January 2008, the day when the Council of the European Union was discussing future cooperation with Serbia, the *Guardian* published an article by Olli Rehn entitled 'Balkans on the Mend'.[45] Among other things, it says that

> people in the Balkans face a stark choice this year: their region could either finally resolve its outstanding problems from the wars of the 1990s or fall back into instability and extremes of nationalism. The first option would take them forward towards stability, prosperity and European integration. But many commentators believe the second is inevitable.

The Balkans can therefore mend themselves, become normalised and escape growing nationalism, only by becoming part of the EU, only by becoming Europe. What is kept concealed when painting such a polarised picture of the two worlds is the contemporary reality of the EU, with many of its members confronting growing nationalism, racism, xenophobia, the strengthening of extreme right political forces and similar 'horrors' – in short, exactly the phenomena that are attributed exclusively to those countries that have a lot of work ahead of them before they can be called European and before they can join the big European family. This type of discourse proposes the following 'time map' of Europe: the EU's present is the Western Balkans' future, with the latter now living not in the present but in a past governed by nationalistic myths. The image in which the reality of the Western Balkans is the reality not of the present but of the past makes the transformation of these countries indispensable and the difference between Europe (the

---

45   O. Rehn, 'Balkans on the Mend', *Guardian*, 28 January 2008, www. guardian.co.uk. The same metaphor of cure/mending was used by Dejan Steinbuch, a columnist for Slovenian free newspaper *Žurnal*, in an article entitled 'How to Cure the Serbs of Nationalism'. Among other things, he wrote: 'Therefore, I think that it is high time we cured our Serbian friends of nationalism and helped them on their way to the future.' *Žurnal*, 23 February 2008, 18.

EU) and the Western Balkans explicit, thus preventing us from perceiving the similarities between the two parts of the continent. Such discourse is not only characteristic of politics and the media, but can also be encountered in academic and other spheres. Maria Todorova's name for the phenomenon where, viewed from the Western perspective, 'the non-westerner is always living in another time, even when he is our contemporary' is chronic allochronism.[46]

On the other hand, in Europe's perception of itself, the idea of progress is inherent to Europe; it is a space characterised by a linear flow of time, as contrasted with the non-European, cyclical perception of time and endless repetition.[47] In addition, Europe sees itself as a community of nations joined together precisely by their ability to face their traumatic past, overcome it and build a better and more ethical society through such catharsis.[48] By contrast, the Balkans live in the past, are obsessed with the past, and on top of that are unable or unwilling to face that past. Since as such they seriously threaten Europe's self-image, it is appropriate to place the Balkans beyond European borders. In 1999, Étienne Balibar pointed out in his lecture given in Thessaloniki, that 'the fate of European identity as a whole is being played out in Yugoslavia and more generally in the Balkans (even if this is not the only site of its trial)' and that Europe has two options:

---

46   M. Todorova, 'The Trap of Backwardness: Modernity, Temporality, and the Study of Eastern European Nationalism', *Slavic Review*, vol. 64(1), 2005, 140–64, 155.

47   'The tragedy of Africa is that the African has not satisfactorily entered history . . . In this imaginary world where everything starts over and over again there is no place for human adventure or for the idea of progress. The man never looks towards the future. Never breaks the repetition cycle . . . That is the problem of Africa', said President Sarkozy addressing young Africans in Dakar. In Š. Š. Tatlić, 'Mikrob v Evropi', *Reartikulacija*, no. 2, 2007/2008, www.reartikulacija.org.

48   In his study of twentieth-century European history, Mark Mazower convincingly deconstructs this European narrative about the cathartic confrontation with the past and points out that Nazism was 'a nightmarish revelation of the destructive potential of European civilization – turning imperialism on its head and treating Europeans as Africans'. M. Mazower, *Dark Continent: Europe's Twentieth Century*, London: Penguin Books, 1998, xiii.

Either Europe will recognize in the Balkan situation not a monstrosity grafted to its breast, a pathological 'after effect' of underdevelopment or of communism, but rather an image or effect of its own history, and will undertake to confront it and resolve it and thus to put itself into question and transform itself. Only then will Europe probably begin to become *possible* again. Or else it will refuse to come face-to-face with itself and will continue to treat the problem as an exterior obstacle to be overcome through exterior means, including colonization.[49]

A deeper look into the European discourses on the Western Balkans shows that today Europe is no more 'possible' than it was over a decade ago when Balibar made the remarks quoted above. With the unfolding of the euro crisis, one could even argue to the contrary. The means used to constitute the Western Balkans (and increasingly the European southern periphery in general) as an area outside Europe have become even more explicit; the use of well-known mechanisms of supervision and colonisation is characterised by an even greater lack of reflection. As to the EU as a whole, this colonisation enables it to continue building and maintaining a self-satisfied image of Europe while shunning, or ascribing to those outside everything that might possibly challenge such an image. In this kind of Europe there is no room for 'peaceful, managed and nurtured diversity',[50] and this kind of Europe is not capable of self-reflection. There the media repeat on a daily basis politicians' statements echoing the well-known patterns that marked the darkest periods of European history. Because of this, it is difficult to avoid an unpleasant feeling of repetition – despite the generalized and deep-rooted opinion that repetition is a problem of the African man and of the Balkan peoples, and by no means of Europeans.

---

49   E. Balibar, *We, the People of Europe?*, Princeton, NJ: Princeton University Press, 2004, 6.

50   T. Garton Ash, 'Europe's True Stories', *Prospect Magazine*, vol. 131, February 2007.

CHAPTER 6

Children of Post-communism[1]

Boris Buden

A curious set of metaphors marks the jargon of post-communist transition: education for democracy, classrooms of democracy, democratic exams, democracy that is growing and maturing, but which might still be in nappies or taking its first steps or, of course, suffering from infantile illnesses.[2] This language of post-communism discloses a paradox that points at what is probably the greatest scandal of recent history: those who proved their political maturity in the so-called democratic revolutions of 1989–90 have become thereafter, overnight, children! Only yesterday, they succeeded in toppling totalitarian regimes in whose persistency and steadfastness the whole so-called free and democratic world had firmly believed, until the very last moment, and whose power it had feared as an other-worldly monster. In the struggle against the communist threat, that world had mobilised all its political, ideological and military forces, its greatest statesmen and generals, philosophers and scientists, propagandists and spies, without ever really frightening the totalitarian beast. Yet, despite that, it calls those who chased it away with their bare hands 'children'. Only yesterday,

---

1   This article was first published as 'Als die Freiheit Kinder brauchte', in B. Buden, *Die Zone des Übergangs: Vom Ende des Postkommunismus*, Frankfurt am Main: Suhrkamp Verlag, 2009, 34–51. The translation is by the author and it was first published in English in *Radical Philosophy*, vol. 159, January/February 2010, 18–25. Another chapter of the book, 'The Post-communist Robinson', is available in the catalogue of the 11th Istanbul Biennial, *What Keeps Mankind Alive: The Texts*, Istanbul, 2009, 169–74.

2   I owe the reference to child metaphors to D. Jović, 'Problems of Anticipatory Transition Theory: From "Transition from . . ." to "Transition to . . .",' presented at the conference 'The Concept of Transition', Zagreb, 22–23 April 2000.

those people got world history going again, after it had been lying on its deathbed, and helped it to walk upright again, after so long. Yet today, they themselves must learn their first steps. Only yesterday, they taught the world a lesson in courage, political autonomy and historical maturity, yet today they must assert themselves before their new self-declared masters as their obedient pupils. Only yesterday, they were the saving remedy for fatally ill societies; today, they themselves suffer from children's illnesses, which they must survive in order to become capable of living. What miracle happened overnight? What wizard turned these people into children?

Of course, it was politics. The child that was suddenly recognised in these mature people is defined neither by an early stage of psychological development that was never really abandoned, nor as a result of the psychopathological phenomenon of infantile regression, but as a political being, a *zoon politikon* par excellence.

An Ideology Called 'Transitology'

The human being as a political child offers itself as the almost perfect subject of a democratic restart. Untroubled by the past and geared totally to the future, it is full of energy and imagination, compliant and teachable. It emanates freedom as though its pure embodiment, but actually it is not free at all. A child is dependent; it must be guided and patronised by adults. However, this only makes it all the more suitable for serving society, as the perfect ground for a new beginning. It neutralises all the contradictions that the sudden irruption of freedom lays bare in society, above all between those who rule and the ruled. There is no relation of domination that seems so natural and self-evident as the one between a child and its guardian, no mastery so innocent and justifiable as that over children. One does not take their freedom away, but suspends it temporarily, postpones it, so to speak, for the time being. A patronised child as political being enjoys a sort of delayed freedom. And in case one day the promise of freedom turns out to be a delusion, one can always say that it was just a children's fairy tale. The repressive infantilisation of the societies that have recently liberated themselves from communism is the key feature of the so-called post-communist condition. It comes to light in the ideology of the post-communist transition, a peculiar theory that addresses itself to the task of understanding and explaining the post-communist transition to democracy. Here, cynicism becomes (political) science. From the perspective of this political science, post-communism is understood above all as a phase of transition – that is, as a process of transformation of a 'really existing socialist' (*realsozialistisch*) society into a capitalist democratic one.[3] Political science finds no reason to understand this transition in terms of a specific historical epoch. It lacks basic identity features: a specific post-communist political subject or system, for instance, and a specific post-communist mode of production, or form of property. In fact, political science does not need the concept of post-communism at all. It prefers instead the aforementioned concept of 'transition to democracy' and it even develops within this framework a special discipline with the task of studying this process: 'transitology'. It is based on the cynical idea that people who won freedom through their own struggle must now learn how to enjoy it properly. The meaning of this paradox goes far beyond the historical situation in which the post-communist societies in Eastern Europe found themselves after 1989.

The concept of transition was introduced by orthodox political scientists in the late 1960s and early 1970s to explain various cases of regime change, principally in South America and southern Europe. 'Transition' originally meant nothing more than 'an interval between two different political regimes', as a minimalistic definition from 1984 put it.[4] This transition was always a 'transition from': 'from authoritarian rule', for instance,

---

3 Here I draw again on Dejan Jović's lecture. I thank the author for providing me with its full text.

4 G. O'Donnell, L. Whitehead and P. Schmitter, eds, *Transitions from Authoritarian Rule: Tentative Conclusions about Uncertain Democracies*, Baltimore, MD: Johns Hopkins University Press, 1986, 3.

in the title of the book by O'Donnell, Whitehead and Schmitter. Basically, at that time, political science always reflected on the phenomenon of regime change retrospectively. It tried to draw lessons from historical experience *ex post*. It was not so interested in the future because the outcome of this sort of transition was more or less open. It did not necessarily end in a democracy; an authoritarian regime could be transformed into another form of authoritarian rule. At that time, it was still conceivable that a military dictatorship in South America might be replaced by a Marxist or even a Maoist dictatorship. The Chilean people, for example, democratically decided to embark with Allende on a form of 'socialist democracy', but the military junta turned them in a completely different direction.

In those days, for political science, the world was still quite complex: there were not just two competing ideological–political systems and military blocs, but also a series of anti-colonial movements in the 'Third World', providing for a certain contingency of the political. At that time, it still seemed as though there was a choice, as though history had an open end. By the end of the 1980s something had changed, and transitology began to understand its topic differently. The process of political transformation was now to be determined in advance. Its goal is always already known – incorporation into the global capitalist system of Western liberal democracy. From that point on, the concept of transition has been almost exclusively applied to the so-called post-communist societies and denotes a transition to democracy that began with the historical turn of 1989–90 and continues, more or less successfully, mostly in Eastern Europe. This condition is familiar to the 'children of communism'. They grew up with the logic of historical determinism. Then, however, it was the moving force of class struggle that was manoeuvring society into a better, classless future. To be free meant, at that time, to recognise the iron laws of history and to yield to them. The trail to a better communist future was not only clearly blazed but also unavoidable.

Nowadays, they are told they must have a similar experience; only this time, it is the General Law of History they have to obey unconditionally. The goal is clearly and distinctively set and its final attainment is guaranteed in advance. According to the new ideology of transition, there are no major obstacles on the way to democracy, so long as one strictly adjusts to the objective, external factors – economic, cultural, institutional, and so on. Sometimes a geographical position will suffice. 'Geography is indeed the single reason to hope that East European countries will follow the path to democracy and prosperity', writes one of the transitologists, who understands politics only as a struggle for control over external factors: 'if we really control economic growth and the institutional setting, it is very likely that democracy will occur'.[5]

Others go a step further. Our way to democracy is determined by nature itself. It is 'a natural tendency and therefore not difficult to achieve'.[6] Even the very idea of politics is based on Charles Darwin's theory of natural selection.[7] The author of this Darwinist theory of democracy, Tutu Vanhanen, also believes that democracy is universally measurable. So he introduced the so-called Index of Democratisation (ID) that shows us on which level of democratisation a society is situated. Accordingly, he also constructed a ranking of democratic societies. In this list, created shortly before the collapse of communism, he classified sixty-one countries as democracies, five as so-called semi-democracies and eighty-one as non-democracies. Only countries that earned more than five ID points were classified as truly democratic. Those under that level were authoritarian. The two poles, 'authoritarian rule' and 'really existing freedom' (i.e. liberal democracy), define a clear line of historical development: from authoritarianism to democracy. The transition is now teleologically determined – that

5   A. Przeworski, *Democracy and the Market: Political and Economic Reforms in Eastern Europe and Latin America*, Cambridge: Cambridge University Press, 1991, ix.

6   J. Mueller, 'Democracy, Capitalism, and the End of Transition', in M. Mandelbaum, ed., *Postcommunism: Four Perspectives*, New York: Council on Foreign Relations, 1996, 117.

7   T. Vanhanen, *The Process of Democratization: A Comparative Study of 147 States, 1980–88*, New York: Crane Russak, 1990, vii.

is, designed from the perspective of its intended result – and consists of climbing up the scale of democratisation to the top, the condition of realised freedom in the system of liberal democracy. One only has to follow the law of nature. Authority on one side and freedom (i.e. autonomy) on the other – these two poles also determine the ideal of an enlightened, modern education: the development of an immature child, still dependent on an authority, into an autonomous, mature citizen of a free society.

According to Vanhanen, the most important factors that affect his Index of Democratisation are competition and participation. His formula is simple: the more democratic the system, the higher the level of participation and competition. The latter stands for the openness of political possibilities, for a pluralism of interests – that is, of political and ideological options. Under 'participation' we should understand the voluntary involvement of citizens in political life and in making political decisions. A fully mature democracy requires mature democrats capable of autonomous thinking and acting.

On these conceptual premises, the process of post-communist transition appears as an educational process following the ideal of education for maturity and responsibility. However, it also reflects all the contradictions of this old Enlightenment concept.

Education for Immaturity and Irresponsibility

The analogy between the historical development of humanity and the growing up of a child (its consciously controlled education) is, as is well known, an invention of the Enlightenment. Indeed, enlightenment is nothing but a transition from immaturity to maturity, or, as we read in the first sentence of Kant's famous essay from 1784, 'man's emergence from his self-imposed immaturity', which he defines as the 'inability to make use of one's own understanding without direction'.[8] In the same

---

8   I. Kant, 'An Answer to the Question: "What Is Enlightenment?"', in *Practical Philosophy*, Cambridge: Cambridge University Press, 1996, 17.

sense that the immaturity is 'self-imposed', the maturity too should be achieved as a result of one's own action. One cannot simply be declared mature – that is, released from tutelage, be it that of nature, God or some master, which is the original meaning of the idea of emancipation as an acquittal, a release from paternal care, being freed from bondage. The Enlightenment idea of a transition to maturity has more of a reflexive sense, as a self-emancipation. Of course, this transition should never be mistaken for a revolution. Kant's concept of Enlightenment implies an emancipation that does not take place through a revolutionary leap, but rather as a reform in the manner of thinking (*Denkungsart*), as a continuous progression which alone is capable of securing the identity of its subject, as the subject of Enlightenment.[9]

In historical developments after Kant, the Enlightenment ideal of maturity – and with it the perception of emancipation as a long-term process with an open end – was pushed more and more into the background. Another idea of emancipation took its place. Emancipation was understood now as an act of liberation from an unjustly imposed domination. The goal of emancipation is no longer a mature man but rather a society free of domination. With this move 'maturity' has lost the emphatic meaning of emancipation.

Curiously, it was not until 1945 that interest in the concept recurred. Of course, this was the time of a historic transition: from fascist dictatorship to democracy. The traumatic historical experience of the masses, who had blindly followed their Führers into the catastrophe, made the idea of autonomous, mature and responsible men and women attractive again. 'Maturity' was now recognised as a precondition for democracy.[10] After a long historical separation, 'maturity' and 'emancipation' met once again. This also influenced post-war philosophical reflection. Habermas, for instance, attached

---

9   M. Sommer, *Identität im Übergang: Kant*, Frankfurt am Main: Suhrkamp, 1988, 123.

10   Ibid., 130ff.

interest in emancipatory knowledge to an interest in maturity. At the same time, pedagogy discovered the concept of 'maturity'; it became the goal of education, the very principle of an emancipatory educational science. The post-fascist transition envisioned the ideal of mature and responsible citizens as the final cause of the construction of a new, democratic society. It is no wonder that the process of post-communist transition finds itself committed to the same ideal. Finally, the new condition understands itself as post-totalitarian – liberating itself ideologically and historically from both 'totalitarianisms', fascist and communist: the so-called double occupation – a retroactive equalisation of two ideologies and political movements that in historical reality fought each other mercilessly.

The post-communist ideal of mature and responsible citizenship has been nowhere so clearly employed as in the development of so-called civil society, which, it is believed, is the true subject of democratic life, the social substratum of all democratic values, justice and well-functioning public and human rights. This civil society is supposed to be very weak in the East European societies liberated from communism. It is still 'in nappies', one might say, which is the reason it has to be first educated, trained, developed, got going.[11] Surprisingly, nobody at the time asked the question: who, if not the civil societies of Eastern Europe, brought the *ancien régime* to collapse? What was Solidarity in Poland if not the paradigmatic institution of a resisting, struggling and radically world-changing civil society par excellence? How has it suddenly become so weak if yesterday it was able to overthrow communism? Who has put the Polish workers in nappies, all those brave men and women who initiated the democratic revolution, withstood the brutal repression of the counter-revolution, and carried the struggle for democracy on their shoulders until the

---

11   Those democratic activists in Eastern Europe who tried during the 1990s to get financial support from the West for their projects simply could not avoid the phrase 'development of civil society' in their applications. It was as though this phrase was a sort of universal key for opening the cash boxes of the 'free and democratic world'.

final victory? Who – and in whose interest – has put them thereafter in children's shoes, diagnosed their children's illnesses, sent them to school and set them exams?

These were the cynical ideologues of transition, the master-minds of the post-communist transformation, as we can call them. However, their cynicism has followed a logic, the logic of domination. If 'education for maturity and responsibility' is propagated in the interest of domination and thereby turns into an endless process about whose possible conclusion the educators alone decide, then the call for 'maturity and responsibility' no longer serves, as Robert Spaemann writes, 'to enlarge the circle of the mature, but rather the circle of those who are for now declared immature'.[12] Thus the child metaphors that are so typical of the jargon of post-communist transition turn out to be a symptom of a new power relationship. They point clearly to a repressive incapacitation or putting under tutelage of the true subject of the 'democratic turn' and to its retroactive des-ubjectivation. We are talking about a constellation for which those words of Adorno, from his radio talk on 'Education for Maturity and Responsibility', still hold true, namely that 'in a world as it is today the plea for maturity and responsibility could turn out to be something like a camouflage for an overall keeping-people-immature'.[13]

Again, in whose interest does this happen? Who puts the protagonists of the historical change under tutelage, who robs them of their subject status? The question is as old as the Enlightenment concept of maturity. Hamann put it directly to Kant: 'Who is . . . the vexed guardian [der leidige Vormund]?'[14] He saw him in Kant himself, or, more precisely, in the gestalt of

12   R. Spaemann, 'Autonomie, Mündigkeit, Emanzipation. Zur Ideologisierung von Rechtsbegriffen', Kontexte (trans.), vol. 7, 1971, 94–102, 96. Quoted in Sommer, Identität im Übergang, 133.

13   T.W. Adorno, Erziehung zur Mündigkeit (trans.), Frankfurt am Main: Suhrkamp, 1970, 143; T.W. Adorno and H. Becker, 'Education for Maturity and Responsibility', History of the Human Sciences, vol. 12(3), 1999, 21–34.

14   J.G. Hamann, Briefwechsel (trans.), vol. V, ed. V. W. Ziesemer and A. Henkel, Wiesbaden: Insel Verlag, 1955ff., 289–92. See Sommer, Identität im Übergang, 125.

the Enlightener. Today, these are the Western onlookers who did not take part in the democratic revolutions of 1989–90. Far from meeting the deeds of the protagonists of the East European democratic revolutions with the 'wishful participation which borders on enthusiasm',[15] with which Kant's passive spectators once welcomed the French Revolution, they reacted to the over-throw of communism with a cynical 'participation' that revealed the wish for power and domination. In fact, they recognised in that historical event, like Kant's spectators of the downfall of the feudal absolutism of 1789, a 'progress in perfection' in terms of a 'tendency within the human race as a whole', but at the same time regarded this same tendency as having been long ago ful-filled in their own reality and therefore, speaking Hegelian, already historically sublated. 'You want a better world, but the better world is us' was the Western spectators' answer to the democratic revolutions in Eastern Europe. In this sense, they are completely different from those who in 1789 so enthusias-tically welcomed the news from Paris. While the latter caught sight of their own dream in the revolutionary reality of others, the former recognised in the revolutionary dream of the other nothing but their own reality.

The consequences of this difference could not be more rad-ical. Those who finally crowned their struggle for freedom with victory in Eastern Europe have become, almost overnight, losers. This was not an effect of black magic but rather of hegemony. It is hegemony that made true winners out of the Western spectators, not only winners over communism but at the same time also over the protagonists of the revolution that brought down communism. Let us hear the declaration of vic-tory in the words of this hegemony itself:

> The armies of the winners did not, it is true, occupy the territory of the losers. Still, given the nature of the conflict and the way it ended, it was logical for the losers to adopt

---

15   I. Kant, *The Conflict of the Faculties* [1798], trans. M.G. Gregor, New York: Suhrkamp, 1979, 153.

the institutions and beliefs of the winners. It was logical in particular because the outcome represented a victory of the West's methods of political and economic organization rather than a triumph of its arms.[16]

It is no coincidence that Michel Mandelbaum, the author of these words, and his colleague, the political scientist John Mueller, speak explicitly of imitation as being the best way to democracy.[17]

It could not be worse: not only are the protagonists of the democratic revolutions robbed of their victory and turned into losers; at the same time, they have been put under tutelage and doomed blindly to imitate their guardians in the silly belief that this will educate them for autonomy. It is not only the arbitrariness of the new rulers, but above all the logic of their rule, that reveals itself here.

Education for Stupidity

The notion of 'children of communism' is therefore not a metaphor. Rather it denotes the figure of submission to the new form of 'historical necessity' that initiates and controls the process of the post-communist transition. On these premises, the transition to democracy starts as a radical reconstruction out of nothing. Accordingly, Eastern Europe after 1989 resembles a landscape of historical ruins that is inhabited only by children, immature people unable to organise their lives democratically without guidance from another. They see themselves neither as subjects nor as authors of a democracy that they actually won through struggle and created by themselves. It has been expropriated from them through the idea and practice of the

---

16   M. Mandelbaum, 'Introduction', in Mandelbaum, ed., *Postcommunism*, p. 3.

17   Mandelbaum: 'Where intense competition is the rule, [imitation] is the best formula for survival' (ibid., 30). As a comment on the process of transition in Eastern Europe, Mueller writes: 'Imitation and competition are likely to help in all this.' Mueller, 'Democracy, Capitalism, and the End of Transition', 138.

post-communist transition, only to return now from the outside as a foreign object that they must reappropriate in a long, hard and painful process. In the strange world of post-communism, democracy appears at once as a goal to be reached and a lost object. Thus for the 'children of communism' the prospect of a better future opens up only from a melancholic perspective. No wonder, since their post-communist present so remarkably resembles their communist past. It does not give them free choice. The 'children of communism' remain what they once already were, namely marionettes in a historical process that takes place independently of their will and drags them with it into a better future. So they are very familiar with this strange form of social life we call 'transition'. As is well known, so-called actually existing socialism was, according to its ideological premises, nothing but a sort of transition society from capitalism to communism. Thus, one form of transition has replaced another. However, both the absolute certainty and the pre-given necessity of the historical development have remained the constant of the transition.

As a result, the question of the future in post-communism is considered as already answered, and the question of the past does not make sense. One does not expect the children of communism to have a critically reflected memory of the communist past. It is precisely for this reason that they have been made into children, namely in order not to remember this past. As children, they do not have one. Paradoxically, it is only in post-communism that one gets a dubious impression that communism actually never existed. Already, in 1991, Jean-Luc Nancy spoke about the anger one is overwhelmed with when hearing all this empty talk about 'the end of communism'.[18] The belief that history is now finally finished with Marxism and communism, and simply so, he found ridiculous:

---

18   J.L. Nancy, 'La Comparution/The Compearance: From the Existence of "Communism" to the Community of "Existence"', trans. Tracy B. Strong, *Political Theory*, vol. 20(3), 1992, 371–98, 375.

As if history, our history, could be so inconsistent, so phantasmic, so flaky [*floconneuse*] to have carried us along for one hundred and fifty years on clouds that dissipate in a moment. As if error, pure, simple, and stupid error could be thus corrected, regulated, mobilized. As if thousands of so-called 'intellectuals' were simply fools, and especially as if millions of others were even more stupid as to have been caught in the delirium of the first.[19]

It is not so much the suppression of communism as a historical fact, the erasure of the communist past with all its intellectual and political complexity from the historical consciousness of post-communism, that evokes Nancy's indignation and concern, but rather the immense ignorance with which the post-communist world refuses to wonder about this past and its afterlife, or to ask: 'Why did this all happen?' Nancy sees in this the true, almost epochal stupidity of the post-communist turn.

Of course, children are not stupid. However, one can make them stupid, or, more precisely, one can educate them for stupidity. In this respect, a hundred years ago, Freud wrote of intellectual inhibitions that culture implants in its pupils through education to make them more obedient and compliant. He differentiated three types of such thought-blockage – the authoritarian, the sexual and the religious – to which correspond three 'products of education', namely the good subjects, the sexually inhibited and religious people. He understood these forms of intellectual atrophy (*Verkümmerung*), as he also called it, as effects of *Denkverbot*, a ban imposed on men and women in their childhood, a ban on thinking about what was most interesting to them. In Freud's time, it was above all the suppression of sexuality that had become the self-evident task of education. Once the *Denkverbot* was successfully implemented in the realm of sexuality, it was extended to other spheres of life, becoming in this way the most important character trait of the whole personality.

---

19   Ibid., 376.

What was at that time sexuality has become, in the world of post-communism, politics itself. While the children of communism are virtually encouraged by their educators to liberate themselves sexually and to come out, as loudly as possible, with their hitherto suppressed sexual identities, to embrace unconditionally all secular values, and to become (instead of good subjects of the totalitarian state) self-conscious, free acting members of a democratic civil society, their liberated intellect seems to have no business being in the realm of the political. It is as though there is nothing there it can wonder about. As though all political questions have been correctly answered long ago; as though the only thing left to think about is how properly to implement these answers, how to imitate, as truly as possible, the pre-given role models and how to obediently follow the wise word of the guardian. It seems that the well-known dialectic of enlightenment, now from its political side, has caught up with the world of post-communism. From being an education for maturity and responsibility that had been implemented to serve the new power, it has become an education for political stupidity. It has turned Kant's ideal upside down and puts its trust in precisely those people who are not able to use their intellect without guidance from another. Thus, the stupidity that Nancy ascribes to the post-communist turn is actually an effect of this *Denkverbot* that has been imposed on the political ratio of post-communism. It is above all in a political sense that people in post-communism have been put under tutelage, made into children, and finally made into political fools.

This insight does not have to be taken as a reason for indignation but should rather motivate maturity. The 'child' as the leading political figure of post-communism is much more than simply an instrument of the new hegemony. It is of structural importance for the fantasy of a new social beginning that shapes the world of post-communism so decisively. As a sort of biopolitical abstraction of the transitional society, it takes over the role of a subject that is freed from all the crimes of the communist past, so that it can enter any new social relation (including that of domination) morally clean. Moreover, as a 'child' it does not have to take responsibility for the crimes of post-communism itself: for the criminal privatisation in which the wealth of whole nations has become the property of the few, almost overnight; for the new, post-communist pauperisation of the masses with all its social and individual consequences; for historical regressions that in some places have thrown the post-communist societies, economically, culturally and morally, back below the levels that had already been reached under communism; and, finally, for all the nationalism, racism, fascism, bloody civil wars, and even genocide. All these phenomena appear today as unavoidable childhood illnesses, or, to put it bluntly, as unpleasant but harmless dirt on the nappies of the newborn liberal democratic society.

Do not Forget: Contradiction and Resistance

The 'child' in post-communism is a sort of ground zero of society on which every catastrophe, the one inherited from the past as well as the new, self-created one, can be recompensed. It is an instance of a primal social innocence thanks to which it becomes possible to integrate everything that happens, including 'the inadmissible, the intolerable' (Nancy), into a new heroic Robinsonade; and to retell it as a universally comprehensible narrative about an innocent restart. In the ideological figure of the innocent child, liberal democratic capitalist society enters the age of its unconditional ideological reproducibility. Even the most distant island can become for a time its cradle, no matter what the cost. Finally, infantile innocence has a constitutive effect for the whole horizon of individualistic (juridical) bourgeois ideology in the era of its globalisation. It helps to reduce the antagonistic, political truth of human history to a relation that is structured according to the juridical pattern, the relation between perpetrators and innocent victims. One looks into history only with a sort of forensic interest, as into a corpse that can provide useful information for the court proceedings.

Hegel knew that only a stone, as a metaphor of 'non-action'

('not even . . . a child'), is innocent.[20] In this sense the fantasy of the innocent new beginning of post-communist society is possible only from the perspective of a historical development that has been brought to a standstill and has frozen in the figure of a child as its political subject. Here, in the moment of historical transition, non-freedom is being replaced by a freedom that needs children, but only to deny itself to them.

It is therefore no wonder that, as Nancy emphasises, one reacts to the cynicism of the time with anger. In the anger that post-communist triumphalism provokes he saw the political sentiment par excellence, concretely, a reaction to 'the inadmissible, the intolerable'.[21] It is the expression of a refusal, of a resistance that goes far beyond what is reasonable. The anger Nancy talks about is political because it is enraged over the reduction of the political to an 'accommodation and influence peddling' that in post-communism determines the frame of the historically possible. The anger opens a dimension of the political that unfolds only in breaking out of that frame. It is therefore the true messenger of a maturity to come that alone can put paid to the post-communist tutelage.

It is in an 'education for protest and for resistance' that, according to Adorno, the 'only real concretization of maturity' lies.[22] He ended his talk on education with a warning – which remained literally his last public words, since he died a few weeks later – a warning that can serve as a postscript to the ideology and practice of the post-communist transition. It is precisely in the eagerness of our will to change, which we all too easily suppress, Adorno argued, that the attempts to actively change our world are immediately exposed to the overwhelming force of the existent and doomed to powerlessness. Thus 'Anyone

---

20   'Innocence, therefore, is merely non-action, like the mere being of a stone, not even that of a child.' G.W.F. Hegel, *Phenomenology of Spirit*, trans. A.V. Miller, Oxford: Oxford University Press, 1977, 282. If this warning doesn't suffice, one should remember Roberto Rossellini's 1948 film *Germany Year Zero*.

21   Nancy, 'La Comparution', 375.

22   Adorno and Becker, 'Education for Maturity and Responsibility', 30–1; translation amended.

who wishes to bring about change can probably only do so at all by turning that very impotence, and their own impotence, into an active ingredient in their own thinking and maybe in their own actions too.'[23]

The repressively infantilised child in us is nothing but a pure embodiment of our political and historical powerlessness in the ideal world of post-communism, which, in a seizure of epochal megalomania, mistakes itself for the realisation of all dreams about freedom. The only possible exit from this self-inflicted immaturity is to protest against it and to resist.

---

23   Ibid., 32.

PART III

Two Decades After Yugoslavia: Bitter Fruits of Transition

CHAPTER 7

The Silence of Lamb-eaters: Transition as a Post-war Crime

Andrej Nikolaidis

In January 1989, the workers of the Radoje Dakić Construction Machinery Factory in Podgorica, known between 1946 and 1992 as Titograd, the capital of the Socialist Republic of Montenegro, left the factory grounds and set off for the parliament. There they joined a crowd of other demonstrators demanding the resignation of Montenegro's communist leadership. The protesters called for new faces at the top of the League of Communists of Montenegro – ones more attuned to the interests of the workers and the Serb people, above all in Kosovo. They accused the Party leadership of having lost touch with the people, of selling out workers' and national interests, and of bureaucracy and corruption. The accusations of corruption included the alleged misuse of government cars for private purposes and attending official lunches to dine on roast lamb. It was this latter detail that made the demonstrators label the Party leaders *jagnjofuci*, 'lamb-eaters'.

In the wake of this event, dubbed the 'anti-bureaucratic revolution', the existing communist leadership resigned and was replaced by leaders whom the people, in a flight of post-revolutionary euphoria, endearingly called 'young, handsome and smart'. A little-known official, Momir Bulatović, became president. His bushy moustache was considered a guarantee of earnest in Montenegro, whose dynastic rulers had all had beards and moustaches. A striking young man of basketballer physique by the name of Milo Đukanović, who in time would develop an impressive taste for British suits and Swiss watches, was made premier – his first paid position. And the position of chief ideologue went to Svetozar Marović, who had attended the Party school in Kumrovec, the birthplace of Josip Broz Tito. Apart from Marx, Marović also liked to quote Hegel. It turned out that he had also attentively read Carl Schmitt, who explains in his essay 'The Crisis of Parliamentary Democracy' that pacifists determined to defend peace would ultimately have no choice but to wage war against those determined to use war as a way of resolving conflict. When Montenegro attacked the Croatian city of Dubrovnik in 1991, Marović termed this offensive a 'war for peace'.

The anti-bureaucratic revolution in Montenegro was masterminded by Slobodan Milošević. The ousted Montenegrin communist leadership had withstood the blows from Belgrade for months up until the demonstrations in front of the parliament, partly thanks to the strong support it received from the communist parties of the other Yugoslav republics. A quarter of a century after the so-called revolution, the Radoje Dakić factory has been closed down. Its workers, who had spearheaded the anti-bureaucratic revolution and thus paved the way for parliamentary democracy and the *transition* (that catchword of our time!) from a socialist planned economy to a capitalist free market in Montenegro, were among the first to be mobilised for the 'war for peace'. Later, during the hyperinflation caused by the sanctions of the 'international community' against Serbia and Montenegro, their monthly wages of around 1,000 deutschmarks at the time of their demonstration plummeted to just 2 deutschmarks. Later, they lost their jobs. Today big developers are negotiating with representatives of the former workers on purchasing the factory site to build commercial apartments.

The reformed Communist Party, which today calls itself the Democratic Party of Socialists, is still in power in Montenegro (amounting to an impressive record of uninterrupted rule from 1945 to 2013). This party, a member of the Socialist International, has won all the elections in Montenegro since the introduction of the multi-party system, and by a tiny margin yet another presidential election in April 2013. Momir Bulatović was president of Montenegro for over seven years and also had a spell as president of rump Yugoslavia. Today he has retired from politics and deals in alcoholic drinks. Svetozar Marović remains a powerful figure in the Party – its vice-president. Milo Đukanović is still prime minister. In the mid 1990s he committed political patricide by rejecting Milošević and his politics: he had come to power riding the wave of Serbian nationalism in 1989, but then he figure-headed Montenegro's independence, which was sealed by referendum in 2006. The independence movement was a reaction of Montenegrin anti-war activists and the autonomous-minded part of society to the attempts of the Serbian political elite to keep Montenegro under Belgrade's control for good. Đukanović was a central figure in both processes, and that is only one of the paradoxes of his long rule.

The anti-bureaucratic revolution was really a counter-revolution. Immediately after installing the new communist leadership, it swapped class rhetoric for ethno-nationalism. The two years that followed saw an unchecked spread of fascism in society as an ideological groundwork for the wars in Croatia and Bosnia-Herzegovina. Walter Benjamin's maxim proved to be correct: the rise of fascism bears witness to a failed revolution (in this case a phoney one). The Yugoslav wars and the sanctions were exploited to accelerate what lay at the heart of the dissolution of Yugoslavia – the transition from socialism to capitalism. The socio-economic processes of the last quarter of a century are today ideologically photoshopped and proclaimed to be the entry into an age of parliamentary democracy, transition, independence, and integration into the EU and NATO, but their real ramifications are quite different: widespread fascist tendencies in society, war, growing unemployment, the eradication of workers' rights, privatisation (a synonym for plunder), commercialisation of the health and education sectors, flourishing inequality, deindustrialisation and desecularisation.

The communist elite was comprised of the children and grandchildren of those who carried out the revolution of 1941–5, yet they sullied every one of the ideals which had once lent moral authority to the ascendant Communist Party. The emerging new class in Yugoslav socialism, which Milovan Djilas warned about in the late 1940s, morphed from a privileged communist class into a new political-financial elite and used the transition phase to increase its power and wealth. The anti-bureaucratic counter-revolution, the spread of fascism and the change of the political and economic system were put into effect, de facto, by the League of Communists of Montenegro itself! If the Montenegrin communist leaders of 1946 were to pass judgement on today's 'reformers', the verdict would definitely be high treason.

Fairy Tales About Transition

One of the secret internal memorandums of the US strategic analysis institute Stratfor from 2009, published on WikiLeaks, states that the International Monetary Fund (IMF) bears part of the blame for the war in the former Yugoslavia. Stratfor analysts considered that the austerity measures imposed on Yugoslavia by the IMF in the pre-war period provoked the social unrest which was partly to blame for the war:

> Due to the global recession any economic indicator from the region is very important. Take special attention of any unrest caused by the crisis involving workers, unions. Do not forget that the austerity measures the IMF imposed on Yugoslavia are partly to blame for beginning of the war [sic]. We must take account of any economically motivated social discontent.[1]

The problem with Stratfor's analysis of the cause of the Yugoslav wars of the 1990s is not only that it is inaccurate – it is also cynical in its inaccuracy.

Yes, the IMF was one of the culprits of the war in Yugoslavia, but not because its austerity measures made workers and unions

---

1   See Balkan Insight, 'WikiLeaks: The IMF's fault for Balkan Wars', 2 March 2012, at www.balkaninsight.com.

take to the streets and then go to war to vent their frustration. Stratfor makes it sound as if the discontented workers dashed straight from the social protests to swell the ranks of national armies and immediately started singing Serbian and Croatian nationalist songs instead of the Internationale. But the war was not caused by the losers who ended up on the streets due to the IMF measures. Rather, it was triggered by the nationalist elites, from which the future 'winners of transition' were to emerge, led by the tycoons. They succeeded precisely because the protests of the workers and unions did not, and so the class conflict was masked by ethnic wars, and the workers magically disappeared, to be replaced by Serbs, Croats, Bosniaks, Montenegrins, etc. War and transition in the former Yugoslavia are inseparable parts of one and the same process, the military aspect of which is being arbitered by the International Criminal Tribunal for Yugoslavia in The Hague, while the transition-related part is firmly under the aegis of the European Bank, the IMF and the European Union. This *Troika* bears responsibility not for provoking the war, but for failing to prevent it, and also for legitimising wartime and post-war plunder.

We, the people of the former Yugoslavia, learned – or should have – that transition also means the evolution of thieves into businessmen. From the EU's perspective, Balkan thieves are much more desirable as partners than Balkan Reds. This is because thieves respect 'sacred' private property. They value it so highly that they risked their own freedom to accumulate property illegally, while Reds want the freedom to take that property away from them. And when the thieves succeeded in gaining control over the desired property, no one was more interested in establishing a legal system, maintaining the new status quo and averting any potential revolution. Those who have accumulated capital *illegally* now have all the *legal* instruments at their disposal to protect that property. Thieves are thus the main supporters of the current system because no one is more determined to prevent the emergence of ideas about the redistribution of wealth.

Furthermore, transition means the evolution of fascists into democrats. The regimes in power in the ex-Yugoslav countries in the 1990s were fascist in all but name. Transition began when the first war broke out, and it was still going strong when the wars in Croatia, Bosnia-Herzegovina and Kosovo ended. It transformed itself into a fourth Yugoslav war, which, although undeclared, was no more humane than the others: a *total war* against the poor.

In the initial phase of capital accumulation, which is obviously a euphemism for daylight robbery, only those close to one of the fascist regimes could get rich. Today, mouthpieces for the wealthy are posted at strategic locations and emphasise that they were able to accumulate capital due to their skills. This is patently false: they got rich through privilege, and they despise the idea of equality because they earned everything they own through inequality. The ideology of today's local elites is neither nationalism nor religious fanaticism but a home-grown combination of Social Darwinism and neoliberalism. The ruling elites are more or less unanimous in their declarations condemning fascism. Governmental and parliamentary bodies are expected to follow the advice of EU colleagues, and they adopt numerous projects, laws and regulations intended to turn the Balkan countries into tolerant societies inhabited by politically correct citizens. With the end of war, the ruling class has peacefully transformed itself into a caste of successful Europeans.

There is something inherently fascist in Social Darwinism. The idea that life revolves around competition gives rise to the idea of 'winner takes all'. The loser is disempowered and takes nothing – except what the winner might feel like giving. The conclusion is that the loser is worthless. This line of thinking leads to the notion that we need to get rid of human ballast, also known as cutting expenses or laying off excess workforce. During the last war in Yugoslavia, more than one army came to the same fascist idea of how to get rid of the human ballast: ethnic cleansing. Applied Social Darwinism has been a continuation of war by other means. Today's financial elites in the countries of the former Yugoslavia, as we have said, were born during the fascism of the 1990s. Fascism of one shade or another is their natural habitat, and their compatriot 'partners' are the very people they once pillaged – a perfect crime! In short, transition is the last in a series of war crimes on the territory of the former Yugoslavia. The accession of our countries to the EU will be the final episode of this crime: the one to place a rubber stamp on its consequences and acquit the culprits. Accession marks the beginning of a new era, in which the crimes of the past will be erased.

The democratisation of our societies and membership in the EU is primarily of interest for our ex-fascist thieves: democracy will best preserve their interests. Since the EU's institutions protect capital far bigger and bloodier than their own, they realise that these institutions will also look after their capital – and do it much better than any system they could ever imagine or create.

That is why the people of the former Yugoslavia not only have to reject the idea that 'the West is to blame for everything' (a phrase used by nationalist elites who always blame others for the wars and the destruction of Yugoslavia), but by the same token also have to reject the idea that the West is a benevolent civiliser. After all, it stood by and watched our savagery and wars with an enormous dose of sadness and trepidation before finally deciding to intervene and cultivate us, make us humane, enlighten us, and, in the end, invite us to join their paradise of democracy and capitalism – the EU.

In this EU fairy tale, the IMF is a kind of Wise Man from the East, who actually comes from the West (not a paradox here!). Before we can defeat the dangerous enemies of the open market and society, the Wise Man teaches us, we must first conquer ourselves. He teaches us the importance of harmony: we have to overcome our own inhibitions, which are the product of a socially sensitive state, before we reach a level where we can become one with the everlasting market. We have to overcome our instincts and urges, which are nothing more than the slackness of tired and impoverished workers. We have to overcome our own antagonisms manifested in social struggle. When we are done with ourselves and can resist the final temptation, and when the Wise Man realises we are ready . . . then, what then? We must resist these pitiful mind games of mainstream liberal demagogy with their insistence that 'our' Balkan capitalism is bad, while the US or EU form of capitalism is good and uncorrupted. This ideology tells us that as soon as we get rid of corruption and implement 'real', genuine capitalism, everything will be fine.

The EU as an Empire

The process of EU enlargement is primarily an imperialist project. Accession to the empire follows the principle of 'standards first, then membership', and the genius of the concept is that membership is perceived as a privilege. It is seen as a series of qualifying examinations which we have to pass so the empire will recognise our worthiness as a future member of the EU. We have to be diligent, and then the benevolent empire will admit us into the club. Imagine if the British Empire demanded that India pass seven exams if it wanted to be part of the Empire. Or if France dictated the conditions under which Algeria deserved to become a French colony.

In his book *Empires*, Herfried Münkler writes that every empire goes through two phases: expansion and consolidation, where the second phase is a 'civilising' phase. During the expansion phase, an empire establishes its military and economic superiority, while during the civilising phase it cements its power in the political and ideological domain. As Michael Mann aptly diagnosed: 'The American Empire will turn out to be a military giant, a back-seat economic driver, a political schizophrenic and an ideological phantom.'[2] Indeed, hardly anyone still believes that the United States is a beacon of democracy and an authorised distributor of human rights. The US neoliberal economy is in tatters, and the political dissemination of American values has been taken over by military expansion. American ideology is a has-been.

---

2   M. Mann, *Incoherent Empire*, London: Verso, 2005, 13.

According to Münkler, the US is on a one-way path to obso-
lescence. The EU will take its place as the great empire of the
West, just as the US took over from the British Empire. That is
why the last chapter of Münkler's book is entitled 'Europe's
Imperial Challenge', and the last sentences read:

> the EU's external borders are not the same as those of the
> Schengen area, or those of the Eurozone. This model [the
> imperial model of borders] must be developed further to
> make Europe's external frontiers at once stable and elastic.
> This will include exercising influence in the periphery of
> the EU, in ways that have a greater affinity with the require-
> ments of empire than those of an interstate system. For
> Europe's future will not be able to do without borrowing
> from the imperial model.[3]

Alice in Peripheryland

The countries of the former Yugoslavia have governments
placed in power by 'fair and democratic elections', but the political, economic and social life of these countries is controlled by
the United States and the Troika. In the lead-up to 'full membership in the prestigious club', as envoys of the EU explain
membership to the local population on television, the US and
the Troika are carrying out a unique social experiment of dual
cleansing. On the one hand, 'anti-corruption initiatives' are
being implemented with the aim of transforming our corrupt,
transitional capitalism into the allegedly clean, non-corrupt
Western type of capitalism. On the other, a process of reconciliation and 'coming to terms with the wartime past' is taking
place. This initiative aims to normalise the consequences of war,
while the anti-corruption initiative seeks to normalise transition (which, as we have said, is itself a consequence of the war).
Needless to say, both forms of 'cleansing' are strictly performative and detached from questions of truth and justice.

---

3   H. Münkler, *Empires*, Cambridge: Polity Press, 2007, 167.

A classic example of the performativeness of the initiatives for coming to terms with the past is Srebrenica. World leaders go there to make moving speeches and bandy about pompous pledges such as 'Never again!', an impressive memorial centre has been built, etc. But Srebrenica remains part of Bosnia's Serb-controlled entity called Republika Srpska – an indelible consequence of the military operations of the Republika Srpska army, during which that genocide was committed. The politics of coming to terms with the past do not envisage a reversal of the political-territorial fait accompli of the Srebrenica massacre, for example a removal of Srebrenica from Republika Srpska, or the abolition of that entity founded on genocide and the politics of ethnic cleansing, systematic mass rape and the indiscriminate shelling of towns and cities.

As far as transition is concerned, it is clear that there can be no talk of justice without (re)nationalisation, which would reverse the consequences of transitional plunder and the privatisation of common assets. But it is equally clear that there will be no talk of nationalisation – can anyone imagine the EU supporting a Balkan government which implemented a policy of nationalisation? That would definitely be interpreted as a grave deviation from the so-called European path.

How then have these two performative endeavours fared in practice: the struggle for truth about the wartime past and the struggle against corruption? It must be said that both have been very successful in achieving their core intention – to institute changes, after which everything will stay the same, and that will mean the completion of the process of normalisation.

From the vantage point of spring 2013, let us look at what the process of cleansing the wartime past has brought in Serbia, which pursued the most aggressive military policies in the 1990s and launched hostilities against two neighbouring countries – Bosnia-Herzegovina and Croatia. Serbia is currently governed by a coalition of the Socialist Party of Serbia (SPS), the party of the now-deceased Slobodan Milošević, and the right-wing Serbian Progressive Party, which developed out of the extreme-right Serbian Radical Party (essentially a radical wing of the SPS during the belligerent 1990s). The ironic result of the innumerable 'initiatives for reconciliation and truth' about the war is that those who waged the war have returned to power. And they have done so with the full support of the EU because they are now pursuing the politics of EU integration, not of war. When it was recently revealed that the Serbian premier Ivica Dačić, former speaker and current president of the SPS, had contacts with the biggest narco clan in Serbia, the EU supported the premier and claimed the affair was a politically motivated attempt to sabotage EU integration efforts.

Things are similar with anti-corruption cleansing. The anti-corruption struggle in our Balkan democracies is as permanent as purges were under Stalinism. If liberal democracy keeps insisting on the struggle against corruption, is that not because corruption is inherent to liberal democracy? The anti-corruption struggle will never end and corruption will never be stamped out. And how could it be, when this civilisation constantly battling corruption is centred around banks – those most corrupt institutions in human history? What would an alien who, like Alice in Peripheryland, landed in the post-Yugoslav countries be able to tell about the anti-corruption struggle here? The enemy is not visible, but no less dangerous . . .

It is not enough for the state to be involved in the struggle against corruption. No, success ultimately depends on the people joining in. Personal initiative is required. A whole gamut of newspaper ads, billboards, TV, radio and internet sites call on the citizens to detect and report corruption. Cities are chock-full of appeals to the public to be an informer, thus creating a latter-day version of Christ's commandment: *denounce thy neighbour*. More arrests are demanded time and time again as European officials beam missives to the people of the Balkan countries, welcoming every new arrest and adding that they expect more.[4] It could seem blatantly cynical to say: the paradox

---

4   See Montenegro NewsBlog, 'France and Germany Set Additional Conditions for Montenegro's Opening of Negotiations', 4 November 2011, at http:// montenegro.blogactiv.eu. See also Limun.hr, 'Brussels Requesting Arrests and Verdicts for Crime and Corruption', 19 May 2011, at www.limun.hr.

is that more arrests means a more successful struggle against corruption. If there are no arrests, that does not mean a drop in the crime rate or that corruption has been stamped out, but that there is a lack of anti-corruption initiatives. The goal is not a society where there will be no arrests because there is no longer any reason to arrest, but exactly the opposite: a society which will keep arresting because there is always a reason. Ultimately, the arrests must never stop and the system's process of self-cleansing must never end. And when this system calls on us to denounce doctors and civil servants who demand bribes, or to report retailers who haven't given us an official invoice, would it be cynical to say: 'Our police officers, government ministers, leaders and the whole political class are irrevocably and unacceptably corrupt, one has to agree. But all of them are just expendable servants of speculative capital, which remains outside the law . . . OK, how about we arrest our corrupt leaders, as you suggest. And when we've done that we can move on to the EU-based bank managers, pumping our money out of our countries . . . What, that's not on?'

The Coming Insurrection?

The 'truth' arrived at through dual cleansing under the patronage of the US and the Troika is therefore neither binding nor effective. And just as the truth about war crimes does not reverse the political consequences of those crimes, the truth about *transitional* corruption does not reverse the consequences of *transition*. When WikiLeaks happened, people in the former Yugoslavia had the opportunity to convince themselves of the colonial status of their countries, even if they did not know this beforehand. This gave rise to aspirations, but this truth had no real impact either. So truth was all around us, but there was something fundamentally false in its universal triumph which told us that truth had not won out after all – truth was the missing ingredient in this story about truth.

Another noticeable upshot of the project of coming to terms with the truth about Yugoslavia's wars is the absence of a common truth: Serbs, Croats, Bosniaks and ethnic Albanians all have their own truths about what happened and who is to blame. As usual, the others are to blame. Now we have separate, democratic states, and that is how things are with democracy, its rule of law, and truth. As Alain Badiou remarks in *Of an Obscure Disaster*, the main feature of the modern constitutional state is universal conformity with the law, not with truth. Democracy is an attempt to transcend antagonisms: you tell me your truth and I'll tell you mine, we'll talk about how true it is that there's no truth; if we have a serious problem we'll set up a commission of inquiry to present a series of conclusions which everyone will be able to interpret as they like, though we should definitely talk about them and listen to expert opinion . . . Postponements and calls for dialogue can only delay *polemos* and *stasis*, not stop them. We saw in the wars for dividing up Yugoslavia what happens with supposedly transcended antagonisms, when suppressed animosities and unsettled scores from the Second World War came to the surface.

So what remains of Yugoslavia's seemingly rock-solid state truth after the catastrophe of the 1990s? The fascist brood have eaten away at the truth of the Second World War national liberation struggle, and today's newspapers, books and encyclopaedias are full of their balderdash. National reconciliation within the individual post-Yugoslav countries made the wars between our nations possible in the first place. The calls for inner reconciliation were just part of the preparations for war.

The idea now is to establish the truth about our crimes – the truth about *us* – under the patronage of Europe, to enter the EU, and thus to consummate our history. It is no coincidence that our politicians speak about accession to the EU as 'returning to where we always belonged'. But what if the imaginary Mother Europe, whose womb we're supposed to return to, is actually a monster? We are caught between a rock and a hard place – between such a 'mother' and the code of fathers who have drafted the contours of a new Balkan bloodbath. When the order of the commissions of inquiry collapses, the future 'we's' and 'they's' will be pigeonholed and ready. Given the suppressed wartime antagonisms and the terrible amount of injustice which transition has brought, the possibility of catastrophe is quite real.

But another possibility is also real. The coming insurrection could head in a different direction this time: towards a change for the better. As in the fairy-tale gone really bad, for almost two decades the transitional winners in post-Yugoslavia acted like wolves, while the citizens acted like lambs. What if the citizens know better now: know who actually benefited from the war, who ate up the commons, and who the real lamb-eaters are today? What if the authentic, emancipatory left in post-Yugoslavia has been silent long enough? What if the time has come to silence the lamb-eaters?

Translated from the Serbo-Croatian by Will Firth

CHAPTER 8

Kosovo:
The Long Independence Day[1]

Agon Hamza

Stating the Facts

This chapter reconsiders the main political and ideological con-juncture in Kosovo, which took shape in the aftermath of the NATO intervention in 1999, via the UN Mission in Kosovo (UNMIK) administration (1999–2008), and which culminated in the declaration of independence of Kosovo in February 2008. This conjuncture has foundations that are neo-imperial, and it can be understood in structuralist (Althusserian) terms. The political and ideological predicament in Kosovo is a 'merely structural effect' of the conjuncture that has dominated Kosovo's citizens since 1999. Five years have passed since the country declared independence on 17 February 2008, yet in the Republic of Kosovo the state of affairs has remained largely the same as before.[2] Following a few years of unsuccessful negotiations with Serbia, the Assembly of Kosovo declared independence based on the Comprehensive Proposal for the Kosovo Status Settlement (known as the 'Ahtisaari Plan'),[3] which foresaw the

---

1 A substantially longer version of this essay was published in S. Žižek and A. Hamza, *From Myth to Symptom: The Case of Kosovo*, Pristina: KMD, 2013. I owe the title of this chapter to Slavoj Žižek.

2 Around 100 countries have recognised the independence of Kosovo, including twenty-two out of twenty-eight EU member states. To date, Kosovo is only a member of (what else but) the World Bank, the International Monetary Fund and the European Bank for Reconstruction and Development.

3 UNOSEK, 'Comprehensive Proposal for the Kosovo Status Settlement', 26 March 2007, at http://unosek.org.

formation of an independent Kosovan polity, supervised initially by the international community.[4]

In Kosovo, political freedom is highly limited by international pressure and intervention, as well as by the corrupt 'local'[5] elite. The economy is profoundly fragile and vulnerable to neoliberal experiments, as well as dependent on foreign aid (mostly restricted to remittances). Added to these challenges, the hegemonic tendencies and aspirations of Serbia remain highly problematic.[6] As a result of this constellation of challenges, the question of sovereignty must be raised first against the 'Western' neo-imperialist interventions, and second against the hegemonic aspirations of the state of Serbia, especially regarding the north of Kosovo. Far from praising sovereignty as the highest aspiration for a country (in a distorted Fichtean sense of 'internal borders'), in the case of Kosovo, the struggle for sovereignty has to be understood as an anti-imperial struggle. The present history of Kosovo is being written according to a neoliberal set of reforms based on the privatisation of all spheres of society, politics and culture. In other words, contemporary Kosovo is a synthesis of neo-imperialism and heavy bureaucracy, or to put it differently, it is the synthesis of the 'American' and 'European' forms of cosmopolitanism.

What the Republic of Kosovo has inherited from socialist Yugoslavia, of which it was a constituent part, while at the same time an autonomous province within the Socialist Republic of Serbia, is its worst feature – poverty. Kosovo still remains the poorest country in the region. According to the best available

---

4   On 31 January 2011, the Kosovo Parliament passed a resolution according to which the supervised (conditioned) independence was to be over by the end of 2012. It duly came to an end in September 2012.

5   The word 'local' has a peculiar meaning in Kosovo. Coined by the 'internationals', it is meant to be a politically correct term for drawing a distinction between the people of Kosovo and the foreigners working for the international administration. It goes without saying that the social implications of the word 'local' are derogatory.

6   See the recently approved Serbian platform on Kosovo, 'Tekst usvojene Rezolucije o Kosovu i Metohiji' (trans.), 14 January 2013, at www.e-novine.com.

figures, the unemployment rate in the country lies between 43 and 45 per cent,[7] while poverty has increased during the last couple of years.[8] The neoliberal reading of this predicament only manages to veil and mystify the structural causes of poverty and unemployment. There is no secret meaning behind the Kosovo case: its 'underdevelopment', poverty and political problems are not due to some 'ancient' force persisting in the present predicament; rather, the actual state of the situation is a result of the twin forces of global capital and neo-imperial plunder. Even though there are certain and 'specific' conjunctural problems with specific political histories, the basic problems that characterise the country are not peculiar to Kosovo as such, but are the immediate forms of the general global concerns of capital itself.

There is but one political paradigm by which the country is ruled: stability. Stability at any cost, that is.[9] Neo-imperial interventions include EU missions such as EULEX, NATO, the International Civilian Office, the World Bank and IMF, the United States embassy, non-governmental organisations,[10] governmental agencies for international development, including

---

7   See the regular reports of the Kosovo Agency of Statistics at http://esk.rks-gov.net.

8   According to reports from the UNDP and other international organisations, about 34 per cent of the population lives in poverty – below the line of 1.42 euros a day – and over 18 per cent live in extreme poverty – below the line of 93 euro cents a day. According to the Statistical Office in Kosovo, the average wage in Kosovo is 220 euros, whereas the GDP per capita is 1,800 euros. One should compare this with neighbouring countries: in Bosnia-Herzegovina and Albania, GDP per capita is 6,000 euros, in Montenegro it goes up to 7,000 euros, whereas in Serbia it is 8,000 euros. See the regular reports at www.ks.undp.org.

9   A good deal of the same arguments on political, social and other problems that emerged after the break-up of Yugoslavia can also be applied to the current situation in Bosnia-Herzegovina, as both countries are 'administered' by the 'international community'.

10   In these reports, the analysts like to measure whether we have an 'independent judicial system and judges', an 'independent media', 'free elections', etc., taken as the indicators of 'real progress towards a sustainable and true democracy'. In this sense, even though it is not an NGO, it would not be too much of an understatement to claim that the entire nature of the OSCE Mission in Kosovo is based precisely on 'analysing' reports. For a rather obscene description of their mission, see www.osce.org/kosovo.

USAID, etc. As a result of this vast web of organisational manip-
ulation, the space of political intervention has been significantly
diminished. The sovereign will of the people is completely marginalised, if not repressed. As the apartheid of the 1990s was
dismantled, from 1999 onwards, the country experienced a
collective excitement and enthusiasm. This collective enthusiasm defined the country in the aftermath of the war, but it
withered away under the new policies presented and implemented by the 'humanitarian governmentality' of UNMIK.[11]
What followed this period was a series of reactionary events. As
independence was declared, the people of Kosovo were hoping
for 'a new beginning':[12] that is, after nine years of UN administration which installed the sort of governance that Peter
Hallward would call 'imperial democracy', we would finally be
able to democratise the country.

The aftermath of the declaration of independence did
nothing but amplify despair and disillusionment. If anything,
independence has brought more imperialist constraints, further
limitation of political space, and economic decline. In this
sense, it is worth recalling the very beginning of Marx's
Eighteenth Brumaire of Louis Bonaparte: translated into the context of Kosovo, the liberation of the country from Serbian rule
in 1999 turned out to be a *tragedy* (humanitarian administration, introduction of a market economy, privatisation, etc.),
while the independence of 2008 was simply a *farce*. Currently,
international organisations 'helping/advising' the government
lead to an international isolation of the country and its

---

11   See www.unmikonline.org. It should be noted that UNMIK has offices
in Pristina and in Mitrovica in the northern part of the country (mostly controlled
by the government of Serbia). It is interesting to note that most UNMIK employees
have switched to EULEX in the aftermath of the UNMIK downsizing.

12   The hope for 'something new' has been repressed and transformed into
what I would call 'The New Born Ideology'. On the day of Kosovo's declaration of
independence, an art project called the 'New Born obelisk' was located in the centre
of Pristina. Despite all the political, media and other ideological campaigns, which
try to convince us that a new era has begun, the independence of Kosovo does not
mark a new era in itself. It is rather the continuation of the 'old within the new' that
legitimises the entire political process in Kosovo from 1999 onwards.

citizens,[13] and further exacerbate ethnically based divisions. This should by no means be read as an attempt to mock the liberation struggle of the late 1990s, or the resistance to the oppressive regime of Slobodan Milošević that took place throughout that decade. The thesis that I want to defend here is that neither this resistance nor the declaration of independence was radical or emancipatory enough.

It's Political Struggle, Stupid!

There was something peculiar in the response of the West to the violent dissolution of Yugoslavia. The usual reaction with respect to the violence in the Balkans was to chalk it up as an outburst of the old 'primitive Balkan passions'. From the perspective of the West, the Balkans remains nothing more than the Other vis-à-vis the civilised West, the cradle of a savage beast in which old myths are resuscitated and replayed every now and then. Against this blatantly racist approach, one should recall Mladen Dolar's quip: 'the European unconscious is structured like the Balkans'.[14] The Balkans symbolises the place where the repressed truth of Europe is brutally revealed.[15]

Given this perception of the region, there have never been as many scholars as interested in the former Yugoslavia as there are now. Apart from a few honourable exceptions, most of the scholars dealing with Kosovo are obsessed with the myths,

---

13 The Republic of Kosovo is the only country in the region that is not included in the so-called White Schengen Zone. With a Republic of Kosovo passport, one can travel visa-free to only five countries: Albania, Montenegro, Macedonia, Turkey and Haiti.

14 Quoted from S. Žižek, *The Parallax View*, Cambridge, MA: MIT Press, 2006, 377.

15 Nowadays it is fashionable to exoticise the region: everyone from anthropologists to artists likes to visit to 'experience the real life in the region', to 'get to know/understand the culture', as was the case with a group of Finnish artists visiting Kosovo as a part of an artistic project. Their racism came out spontaneously, as it were: they enjoyed being in a country that is not (yet!?) subjected to the alienated and commodified life of the 'first capitalist world'. On the other side, the ultimate form of racism is that which argues that the Balkans is the place where European civilisation meets oriental despotism.

cultures and the past of our nations; dozens of conferences are organised every year on these topics in universities all over Europe and the United States, and as many books are published.[16] What they all have in common is a culturalist obsession with myths as a way of discovering something about the country.[17]

Against this perception of the Balkans, and therefore the racist perception of the wars that erupted with the disintegration of Yugoslavia, one should recall a scene from a debate that took place a few years ago on an Austrian TV programme, between an Albanian, a Serb and an Austrian pacifist. As Žižek reports,[18] both the Albanian and the Serb were rational and consistent within their nationalistic logics. At one moment during the debate, the Austrian peacenik interrupts them, in an attempt to make an impassioned plea: 'Whatever you do, please promise that you won't kill each other; you should do your best to resist the terrible temptation of hatred and vengeance!' As the story goes, 'at this moment, something [not so] unique happened: the two official "enemies" briefly exchanged gazes of solidarity as a gesture of shared perplexity, as if to say: "What is this idiot doing here? What is he talking about?"' Following this line of thought, one should say that this very exchange of gazes between the Albanian and the Serb gives us a glimmer of hope: 'Let's get together, join forces, and knock off this stupid pacifist, then we will be able to do something together.'[19]

On one level, this story encapsulates the true (or real) nature

16   If one is really interested in the case of Kosovo, I would not recommend the following titles: T. Judah, *Kosovo: What Everyone Needs to Know*, Oxford: Oxford University Press, 2008; T. Judah, *Kosovo: War and Revenge*, London: Yale University Press, 2002; J. Pettifer, *Kosova Express: A Journey in Wartime*, London: C. Hurst and Co, 2005; J. Pettifer and M. Vicker, *The Albanian Question: Reshaping the Balkans*: London: I.B. Tauris, 2009.

17   If there is one pure example of an attempt to 'demystify' one myth by creating another, and in this way creating a political narrative, it is A. Di Lellio, *The Battle of Kosovo 1389: An Albanian Epic*, London: I.B. Tauris, 2009.

18   S. Žižek, *Manje Ljubavi, Više Mržnje* [Less Love, More Hatred], Belgrade: Beogradski Krug, 2001, 8.

19   Quoted from S. Žižek's lecture in Pristina, 'Ideology Between Fetish and Symptom', 19 May 2009.

of the 'Albanian-Serbian question'. Many of the so-called
authorities on the 'Kosovo issue' often refer to that 'question' as
a matter of ethnic, cultural or religious hatred. This reductionist
narrative states that cross-religious and cross-ethnic hatred has
a history that is deeply rooted in the conscience of the two
nations, arising out of certain myths and folkloric tales. The
result of this narrative has been to depoliticise and further 'eth-
nicise' what is fundamentally a political problem. All attempts
to squeeze the 'Kosovo question' into the domain of an ethnic/
cultural problem conceal a form of racism. The proper way to
counteract these representations is to propose the concept of
'the necessity to demystify the demystification of myths'. There
is a large cadre of scholars who write about demystifying the
myths that supposedly underpin the inter-ethnic violence in the
region. These attempts fail, however, not only in demystifying
myths but also in getting at the deeper meaning of the Kosovo
issue because they too miss the essential political dimension to
the conflict. This failure is the 'natural' outcome of what is otherwise an 'academic' endeavour that is out of touch with the
realities of the situation. These studies often perpetuate a cycle
of racism in which even many benevolent 'pro-Kosovo' scholars
find themselves caught.

In the beginning of his rather short but extremely provocative book, *Serbia and Albania*, Dimitrije Tucović (a Serbian
socialist from the beginning of the previous century) writes that
'with the occupying politics employed by the Serbian government against the Albanian people, in the western borders of
Serbia such relations were created, that in the near future we
can hardly expect any peace and normality'.[20] This suggests that
the 'Albanian-Serbian question' is simple – that it is a problem
of the colonised and the coloniser. To put it in the discourse that
was famous during the 1990s in Kosovo, the relation between
Albanians and Serbs is that of the occupied and the occupiers.

---

20   D. Tucović, *Serbia dhe Shqipëria: kontribut në kritikën e politikës push-
teuese te borgjezisë serbe*, [Serbia and Albania: A Contribution to the Critique of
the Occupying Policy of the Serbian Bourgeois], in *Zgjedhje Punimesh II* [Selected
Works II], Pristina: Rilindja, 1981, 262–3.

A few years after Tucović wrote *Serbia and Albania*, Bajram Curri, an Albanian revolutionary,[21] had a short but interesting correspondence with Lenin precisely regarding the right to self-determination for the Albanians. It is reported that Lenin suggested to Curri that the Albanians should unite with the Macedonians in a joint alliance[22] against the Serbian bourgeoisie,[23] since both nations were fighting against the Serbian occupation and for creating their own nation-states.[24] In this sense, it was Lenin himself who denounced the London Secret Treaty,[25] thus preventing the country from further partition.

This brief detour into the 'history' of the Albanian-Serbian question is a counterweight to the revisionist reading of the history that we (in the entire region) have been subjected to

---

21   During the First World War, Bajram Curri organised a guerrilla unit under a movement called the Committee for the National Defence of Kosovo. He was an important figure during the socialist revolution of June 1924 in Albania, known as the June Revolution, led by Fan Stilian Noli. As the counter-revolution succeeded (with the help of forces from Yugoslavia, to where Albania's King Zog had fled), he escaped into the mountains in the north of Albania, where in March 1925 he shot himself in order to escape being captured by Zog's militia. Noli's poem on Curri is one of the most beautiful revolutionary poems in the Albanian language.

22   An excellent job collecting material on the Albanian communist movement and the creation of the Albanian Communist Party has been done by an otherwise reactionary historian, K. Frashëri, in *Historia e Lëvizjes së Majtë në Shqipëri dhe e Themelimit të PKSH-së 1878–1941* [The History of the Leftist Movement in Albania and of the Establishment of the CPA 1878–1941], Tirana: Akademia e Shkencave të Shqipërisë, 2006. References to these developments are from Frashëri's book.

23   Unfortunately, this correspondence remains 'classified' in Tirana's State Archive; however, there have been wide reports, analyses and commentaries on this correspondence, especially during socialist Albania and Kosovo.

24   The Albanian political and intellectual avant-garde of the beginning of the twentieth century had a great respect and admiration for the Soviet Union and for Lenin: this was expressed by Fan S. Noli himself in his speech in November 1927 at the conference 'Friends of SSSR' in Leningrad. See, F.S. Noli, *Artikuj, ligjërime* [Articles, Presentations], Pristina: Rilindja, 1981.

25   The London Secret Treaty was signed on 26 April 1915 by the four world powers of the time (England, France, Italy and Russia). These countries pledged that after the First World War, parts of Albania would be divided between Serbia, Montenegro and Greece. The remaining part of the country was to come under Rome's protectorate.

over the last twenty years. It is very symptomatic that most scholars seldom mention these facts.[26] By now the 'status' of the myths (and their relation to the wars of the 1990s) has been clarified enough: the wars in the former Yugoslavia were *by no means* the consequence of our inability to distinguish between our myths and so-called existing reality. We in the Balkans are *by no means* hostages to our own myths or our own history, nor a region of philistine gangs that cannot overcome their own past, but necessarily revive our myths and folkloric tales and let them rule our lives. The exact opposite is true. It was precisely when the wars started that these myths were resurrected, but then they had a precise function: that of an ideological supplement to what was happening in the present. One seeks refuge in myths only when 'reality' is unable to rationalise the present.

The function of the cadre of scholars is reminiscent of Chesterton's theory of the policemen of mythical tales: trying to detect the deeper meaning of cultural/national differences, they seek to project their 'discoveries' onto a crime *to be* committed. In this sense, these academics function as an ideological support to the ruling ideology of Kosovo. Do they not resemble the continuation of the utterly racist agitation of the KFOR forces? Recall the infamous poster issued by KFOR, depicting a dog and a cat followed by the message: 'if they can do it – so can you'. This stands as a pure example of interventionist racism par excellence: leaving aside the disgusting treatment of

---

26   For a succinct analysis of the position of the Albanians in the Kingdom of Serbs, Croats and Slovenes, and in the SFR of Yugoslavia, see B. Stojanović, *State and Contemporary Art*, Belgrade: Prelom, 2006, 197–203. It is important to emphasise that the issue of the Albanians was not resolved in either the Yugoslav Kingdom or in socialist Yugoslavia. The Resolution of the Bujan Conference (December 1942–January 1943) and the Anti-Fascist Council of the People's Liberation of Yugoslavia's (AVNOJ) Resolution, in which the right of self-determination for the Albanians had been recognised, was denied after the Second World War. However, it is interesting to recall the claim made by many leaders of the Kosovo Liberation Army (KLA) that their liberation struggle was a continuation of the anti-fascist national liberation struggle. For more on the partisan struggle in Kosovo, see A. Hamza, 'Politika Partizane, ose krijimi i univerzalizmit' [Partisan Politics, or the Foundation of Universalism], *Koha Ditore*, Pristina, 23 July 2010.

Albanians and Serbs as animals, the discourse of liberal multi-cultural tolerance, as portrayed in KFOR posters, is here advertised as a 'natural' coexistence between the cat and the dog. The poster renders visible not only the limits of multi-ethnicity (in its liberal/neo-imperial configuration), but also the racism of cultural studies scholars dealing with the region.

Going back to the TV show mentioned above, there is indeed an Albanian-Serbian question and it is a political question par excellence. This brings us to the crucial point: the independence of Kosovo. To put the question in Badiou's terms, what is independence the 'name' of? From whom, and for what, is independence being sought? To formulate an answer in schematic fashion, the independence of Kosovo is a name for equality. It is not an empty name, a word deprived of its 'positive content', but has a precise political meaning. It is the name of the national liberation struggle. By national liberation, one should understand the struggle against Serbian government oppression between 1989 and 1999, a period that can justifiably be called a period of apartheid. Albanians in Kosovo were organised under the so-called parallel system, which included the parallel organisation of education, health care, etc., whereby workers, teachers, doctors, nurses and public administrators of Albanian nationality were expelled from their jobs in the course of only a few months in 1990. According to the best available estimate, just over one million Albanians lost their jobs. Private houses were used as schools (at all three levels: primary, secondary and university). It is worth recalling two other telling details. During the 1990s, it was prohibited for more than three Albanians to walk together in the street: this was considered a threat to public order and a separatist gathering. On the other hand, a new version of the Albanian language was developed during that period: an inverted 'self-censored' language, which served as a means of free communication hidden from the Serbian police, secret service and other repressive apparatuses.

The struggle for independence is the name for the struggle against unequal national status within the Socialist Federal

Republic of Yugoslavia (SFRY) and then the Republic of Serbia. Its legal-political status was peculiar: Kosovo was a constitutive element of the SFRY, but at the same time, an autonomous province of the Republic of Serbia. Unlike the other nations, Kosovo's legal status in the Yugoslav Federation was that of a *nationality* (*kombësi, narodnost*). Being the poorest and the most underdeveloped part of the SFRY, the struggle for independence included in itself the struggle for economic equality as well. Last but not least, the struggle for independence is an anti-colonial struggle (in Tucović's sense).

The struggle for independence is neither a psychological state of mind, nor the eternal drive of the Albanian separatists (as politicians and media of the state of Serbia prefer to understand it). Independence is the name for emancipation, equality and liberation. This is where the Western left got it wrong. It was fashionable and all too easy to criticise the NATO bombings. Max Horkheimer wrote in 1939, 'whoever is not prepared to talk about capitalism should also remain silent about fascism', and the same should apply to the (Western) left: 'whoever is not prepared to talk about the apartheid of the 1990s, should also remain silent about the NATO bombing'.

What Is to Be Done?

The present political and ideological conjuncture of the Republic of Kosovo is mostly a result of 'humanitarianism'. That is to say, the independence of Kosovo is problematic mostly due to the *way in which it was brought about*. In 1999, we experienced a 'humanitarian intervention' against the Federal Republic of Yugoslavia (Serbia and Montenegro), and in 2008 Kosovo declared its independence based on 'humanitarian premises'. This humanitarian dimension resulted in the event of independence being a ruthlessly depoliticised act. To state it in Žižek's terms, the act of the declaration of independence was *decaffeinated*. The declaration of independence was further depoliticised with the Ahtisaari Plan, a document that stands for an arrogant negation of any notion of 'the will of the people'[27] which it purports to support and maintain. The independence of Kosovo, although proclaimed by parliament,[28] sprang out of a 'package' (as some refer to the Ahtisaari Plan) – or, to put it in less prosaic terms, the independence of Kosovo has the status of an imperial imposition. It is no wonder that the Ahtisaari Plan was never the subject of a referendum. During the time of negotiations with Serbia over the so-called final status of Kosovo, the entire range of solutions offered remained within the liberal-democratic horizon: from 'Kosovo je Srbija' ('Kosovo is Serbia': the official state slogan of Serbia), to the partition of Kosovo, multi-ethnic Kosovo, independence, etc.

On the other side, precisely during this time, the then political movement Lëvizja Vetëvendosje! launched its slogan: 'Jo Negociata – Vetëvendosje!' ('No Negotiations – Self-determination!'),[29] thereby opposing the negotiations on Kosovo's political status. The problem with this slogan, however, was that at a certain point during the negotiations it was clear that a form of independence would be designed in the Final Plan, and thus the slogan was no longer operative. With this in mind, Besnik Pula proposed perhaps the most radical solution at the time, maintaining that we should radicalise the political slogan proposed by Vetëvendosje. He insisted on going beyond 'independence', and proposed the slogan 'No to Independence – Yes to Self-Determination'.[30]

The political, economic and ideological situation in the

---

27   As developed in P. Hallward, 'The Will of the People: Notes Towards a Dialectical Voluntarism', Radical Philosophy, vol. 155, 2009, 17–29.

28   Before 2008, Kosovo's institutions were founded upon the so-called Constitutional Framework for Provisional Self-Governance. UNMIK, Regulation No. 2001/9 on a Constitutional Framework for Provisional Self-Government in Kosovo, Pristina, 15 May 2001, at http://assembly-kosova.org.

29   This graffiti has appeared all over Kosovo, while many activists of the movement were arrested during the action that lasted for months. Vetëvendosje! transformed itself from a movement into a political party and shifted towards the right.

30   B. Pula, 'Pavarësia pa vetëvendosje e Ahtisaarit' [Ahtisaari's Independence Without Self-Determination], February 2007, at http://besnikpula.wordpress.com.

Republic of Kosovo is highly irrational precisely because of the 'coexistence' of neo-imperial structures. The will of the people is a pure negation of the neo-imperial agenda and this tension produces a continuous antagonism. In each of these areas, the space is open; no 'final' solution has been achieved. The process of privatisation of public enterprises is ongoing;[31] the country is in a permanent state of exception (with KFOR as its eternal guarantee); the so-called European model of decentralisation is only a euphemism for an ethnically differentiated society,[32] or an ethnic partition of the country; negotiations with Serbia on the so-called technical/practical issues are completing what has been often referred to as the 'Bosnianisation of Kosovo'; and the list goes on. In this sense, in the existing structural config-uration of the state of Kosovo, there can be no possible solution to all of these problems in any foreseeable future. All the obsta-cles and problems that confront us are not only accidental disturbances; the malfunctioning of the state as such is struc-turally necessary.

Taking all of these dynamics into account, one should insist more than ever on the idea of going *beyond independence*. To state it simply: the proclamation of independence was necessary as an attempt to mark a break from the past; independence is the 'condition of the possibility' for something else. Therefore, every move beyond independence should either begin from or go through independence. In 1991, Jean-Bertrand Aristide insisted that 'only a complete revolution can change Haiti'[33] – a

---

31   I do not think it would be much of an exaggeration to repeat what Peter Hallward wrote apropos Haiti after the earthquake of 2010: 'punitive international trade and financial arrangements ensure that such destitution and impotence will remain a structural fact of Haitian life for the foreseeable future'. See P. Hallward, 'Our Role in Haiti's Plight', 13 January 2010, at www.guardian.co.uk. For an excel-lent analysis of the imperial intervention and its catastrophic outcome in Haiti, see Hallward's *Damming the Flood: Haiti, Aristide and the Politics of Containment*, London: Verso, 2007.

32   One should be aware of the terminology that is used by the so-called international community in Kosovo: the people of Kosovo do not constitute a nation, rather we are reduced to the level of 'ethnicities', or a community of ethnic groups.

33   Quoted in Hallward, *Damming the Flood*, xxxvi.

complete revolution, which would begin from (the proclamation of) independence, go through it and radically transform it.
This same insight is applicable to Kosovo, and indeed, is the
only means by which it can effectuate political change. To put
the issue in a more schematic fashion, going *beyond independence* is the name for the negation of the actually existing
predicament and the opening up of political possibility, so far
closed down by the ruling international and local elites. If we
are honest, we will rarely find anyone who *really* believes that
the independence of Kosovo, in its actual form, is the long-term
solution. Many proposals have been made on the future of the
country: from unification with Albania,[34] to return to Serbia,
or a regional federation or union. It is worth recalling Tucović's
idea of the Federation of the Balkan States as one of the possible
solutions for the region.[35]

The revolutionising of Kosovo at all its different levels –
from democratising the 'imperial democracy', to dissolving
neoliberal economic experiments, to taking the fate of the
country into our own hands – is the basis for a possible opening
of the space of political emancipation. Differently put, the complete revolutionising of the Republic of Kosovo should be read
as a call for intervening in the openness of the political and
economic situation, transforming and 'democratising' the
existing democracy, which has neo-imperial foundations and
'values'. The paradox in this situation is that the very structures
put in place 'to promote and install democracy' are effectively

---

34   This is what Lëvizja Vetëvendosje!, the third biggest political party in
Kosovo, argues for. See www.vetevendosje.org. This idea has also been developed
by Slavoj Žižek, although one should emphasise that Vetëvendosje's and Žižek's
understanding and argumentation for this solution come from completely different
positions and angles. See S. Žižek, 'Možda je dobro da se Kosovo udruži sa
Albanijom' [Maybe it's Good that Kosovo Unites with Albania], 9 April 2010, at
www.dw-world.de; S. Žižek, 'West Wants a Decaffeinated Kosovo', interview with
Agon Hamza, *Koha Ditore*, 18 May 2009, Pristina.

35   The wavering between the Balkans and Yugoslavia is not accidental. Due
to limitations of space, it has to remain undeveloped here. When referring to
Tucović's idea of the unification of the Balkan states into one 'Federation/Union',
however, it stretches beyond the borders of the former Yugoslavia.

killing every democratic tendency in the country. Therefore, getting rid of every neo-imperial organisation is a matter of political urgency. Similarly, the aggressive neoliberal policies are transforming Kosovo into a country in which the struggle for survival is the normal predicament for the majority of the people. The privatisation of socially and state-owned enterprises has even failed to realise the promises of the ruling elite. A new economic model is therefore more than ever necessary. Yes, the people of Kosovo live in an ongoing dramatic situation, but the revolutionising of the country means above all a situation in which 'men become the authors and actors of their own drama', to quote a poetic line from Marx's *The Poverty of Philosophy*. This is a precondition for any political move against the reactionary politics that function at the level of the state throughout the region, and this is a political struggle that makes neither the post-Yugoslav region nor Kosovo much different from the rest of Europe.

CHAPTER 9

Mapping Nostalgia for Tito: From Commemoration to Activism[1]

Mitja Velikonja

And smart he was, one-legged cool mate.
Lied much, motherfucker, but we all loved him . . .
From Srdjan Dragojević's film *Pretty Villages,*
Pretty Flames (1996)

'The very curious period of post-communism', as former dissidents Adam Michnik and Vaclav Havel described it in a 1992 interview,[2] has spawned a series of interesting social phenomena and cultural curiosities across the former Yugoslavia. The professional public and ordinary people both refer to them as 'Yugonostalgia', or nostalgia for the late country. Its manifestations are extremely diverse, varying with the region, time, group of people or intentions. It involves pleasant memories of various 'things Yugoslav' rather than things specific to individual nations of the former Yugoslavia. These include its pop culture, films, television series, comedy programmes, the entertainment scene, victories of national sporting teams, formal and informal relationships, travels and holidaymaking, employment opportunities across the former country, various aspects of everyday life, cult consumer products, etc. Titostalgia is part of Yugonostalgia: a lament for *Yuga*, as it is affectionately called,

---

1   An earlier version of this chapter was published as part of the book M. Velikonja, *Titostalgia: A Nostalgia for Josip Broz*, Ljubljana: Peace Institute, 2008.
2   Interview with A. Michnik and V. Havel, 'Prečudno obdobje postkomunizma' [Curious Era of Post-Communism], *Nova revija*, vol. 121–2, 1992, 598–617.

is, as a rule, also a lament for *Comrade Tito*. Titostalgia is a more concrete, direct and essential part of the loose notion of Yugonostalgia, but it nevertheless needs to be examined in a broader context. Over the turbulent decades following his death, the attitude towards Tito of Yugoslav citizens, and later of the citizens of the newly formed countries, as well as of the wider international community, greatly varied.

Nostalgia is not only a complex phenomenon, but also a contradictory one that combines various narratives and practices. Apart from mimetic nostalgia, which is serious, dogmatic, unchangeable, expressly political and continuous, in which Broz's image is the same as it was in the past, there also exists a counter-nostalgia, satirical nostalgia, or 'neostalgia'. Its defining features are a mischievous teasing and a deliberate subversion of the current system by exploiting the problematic past. Such behaviour is not without political connotations, although these are indirect and shifted to another level. The one thing clear is that this enduring and strong affection for *Comrade Tito* cannot be explained in simple terms, as a consequence of one or a few factors. Below I present and reject several such generalised explanations of both materialised and non-materialised *Titostalgia*. In each case, I first present an argument and then my counter-argument, because each argument is valid to a certain extent, but none provides a comprehensive explanation.

Argument One

The 'return of Tito' is a consequence of the catastrophic events over the past two decades or so: wars, slaughter, destruction, destitution, economic and social underdevelopment, political crises, etc. 'Everything has collapsed' was a resigned comment by a Kosovan, who summed up the opinion of many others. Since Broz is idealised as a symbol of friendship, solidarity, prosperity and security, it is seemingly self-evident why people long for that era. Consequently, one would expect to find the strongest expressions of Titostalgia and Yugonostalgia in those parts of the former Yugoslavia where people most suffered and which today radically lag behind their neighbours. In principle, the worse the present seems compared to the past, the stronger the nostalgia. Dissatisfaction and despair inspire and provoke nostalgia, and the past appears as a safe haven when confronted with present-day problems. While this is true, it does not explain the strong presence of Titostalgic elements, narratives and practices in Slovenia, which to a large extent escaped the tragic fate of most other former Yugoslav republics and achieved economic and political progress during the past two decades despite many serious problems. In addition to diachronic causality, it is necessary also to take into account synchronic interrelationships, as Jameson suggests:[3] not only the recent past, but also – or mostly – the contemporary situation in Slovenia. Obviously, there are other factors influencing nostalgia as well.

Argument Two

The enigmatic veneration of the late leader is actually the nostalgia of older generations for *past times*, for their youth, enthusiasm and ideals, meaning the nostalgia of former *Tito's youths* whose best years were lived when Yugoslavia was at its peak and Titoism was a mature phenomenon. 'It will never be better than it was then' is a statement I have heard frequently in various parts of the former Yugoslavia. It is believed that Tito's fans come mainly from the ranks of 'ordinary people', who either met him at one of the many events or receptions organised for children and young people, or who were award winners, relay runners, co-fighters, co-workers and so on. Broz was undoubtedly a populist. He had a feeling for people, loved to mix with them, and in contrast to some of his contemporaries, was not a cabinet leader. Judging by interviews and conversations, but also various other sources, I can establish four 'common denominators' underlying Broz's present popularity

3   F. Jameson, *Archaeologies of the Future: The Desire Called Utopia and Other Science Fictions*, New York and London: Verso, 2005, 88.

with these people: anti-fascism and the liberation struggle; industrial and social modernisation; peace; and global reputation and recognition.

Yet age is not the exclusive factor in nostalgia. Naturally, in one of its forms, nostalgia is a 'positive memory' of the past, but Titostalgia can also be found among the younger generation that was born when Tito was already (long) dead, or among the generation that only vaguely remembers him. They too 'find in the past what they miss in the present'.[4] How, then, can the traditional definition of nostalgia as something *personally experienced* explain teenagers' wearing T-shirts with Tito's image, or self-organised student excursions to Kumrovec or Belgrade in which all the participants were born after 1980? Nostalgia in young people should be understood differently from older people's nostalgia, that is, as *neostalgia*. While some young people are obviously aware that they did not know Tito at all and that they could not possibly know him, others act as if they really remembered him and preserve him in their memory. A survey on Yugonostalgia among Slovenian youth showed that they imagined 'a secure, stable, just and united Yugoslavia', inhabited by a 'simple, satisfied and non-ambitious people who cultivate the values of collectivism, solidarity and equality'.[5] Similar viewpoints could be gleaned from the conversations with young Croatians who attended the Youth Day celebration in Kumrovec. One among them gave a typical answer stating that it was 'undoubtedly better in the past', 'life was more relaxed', 'more human and less stressful', 'men were co-workers, not competitors'.[6]

---

4   L. Pečjak, 'Nostalgija po sedanjosti: oblike, pomeni in vloge nostalgičnega diskurza med mladimi' [Nostalgia for the Present: Forms, Meanings and Roles of Nostalgic Discourse among Young Generations], *Časopis za kritiko znanosti*, vol. 34(224), 2006, 47.

5   Ibid., 46.

6   N. Kovačič, 'Petorica mladih Hrvata putuju u dobra stara vremena' [Five Young Croats Travel to Good Old Times], in K. Mathiesen Hjemdahl and N. Škrbić Alempijević, eds, *O Titu kao mitu – Proslava Dana mladosti u Kumrovcu*, Zagreb (trans.): FF, Srednja Europa, 2006, 328.

Argument Three

It is from here that my next argument arises, namely that Titostalgia (and thus Yugonostalgia) among young people is not a consequence of a mechanical passing down of positive memories through generations. According to one argument, Titostalgic parents presumably educate their children in this spirit, and their children simply accept it.[7] Once again I find this explanation too simplistic, because it ignores the gap between the values and production of the parents' culture and those of the younger generation's culture, lacking virtually any linearity in modern, fast-changing societies. Unlike their parents, many young people of today think of Tito outside any context, seeing him as a completely new figure.

Argument Four

In patricentric (Titocentric?) Yugoslav ideology, Broz embodied practically every character: an unschooled peasant boy, a precarious proletarian, an ordinary soldier, a captive, a political prisoner, a victorious commander-in-chief, a globally renowned statesman and, inevitably, a bon vivant, a hedonist, a womaniser and a 'real macho'.[8] He was simultaneously a 'typical Balkan man', a 'typical Central European' and a 'typical cosmopolitan'. He started out as a member of a lower class, then rose to the petty bourgeoisie, and eventually to the higher class, indeed the highest. Within the post-war political imaginary, he was identified with his state, *Tito's Yugoslavia*, and all its citizens (at least according to one popular slogan of the past – 'We are all Tito!').

---

7   ''Cos you had a good time, I hear about it at home', was how a young man in his twenties explained his nostalgia for socialism to Broz's impersonator Godnič. N. Močnik *Ugledališčena nostalgija* [Nostalgia in Theatre], Ljubljana: Research seminar – FDV, 2008, 11.

8   In America, this would be called *The American Dream*! Actually, it is one of the fundamental liberal myths about the infinite possibilities of vertical mobility – of an individual, not of a class or a group of people – according to which anyone can achieve anything provided that *he/she has talents and puts in enough effort*!

His notorious political contemporaries were presented as his antagonistic counterparts and Broz emerged a winner from every conflict with them.[9] His political acumen, tactical wisdom, military genius, but also his affability, charm, and even physical endurance and vitality were highlighted. It is possible to synthesise all these vignettes into two main ones: in the first, he appears as a *great leader*, a successful, unwavering and just politician, photographed in the company of top world leaders, crowned heads and Hollywood stars, living in immense luxury, hunting, playing with tame leopards, navigating his yacht, etc. In the second, he is 'one of us', *a man of the people*, shown in informal situations, for example picking fruit, taking photos, swimming, playing chess, playing the piano, metalworking, dancing in *kolo*, chatting to ordinary people, workers, children and soldiers. This inflation of images of the leader and his 'phoney closeness' supposedly facilitates people's identification with him – that is how one could sum up the simplified rationalisation of affection for a living or late politician. The more the better, it seems.

Yet even this explanation is not sufficiently convincing, given that the simultaneous humanisation and exceptionality of contemporary politicians is not a new propaganda trick. They are untouchable, but also neighbours; somewhere far away, but also among us. They are something special, but also the same as us.[10]

Moreover, the stress on the celebrity chic surrounding Broz and his life in the lap of luxury at a time when he was the leader of a developing country that was more impoverished than not, is of dubious explanatory value. One would imagine that, in a society in which egalitarianism and communitarianism were both a pre-modern tradition and a socialist propaganda maxim, Tito's blatant monarchical extravagance would be seen as a

---

9   For his admirers, he is, naturally, better than any of his successors, i.e. post-socialist politicians. One among them says: 'My dear Tito, many imitate you but none can hold a candle to you' (in the visitors' book at Tito's mausoleum in Dedinje in Belgrade).

10   R. Barthes, *Mythologies*, London: Vintage, 1993, 91–3.

drawback rather than a positive trait. It is interesting that today's nostalgics do not hold it against him, although they, much like the wider society in post-socialist countries, evaluate negatively contemporary upstarts, tycoons, profiteers and people who have become rich and famous overnight. This double criterion is usually justified humorously, along the lines 'Tito stole but he also gave, those today steal but give nothing.'

Argument Five

Tito was, and still is, esteemed for his political originality. However, Broz's Yugoslavism was just one form of the wider and older South Slavic supra-national ideology. In much the same way, socialism as a political system existed before Broz's time and, after the Second World War, evolved elsewhere in Eastern Europe as well as beyond it. Mass rallies and various cultural, sporting and political events resembling the Youth Day are a reliable part of the ritual repertoire of every authoritarian group: the Church, the state, political parties, etc. Just think of the opening of the 2008 Olympic Games in Beijing. And last but not least, many important elements of the Broz propaganda machine were not without precedent. In 1940, relay races in honour of the then underage King Petar II of Yugoslavia were held, starting in Kragujevac and crossing the whole country. Towards the end of the war it was again in Kragujevac that the idea of a relay race in honour of the new leader, Broz, originated. Furthermore, he took over from the Karadjordjević family the custom of being the godfather to the ninth or tenth child in a family. 'We are Tito's, Tito is ours' is a slogan much reminiscent of the one used by Serbian radicals towards the end of the nineteenth century ('We belong to Pašić, Pašič belongs to us').[11] Finally, Broz's succinct 'last testament', 'Watch over brotherhood and unity, we paid for it in blood!', is reminiscent

---

11   I. Čolović, 'O maketama i štafetama' [On Maquettes and Relay-Batons], in R. Leposavić, ed., VlasTito iskustvo / Past-Present, Belgrade: Samizdat B92, 2004, 140.

of the alleged last words of the Yugoslav King Aleksandar, assassinated in 1934 in Marseille: 'Watch over Yugoslavia!' The obsessive rhetoric of brotherhood is at any rate part of every corporatism – we can also hear it as part of the ideology of the new Eurocentrism.[12]

Furthermore, new mass-culture production, souvenir products and the use of Broz's image in advertising can be explained by purely commercial motives – Tito simply sells well! This was the guiding principle of the Mirna voda company based in Zagreb, which named its new bottled water *Titov izvor* (Tito Spring). 'We named it Tito Spring because Joža [regional diminutive for his first name Josip] can bring profit', was their explanation.[13] The name was suggested to them by an advertising company aiming to bring a breath of fresh air to the market. The commercialisation of Tito is by no means an exception. Other charismatic leaders or personalities are used in similar roles, for example Che (on cigarette packets, vodka bottles, ice cream and bikinis), Stalin (on glasses and in the shape of a candle), Mao (on watches and tags), Gorbachev (a vodka label), and Atatürk (found practically everywhere across the symbolic landscape of the Turkish state).[14] All this adds up to a genuine nostalgia industry. Zala Volčič argues that the use of Broz's image in advertising is 'perhaps the final sign that Slovenia [has] become a full-fledged consumer society freed from anxiety of sliding back toward its socialist past'.[15]

Tito sells well, no doubt, but many of the objects and arrangements mentioned earlier are home-made and intended,

---

12   See examples in M. Velikonja, *Eurosis: A Critique of the New Eurocentrism*, Ljubljana: Peace Institute, 2005.

13   See R. Kajzer, 'Blagovna znamka Tito' (trans.), *Delo*, 21 May 2005, 32, and J. Z/STA, 'Tito se še vedno prodaje' (trans.), *Delo*, 16 May 2005, at www.delo.si. They plan to export bottled water primarily to non-aligned countries.

14   In the words of Marc Lacey, 'In fact, 40 years after his death Che is as much a marketing tool as an international revolutionary icon.' M. Lacey, '40 Years after Che's Death, His Image Is a Battleground', *International Herald Tribune*, 9 October 2007, 6.

15   Z. Volčič, 'Yugo-nostagia: Cultural Memory and Media in the Former Yugoslavia', *Critical Studies in Media Communication*, vol. 24(1), 2007, 21.

as their creators claim, 'for use in the privacy' of one's home. By the same token, many similar activities and events ('pilgrimages' to Kumrovec or to his mausoleum in Belgrade) have no commercial value whatsoever and are not profit-oriented. A large part of this production follows the DIY principle. In support of this thesis, just think of the messages in visitors' books, most of which are very intimate, introverted and self-purposed, or the earlier-mentioned satirical arrest warrants listing Broz's 'crimes'. Titostalgia is not only an effective marketing trick, but also a typical example of 'reflective nostalgia' as defined by Svetlana Boym.[16]

Argument Six

The posthumous informal 'rehabilitation' of Broz is just one among the presently popular obsessions and fascinations with the past, or 'past-ism', to put it concisely. Toying with and replaying history is a strategy frequently used in postmodern narratives ranging from media culture to the arts, all adding to the past a measure of spectacle and pop art and changing it into a thrilling, titillating and trivialised story. This gives rise to the present feverish search for details of Broz's personal life: his love affairs, his favourite dishes, friendships with domestic and foreign film stars, marital scandals, ambiguous origins, etc.[17] Like any other kind of nostalgia, Titostalgia, too, can be a hobby, as it is in the case of the collectors' Nostalgia Institute in Ljubljana. Yet, although this is true in principle, one may ask why some other nostalgic trends in these societies are not equally strong, and why there is no equally obvious nostalgia for other important personalities. Naturally, other such

---

16   S. Boym, *The Future of Nostalgia*, New York: Basic Books, 2001, 41–55. In contrast to restorative nostalgia, which strives for the active reconstruction of the past, reflective nostalgia rests more on the feelings of yearning and loss: it 'lingers on ruins, the patina of time and history, in the dreams of another place and another time' (ibid., 41).

17   See R. West, *Tito and the Rise and Fall of Yugoslavia*, London: Sinclair-Stevenson, 1996, 183.

personalities are the subject of various nostalgias – the 'old demons return', as Adam Michnik put it, in Slovenia and elsewhere in post-socialist Europe. Certain controversial personalities from modern history are venerated again – however, these trends are incomparably less strong than in the case of Broz.[18] Accordingly, Broz has firmly settled in first place on the Croatian top 100 list of historical figures.[19] On the Slovenian list dating from 2003, he occupied fourth place, while the renowned Slovenian politicians Pučnik, Korošec and Krek were well behind.

Broz is said to be respected by his old comrades, Titoists, diehard Yugoslavs, rigid Yugonostalgics, Yugophiles, Yugo-Bolsheviks, cryptocommunists, the stinking guts of Yugoslavia, Udba-men (Udba was a Yugoslav version of the KGB), spies of international Bolshevism, false prophets, army officers' children, the red bourgeoisie, children from ethnically mixed marriages, Yugocomrades, Yugozombies or Partisan fossils. Generally, he is believed to be more popular among anti-fascists and left-wingers, according to the logic 'he was a leftist, too!' There are at least four objections to this argument. First, many of the erstwhile most eager Titoists are today – *ah, cuore ingrato* – the most ardent anti-Titoists. For example: advocates of the huge inscription *Tito* in large white stones on the hilltop above Branik have established that among the desecrators and opponents of the sign are certain people who decades ago actually painted it and then maintained it for a long time.[20] Even the responsibility for the disintegration of Yugoslavia in the late 1980s can be partly attributed to certain groups within the ruling elites, meaning the political party elites in individual republics which swore to *follow Tito's path* but actually diverged

18   A good example is the former dissident and later Polish President Lech Wałesa, who started as a charismatic opposition leader in the 1980s, became one of the leading politicians in the 1990s, but since then has been reduced to a political outsider.

19   'Tito je najveći Hrvat u povijesti' [Tito Is the Greatest Croat in History], *Nacional*, 6 January 2004, 46.

20   An interview with the Slovenian Titoist E. Bizjak, 13 August 2008.

from it. Furthermore, various antagonistic groups from this period referred to him and even staged demonstrations in which they carried his portraits, but their real goals were different (for example, Kosovo Albanians and Serbs in the 1980s). To borrow from Slavoj Žižek: 'Tito has not died for the second time through the agency of an Enemy: his legitimate successors took care of that pretty well.'[21]

The second objection: why is it him (and Che) and not some other left-wing politician, either global (Stalin, Mao, Castro, Trotsky, Subcomandante Marcos) or local (M. Pijade or E. Kardelj, legendary Partisan commanders)? And the third objection – the examples from real life testify to the opposite of what is claimed, given that even some nationalists and right-wing politicians also refer to him. For example, the notorious leader of the Slovenian Nationalist Party, Zmago Jelinčič, placed a monument to Broz in the garden of his villa. The inscription on the plinth reads: 'A son of a Slovenian mother – The victor of WWII – Marshal of Yugoslavia'. It is one of just two new monuments to Tito erected over the last twenty years (the other is in Labin, Istria). At a local election in 2006, a candidate of the right-wing Slovenian People's Party included in his election pamphlet a long quotation from one of Broz's famed speeches and a well-known portrait of him.[22] The Croatian historian Tvrtko Jakovina also writes about the 'first Croatian President F. Tudjman's never fully voiced but nevertheless obvious sympathies for Broz'.[23]

And, last but not least, the explicitly positive image of Broz emerging from opinion surveys should not be attributed solely to secularist left-wingers, as the following two messages picked from many similar ones found in visitors' books illustrate. The first comes from the book in Tito's mausoleum in Dedinje: 'Honorable Josip Broz Tito, may the almighty God bestow on

---

21   S. Žižek, *Druga smrt Josipa Broza Tita* [The Second Death of Josip Broz Tito], Ljubljana: DZS, 1989, 115.

22   *Join Forces! Your Mayor R. Harej*, an SLS candidate in the elections to the municipal council in Nova Gorica, 2006.

23   T. Jakovina, 'Nepoznati Tito iz američkih arhiva' [Unknown Tito from American Archives], *Globus*, 2 May 2008, 53.

you eternal peace and rest!' The second is from the house of his birth in Kumrovec: 'I'm happy that I lived while you were the President, may you rest in God's peace.' In a Bosnia-Herzegovina broadcast on Broz a few years ago, an older woman who was asked what she thought about him and his time replied: 'May God give him a sacred paradise!'[24]

Argument Seven

Some interpret the 'second coming' of Broz through mass culture as being a static, old-fashioned, even technologically backward phenomenon, a reproduction of the past that will soon die together with his ageing subjects, meaning that it will disappear through entropy. A certain continuity with the past undoubtedly exists. At events paying tribute to him, people fly old flags, wear old medals and fragments of uniforms, and the rhetoric is reminiscent of that used during the heroic times of the Partisan resistance and the era of the enthusiastic post-war building of socialism. On the other hand, Titostalgic discourse has also moved to new media. There are several web pages dedicated to Broz, and interesting debates between his supporters and opponents in various chat rooms and blogs. On his birthday, or on the (former) Republic Day, funny greeting cards are distributed by email (e.g. one showing a pretty young woman congratulating him) often including a well-known statement in all Yugoslav languages ('Dear Young Comrades, Happy Youth Day, 25 May!'), or humorous descriptions of those times (e.g. 'Seven Wonders of Socialism', briefly ironising all that was dysfunctional in a system that nevertheless worked). T-shirts and other objects with Broz's image can be bought online from the Josip Broz Tito Shop at josipbroz.com.

The Slovenian bloggers' magazine *Drugi svet* (Other World) and the publisher *Mladinska knjiga* launched an invitation to

---

24   A. Telibečirović, 'Bog mu daj sveti raj' – Lik Tiva v BiH' ['May God Rest His Soul in Peace' – The Image of Tito in Bosnia-Herzegovina], *Mladina*, 24 April 2004, 25.

bloggers to 'write about their views of Tito or an interesting related experience, or send a message dealing with this topic'. The Slovenian company Pimp offers caricatures and funny voices of famous personalities and other unusual sound effects for mobile phones; among others are the tune of the Yugoslav anthem 'Hey Slavs' with the SFRY emblem, and *Comrade Tito* with a caricature of Broz and Jovanka reminiscent of Homer and Marge Simpson. His image is also reproduced on mouse pads: those sold in Ljubljana are in the shape formerly used for street signs with street names (e.g. Titova 244); in Belgrade, he is depicted on a white horse or playing a piano; in Croatia, they bear his image from Partisan times and an inscription alluding to punk: 'Tito Is not Dead', with an encircled A (as in for Anarchy).

Argument Eight

What is involved is the continuation of Tito's personality cult, his charismatic image and narcissistic self-image, cultivated by him and for him ever since the Second World War. In this argument, the emphasis is on his hedonism, luxury, glamour, nonchalance, and his association with important contemporary politicians and the jet set from the world of entertainment. After the war he made 142 trips, visited sixty-two countries, and met practically every world statesman either as their guest or as host. This is also the image usually presented by contemporary newspaper articles, a characteristic description being: 'Tito was a typical bon vivant, actually the epitome of hedonism.'[25] True, but the mythologies surrounding great leaders, 'heroarchy' or 'government of heroes', to use Thomas Carlyle's term, come and go, while the one that developed around Broz not only survived, but also acquired new dimensions in a politically and culturally changed situation. It seems as if Broz has been regenerated for new generations that have only second-hand, indirect

---

25   S. Banjanac Lubej, 'Skrivnosti Titove kuhinje' [Secrets of Tito's Cuisine], *Žurnal*, 30 November 2005, 43.

knowledge of him. Even among the left-wing parties, it is their youth sections rather than the bulk of members that preserve the memory of him, although many such parties arose from the former League of Communists or one of the political organisations that existed under the former regime. A typical example is the Slovenian Youth Forum of Social Democrats, whose representatives regularly attend the ceremonies in Kumrovec and lay wreaths at the monument to Broz, as do their Croatian counterparts from the Youth Forum of the Social Democratic Party. As already mentioned, his image is also frequently found on the alternative and subcultural stage.

Argument Nine

In certain circumstances Broz is still a delicate political topic, particularly in everyday wrangles among political parties – he seems to represent a kind of political divide separating the left wing from the right wing.[26] The right-wing Slovenian columnist B. Nežmah, writing when the ruling parties were the Liberal Democracy of Slovenia and the United List of Social Democrats, accused 'the political and management elite of celebrating the accession to the EU, while perpetuating their contradictory silent admiration of Tito and de facto replication of his attitude towards the opposition.[27] A similarly volatile atmosphere is frequently felt in Croatia, particularly in the rivalry between the two biggest parties, the right-wing Croatian Democratic Union and the left-wing Social Democratic Party. When Zoran Milanović, the SDP leader, said in the summer of 2007 that 'Tito was greater than Tudjman', he provoked an avalanche of accusations from the opposing camp. There were allegations that some wished to restore Yugoslavia, re-establish links among the Balkan countries, and that Milanović was actually a 'fervent

---

26   This also extends to everyday discussions. An older Titoist from Slovenia told me that he embarrassed his acquaintance who has changed loyalties by asking him: 'And who gave you all that, education, job, pension, who – Tito!'

27   B. Nežmah, 'Tito v Brižinskih spomenikih' [Tito in the Freising Manuscripts], *Mladina*, 24 May 2004, 20.

Titoist' who was in favour of 'Yugoslavia and communism', etc. Nevertheless, this is not the rule, as is obvious from the several examples given above revealing that Broz's supporters also come from the right of the political spectrum.

Argument Ten

Titostalgia (and Yugonostalgia) cannot be fully explained by the fact that Yugoslav socialism, i.e. Broz's government, was more humane than other socialist regimes, that his authoritarianism was milder and softer than that of his eastern counterparts, that the Yugoslav living standard was higher, that the state took care of employment, accommodation and social security, and that Broz succeeded in placating the sources of conflict for so long, contributing in this way to peace in the region. To sum up, the nostalgic pastorals claim that 'life under Tito was quite good'. While it is easy to go along with the above arguments, it should be noted that the majority of Yugoslavs never had close experience of life under the real-socialist regimes outside Yugoslavia. The negative images of these regimes were formed on the basis of negative propaganda (claiming that 'our self-management socialism is better than their statist bureaucratic socialism') and sustained through the silent fear that the 'Russians might eventually decide to march into Yugoslavia'. The Yugoslavs had more experience of and more contact with life in the West, so it would not be surprising if they evaluated life in socialist Yugoslavia in worse terms and were critical of it.

Argument Eleven

There have been many attempts to explain the massive presence of Broz's image as pure parody, or a playful subversion of dominant political, cultural and media discourses. Examples of humorous renderings of Broz are many. We can cite a photomontage on the cover of a CD compilation of ex-Yugoslavian pop stars, in which Broz looks like Marlon Brando in the movie

The Wild One (1953); he is depicted as a biker with bared mus-
cular arms, in a sleeveless jeans jacket studded with labels, and
riding an impressive motorbike. Another example appears on a
T-shirt showing him at an advanced age – in the original photo,
he is smoking a cigar, but here it has been changed into a really
big joint; printed alongside is the well-known socialist slogan
'We want nothing that belongs to others, and won't give anything that belongs to us.' A commercial radio in Slovenia
broadcast a humorous programme in which 'Tito' called in
from heaven. *ŠKUC*, the cult exhibition space in Ljubljana, uses
Broz's image for the sign on the men's toilet, and the image of
his wife Jovanka for the ladies'. Various youth clubs organise
parties, concerts and other events on Tito's birthday, while
Yugonostalgic *fešta* parties and retro-parties have become a
familiar item on the entertainment menu across the former
Yugoslavia. This is interpreted as an entirely apolitical type of
entertainment, a stunt or mild provocation, a pretext for
throwing a good party in Tito's memory, although the majority
of young people attending may not know exactly who he actually was.

This comical playing with the past is undoubtedly part of
neostalgia. Yet I believe that it is also a kind of political gesture,
of which its protagonists are not necessarily fully aware.
Naturally, I do not argue that all those who wear T-shirts
sporting Tito's image, or who participate in commemorating
events or parties, or who think of him as a 'good leader', also
adhere consciously to his political legacy or support his political
platform. This kind of loyalty cannot be purchased along with
a T-shirt or a ticket. And yet it is legitimate to ask why the
holiday of the defunct state and the birthday of the late leader
are so widely celebrated in Slovenia, and not, say, Statehood Day
(25 June) or Europe Day (9 May). The answer can be found in
the latent and unconscious – and frequently even obvious and
well-reflected – subversion immanent to this type of nostalgic
discourse. Statehood Day and Europe Day are official national
holidays and part of dominant discursive constructions, so
inevitably it follows that it is necessary to appropriate other

holidays, if only for the simple reason of challenging the official ones.

Finally, we have good reason to assert that Titostalgia is more a rejection of the current political situation and leaders than an uncritical glorification of the politics of several decades ago and of Broz himself. It can, therefore, be understood as a protest, or an effective provocation, or even a defence, particularly on the part of young people, against the aggressive imposition of new ideological trends (e.g. nationalism, the dictate of humble accession to Europe, neoliberalism, conservatism, traditionalism, clericalism, the restoration of the old political situation). This helps us to understand the graffiti 'TITO KPJ' at the entrance to the Split-Makarska archdiocese building that appeared a few years ago,[28] or 'Tito' sprayed over 'Welcome to the Republic of Srpska' written only in Serbian (in Cyrillic) and in English on a large billboard greeting you on entering the Serbian part of Bosnia-Herzegovina, or the graffiti in Labin (Croatia) reading 'We want Tito, not the EU'. The following anecdote from Ljubljana is another good illustration of the underlying motive. During the punk craze in the late 1970s and early 1980s, a graffito based on the official pioneer slogan 'Forward we go with Tito, for our homeland!' appeared, only with 'Tito' substituted with the provocative 'punk' (so the slogan read 'Forward we go with punk, for our homeland!'). Towards the end of the 1990s, when punk had already gained its 'citizenship rights', there appeared a new version of this graffito, with 'punk' now crossed out and 'Tito', by this time already a provocation, reinstated. The message was and is clear: to go against the existing political system and ideology!

The author of a Slovenian web page about Tito claims that young people, resisting the impersonality of capitalist society, 'seek escape in obsolete ideals (Tito, Yugoslavia) because it is a way to kill two birds with one stone. They are interested in something which is not part of today's capitalist world (a revolt against trends, commercialisation, everything that is popular)

---

28   *Feral Tribune*, 1 April 2005, 8.

and which also illustrates times when people were committed to a shared idea and believed in shared goals.'[29] Yet Broz's image and Partisan slogans ('Death to Fascism – Freedom to the People!' etc.) are frequently part of a new political activism as well. The flags of socialist Yugoslavia and its individual republics (featuring the communist red star), the red banners of the former League of Communists and photos of Broz are also seen at various worker and student demonstrations: for example, at recent Slovenian protests against political and financial elites in 2012 and 2013. The exaltation of Broz therefore involves criticism of the present ruling structure, but also offers a different perspective that in many ways comes close to contemporary left-wing trends. Consequently, it is not by chance that the criticism of the current state of affairs (plus matching slogans) and the appeals from young fighters for a more just world (alter-globalists) are almost identical to the criticism and appeals voiced by ageing Titoists, pop-leftists and neo-Titoists. Some venture far beyond simple negation – they also offer alternatives. Neo-Titoists from former Yugoslav republics do not restrict their activity to commemorations in Kumrovec or Dedinje: they also meet regularly in Bihać, Jajce and other places important for the history of socialist Yugoslavia.

Finally, Broz figures as one of the icons of leftist resistance, along with Che, and is presented not only as the founder of a stable state, a peacemaker, a legislator, that is as a 'Solon-like' figure,[30] but also as a warrior, a victor in uniform, symbolising continual struggle and an 'Alexander the Great' figure[31] (a kind of 'Yugoslav Che' from the Second World War, 'Che preceding Che', or 'Che for domestic use'). Taking a sample of forty-five

29   R. Repnik, 'Jugo v naši glavi' [Yugo in Our Head], *Nedeljski dnevnik*, Ljubljana, 19 December 1999, 16.

30   T.R. Girardet, *Mythes et mythologies politiques*, Paris: Éditions du Seuil, 1986, 77–8.

31   Ibid., 75–7. It is not insignificant that after the war there were attempts to link Broz's origins to the insurgency tradition of the region of Zagorje (the great peasant rebellion in 1573); there were also speculations about distant family relations between the sixteenth-century insurgency leader Matija Ambroz Gubec and the Broz family (Ambroz-Broz).

T-shirts, he is most frequently depicted as a Partisan commander (55.5 per cent) and less frequently as the President of Yugoslavia in his later years (29 per cent). The same holds true of other products and souvenirs of the culture of Titostalgia – there, too, the younger 'Partisan' Broz prevails.

True, the motive here is the eternal opposition to the current state of affairs, but there is more to it than meets the eye. In my opinion, it is not just about saying *No!* to the present, but also, or even above all, about reaffirming earlier, now neglected values such as social justice, common property, health and social security, solidarity within society, linking of nations, etc. In brief, what is involved is the promotion of what was positive in 'the lost world of Tito'. For example, his impersonator Godnič says that 'as a Tito youth – and I'm still thankful to him for this – I did not know the racial or religious intolerance that came with the new times'.[32] The famous Roma singer Esma Redžepova, from Macedonia, remembers him as 'the best statesman in these parts, because he linked us together'.[33]

My ultimate conclusion is a little unexpected and seemingly contradictory: the Tito of Titostalgia does not have much to do with the 'real Broz'. In fact, as a historical personality, he is not even very important in that context. This retrospective utopia within nostalgic narratives explains why today we encounter not only the surviving examples, or residues, of the former veneration of Broz, but primarily his new image, recreated in new ways. It tells us that for utopia the *actual experience of his epoch* is not important, so that young people who share with the older generation the vision of a better world can appropriate him too; that various antiques and souvenirs are not only materialised memories whose function is to evoke in our minds a pleasant image of Broz, but they also tell us what kind of image it should be. They are on offer not only because the 'market asks for them' but because supply

---

32   M. Hrastar and V. Pirc, 'Ljubi diktator – Ljubiti, prezirati, častiti ali sovražiti lik in delo J.B. Tita' [The Beloved Dictator – To Love, to Detest, to Celebrate or to Hate the Image and the Work of J.B. Tito], *Mladina*, 24 May 2004, 23.

33   An interview with E. Redžepova, *Nacional*, 6 January 2004, 45.

itself creates the market; or, put differently, memory is not only evoked but also created – what is involved is not simply a 'return of the suppressed', but a kind of new coming into being, not only a reinterpretation, reinvention, redefinition, reappropriation, reconstruction and adaptation, but also the invention and construction of the past as it never existed. It is not solely a shift of meaning, but the creation of meaning; not only decontextualisation, but a completely new contextualisation. Nostalgia has less to do with the embellishment of the past than with its invention, construction and new conceptions. All this does not necessarily have much to do with how the past actually looked and what kind of character it actually had. It is primarily a new composition and not only a positive historical heritage, or the 'legacy' of our beautiful shared past. It is not a *welcome back*, but a *hello to the new*.

To be more concrete, the slogan of Titostalgics – 'Tito is alive!' – should be understood literally: their Broz is a figure of the present, not of the past. Broz in Titostalgia is not the fervently sought second Tito. He has not come back, but was born in nostalgia – distant from his historical image – born anew to a large degree. What is involved is not his redesign, ideological lifting or makeover, to use the lingo of modern popular culture, or a pimp-my-leader project. His replica born out of nostalgic yearnings is in all respects more perfect, better, and more just than the historical prototype. Utopia therefore makes nostalgia a critical, active social notion, not just a passive, defensive and reactionary one, as it is usually accused of being.

In brief, Broz in Titostalgia is a symptom of post-socialist transition, meaning the painful combination of neoliberalism, neo-conservatism and post-colonialism, and not a reappearance of socialism. Of course, the question that arises is why it is Tito and Titostalgia that are present in modern culture, if the historical Broz is not of crucial importance and it has more to do with the search for a utopian society and its just leader. In my opinion, the answer lies in the fact that, for the people in this part of the world, Broz and Yugoslavia, as a social experiment that worked for some time, provide the closest frame of reference for the realised utopian ideals of a just society, meaning just for the most of its members, and of a fair leader. At the same time, it is also a sharp critique, particularly from young people, of present social injustices, economic inequalities, political arrogance and, of course, of nationalism, nation-states and their national cultures as well as other exclusionary practices, because the examples from the past prove that it was possible to live together. Here the historical lesson appears as an alternative to the present.

Practically all post-Yugoslavs know Broz. He is the most accessible and 'borrowed' image of the indeterminable utopian search, or the historical figure that 'goes beyond human boundaries'.[34] As the examples of Titostalgic culture clearly show, any Titostalgic person can create his or her 'own Tito' while pursuing his or her nostalgic hobby. Much like other nostalgicised personalities, things and eras, the notion of Tito is polysemic, polyphonic, unstable; it has neither the same meaning nor the same ring to it for all of its creators and recipients. Jameson arrived at a similar conclusion when he described the 'excitement that identifies a forgotten or repressed moment of the past as the new and subversive'.[35] What is important is that the utopian wish can be attributed to Broz, that is to say, that the ideology of that utopia is materialised in Titostalgic cultural production, to use Althusser's terms. Yugostalgia, as the wider phenomenon, and Titostalgia as the narrower, express precisely that: the nostalgics' wish for better times, a better political system and a better leader, although, unfortunately for them, these belong to the past. To rephrase the cliché: utopia dies last.

In our case, nostalgia 'speaks' the Yugoslav, Titoist language, not only because the reality of that time collapsed before the very eyes of the majority of its citizens, or because of enduring collective and personal memories and testimonies, or because 'certain things survived' the chaotic transition. There is also the

---

34 See E. Bloch, *Princip nada* [The Principle of Hope], Zagreb: Naprijed, 1981, 1180–219.

35 Jameson, *Archaeologies of the Future*, 25.

utopian, transcendent, emancipatory element: a vaguely pro-
filed wish for a better world. For this reason, the introductory
questions 'Why Tito?' and 'Why Yugoslavia?' need to be
reversed. These are not questions but answers. The real questions are the following: Where do we go now? How? Who, in
fact, are today's leaders? In this sense, Titostalgia is a political
discourse, but on another level, not the apparent one. This discourse is not directly and conventionally political in the sense
that it resuscitates Yugoslavia, or takes us back to Tito, etc.,
which is the interpretation favoured by its constantly alert
opponents and one avoided by many of its proponents. The
reason for this is that not only are these implications impossible,
but primarily because Yugoslavia and Tito never existed in the
way they are constructed within Titostalgia and Yugostalgia. It
is not a revisionist or 'restorative nostalgia', not a return of the
past, but rather a return of the utopias of those times.
Re-politicisation therefore occurs on a much more abstract or
meta level, within utopia. It transcends the concrete left–right
political divides, daily politics, actual historical personalities,
circumstances and regimes. It is rather an indefinable wish for
better times, a more just world and incorruptible people which
only later made use of something definable as its reference. It is
a clear message to the present, exposing its deficiencies and
telling it what a better world should look like.

The Yugoslavia of the nostalgic discourse never existed. It
is its utopian simulation, Yugoslavia as it should have been, a
dreamland purified of all weaknesses and mistakes, a kind of
socialist Cockaigne. The same holds true of Tito. It is ironic that
Broz's brave promises, optimism and endeavours to create a
better life for the Yugoslav nations have survived only in the
imagined world of nostalgia. All that remains of the anticipated
'kingdom of freedom' is an inspiring recent past; Bloch-like
'anticipatory consciousness' has been reduced to a retrospective
utopia, a wish for the better that looks back into the past. The
real historical personality became a typical myth. The late politician reappeared as a pop idol, the communist became a
profitable brand name, the 'beautiful future' is behind us, not in

front of us, and the signifiers of the former proletarian state have become modern consumer commodities. Judging by these nostalgic narratives, Yugoslavia was a perfect state and its leader, Tito, a perfect ruler. But as we know, such perfection can live only in nostalgia and exist only as utopia, which, as we also know, is a place that does not exist.

PART IV

Towards a Balkan Spring?
New Political Subjectivities

Insurrections in the Balkans: From Workers and Students to New Political Subjectivities

Michael G. Kraft

By the time Karl Polanyi finished his seminal work, *The Great Transformation*, in 1944, the great economic, social and technological changes of the nineteenth century had already come to a halt. The expansion of the market economy, which had swept away old forms of social organisation in favour of self-regulating markets, did not guide the Western societies into prosperity and peace. The tale of blind progress and material welfare provoked the opposite: the nineteenth-century civilisation had collapsed and had provoked an era of unrest unprecedented in the modern world (the Great Depression, the rise of Nazism, and the Second World War). If we read Polanyi's analyses carefully, it is remarkable how vehemently he warned of the coming convergence of liberal capitalism and authoritarianism and fascism. Polanyi was searching for a solution to the question of how to reconcile human freedom and the 'reality of society', i.e. the market mechanism, capital, economic value and labour. He came to the conclusion that free-market arrangements make it impossible for the individual to assume social responsibility: a society founded on free markets promotes conformity and stupidity, and renders critical and responsible thinking and acting redundant. For Polanyi, to be free is not to be free from duty and responsibility, 'but rather to be free because of duty and responsibility'. It is 'the point at which we take up the unshiftable responsibility of society ourselves'.[1]

---

1   K. Polanyi, 'On Freedom', in M. Cangiani, K. Polanyi-Levitt and C.

Today, in the early twenty-first century, we are faced with similar political and moral issues. In the past few years we have seen a new wave of protest across the world. Polanyi's key question for social freedom has recently been reformulated by various social movements (the recent uprisings in the Arab world, the Occupy movement, the Indignados, etc.). The capitalist cycle of boom and bust, which has finally reached the capitalist core via deregulated financial markets, together with a global shift in power relations and increased capital accumulation in the periphery, has meant increased social inequality and a retrenchment in the welfare state and social security systems. This has been particularly noticeable in the south-eastern periphery of the European Union. Which processes have been initiated in the states formed after socialist Yugoslavia? What has been the dominant discourse describing the transition from 'socialism' to capitalism and which interests did it serve? Which realities have the neoliberal programmes of austerity and the expansion of unfettered markets produced in these countries, and is there a growing resistance against these policies?

First, I provide an overview of the concept of transition by exploring it from historical, economic and political perspectives. Second, I contrast the narrative of transition with the existing realities in order to unmask its contradictions. This adds to an understanding of the emergence of protest and resistance movements, which put matters such as collective decision making, social justice and democratic forms of organisation up front. By exploring various initiatives in Croatia, Serbia and Slovenia, I draw up a counter-narrative of resistance and social emancipation, which for a long time has been – and still is – repressed by the dominant liberal discourse of 'catching up with the West', giving an account of current struggles and mobilisations in these three post-Yugoslav states and mapping the resistance in the Balkans. Finally, I search for what is

---

Thomasberger, eds, *Chronik der großen Transformation III: Menschliche Freiheit, politische Demokratie und die Auseinandersetzung zwischen Sozialismus und Faschismus* (trans.), Marburg: Metropolis, 2005, 147.

common to all these different local movements in the new global protest cycle, and attempt to shed light on the question of whether new political subjectivities are being created in the recent movements, and, if so, to determine what their distinctive characteristics might be.

The Eternal Transition

There is no single narrative in Eastern Europe in general and the Balkans in particular that has been put in place more prominently and one-sidedly in order to justify the institution of market capitalism in the former 'socialist' countries than the concept of 'transition'. At the heart of this narrative lies the idea that democratisation and free elections together with the capitalist path of development will bring about peace, freedom and material well-being for all.[2] In order to better grasp the discourse of transition and its ideological content, I will comment on various components which are comprised within this notion. Take the idea of a savage and uncivilised Balkans. The region has historically been envisaged from a European perspective as a civilisation at a lower level of development that needs external help, supervision and assistance for pacification and democratisation.[3] The Balkan wars of the 1990s and the subsequent unstable political period have been interpreted precisely from within this paradigm.[4] The dominant political discourse regarding the former Yugoslavia has been limited to the ethnic and nationalist dimension of the conflict on the one hand, and the democratic and economic catch-up with the 'developed' European capitalist core on the other. However, this reductionism only repeats the historic, stereotypical image of a savage

---

2   F. Fukuyama, *The End of History and the Last Man*, New York: The Free Press, 1992; J. Kornai, 'The Great Transformation of Central Eastern Europe', *Economics of Transition*, vol. 14, 2006, 207–44.

3   M. Todorova, *Imagining the Balkans*, Oxford and New York: Oxford University Press, 2009.

4   J. Morton et al., *Reflections on the Balkan Wars: Ten Years after the Break-up of Yugoslavia*, New York: Palgrave Macmillan, 2004.

and uncivilised Balkans. It has served as an instrument of domination that has led to a neo-colonial relationship with the European Union, which implicitly presents modernisation along Western lines as normatively desirable. In a 2008 speech delivered at the Conference on Civil Society Development in Southeast Europe, Olli Rehn, former EU enlargement commissioner and current economic and monetary affairs commissioner, had the following message for the people of the Balkans: 'Overall, the western Balkans is making steady progress towards the EU. If the current challenges . . . can be successfully overcome, then the region has a bright future – and that future is in the European Union.'[5] Despite this hope for a bright future, Rehn continued his speech by defending EU policies towards the Western Balkans and demanded more sacrifices and commitment from the side of the local population:

> In the [EU] enlargement countries, people sometimes ask why they should go through substantial, even painful reforms to join the EU. Posing this question sends the message that they do not necessarily perceive these reforms as something that is, first and foremost, in their own interest. I would prefer that people of the region could see themselves not as 'takers' of externally imposed conditions, but rather as 'makers' of their own future. Reforms are not done only for the EU, but primarily for the people of the region. Enhancing democracy and the rule of law, promoting fundamental freedoms and developing a rules-based market economy do indeed improve everyday lives of the citizens.[6]

Rehn's speech is a good example of the argument that the transformation from 'socialism' to capitalism demands human sacrifices and hardships in the medium term that will

---

5   O. Rehn, 'Civil Society at the Heart of the EU's Enlargement Agenda', paper presented at the Conference on Civil Society Development in Southeast Europe 'Building Europe Together', Brussels, 17 April 2008.
6   Ibid.

subsequently be rewarded with prosperity and freedom in the future. The EU's enlargement strategy and its political conditionality towards the Western Balkans guarantees that such policy changes are and will be implemented, regardless of whether it is in the interest of the people. There is no room for discussion or reflection on equal terms.

The same holds true for economic development. Few topics have been so amply researched in Eastern Europe as the economic transformation from 'socialism' to market capitalism. The countless PhD theses and publications funded by Western donors and the creation of numerous departments and research institutes are astounding. For over twenty years, neo-classical economists have tried to solve the myriad transition problems by employing their neoliberal toolbox. Despite little obvious progress or improvement in the lives of ordinary people, the prescriptions still remain the same: deregulation, unfettered markets, cuts to social spending, instituting the rule of law and extending the realm of private property. They still speak of a 'convergence process in Europe'.[7] However, quite the contrary is the case. Although the different Balkan countries had achieved close to common levels of inequality at the end of the 1990s, the development gap relative to the EU remains significant. According to economists Jalal El Ouardighi and Rabija Somun-Kapetanović, the relative average income of the Balkan countries dropped from 40 per cent to 30 per cent of the EU average between 1989 and 2008.[8] If reality does not comply with theory, the consequence drawn by mainstream economists is that the error is to be sought not in the system itself, but in the imperfect implementation of free markets, in political interference, corruption and clientelism, as well as in the ethnic conflicts that

---

7   Transition economists never tire of producing statistics which supposedly measure the time it will take to catch up with Western countries. The convergence time to Western Europe for, e.g., Slovenia, they say, is thirty years. See Kornai, 'The Great Transformation of Central Eastern Europe', 207–44.

8   J. El Ouardighi and R. Somun-Kapetanović, 'Convergence and Inequality of Income: The Case of Western Balkan Countries', *European Journal of Comparative Economics*, vol. 6, 2009, 223.

culminated in the turmoil of the Balkan wars. Their conclusion is to try harder, to take the liberalisation of economic policies still further in order to 'effectively' prepare the way for accession to the EU. Such policies, prescribed by international organisations and the EU, are willingly executed by an EU-oriented political class.

However, if we look at the social, economic and political situation in the post-Yugoslav region in 2013, there is little cause for confidence. Growing unemployment, widespread corruption, low levels of trust in the political class, and a lengthy process of deindustrialisation destroying thousands of workplaces have pushed many people into poverty. The economic crisis which hit the Balkans hard from 2008 onwards has joined an already long-standing crisis of representative politics. Serbia, for example, experienced a significant drop in GDP as well as foreign direct investment as a result of the crisis, and the country struggled to avoid a collapse of its monetary system. Yet it was a crisis that was imported via the previously liberalised banking system, of which some 74 per cent (as of 2012) is controlled by foreign banks.[9] The major banks of the EU were quick to withdraw capital from their Eastern European branches and ceased to extend fresh credit lines. As if the global economic crisis was not already bad enough for the people of Serbia, destroying hundreds of thousands of workplaces and making people redundant when exports declined by some 25 per cent, the loan agreement with the International Monetary Fund stipulated substantial cuts in public expenditure. In the following years, unemployment soared, reaching a regional record high of 27 per cent in 2012.[10] The EU-directed liberalisation policies had manifestly aggravated an already fragile social situation.

For a long time, the 'natural laws' of the free market, the bounded economic rationality and the set-up of the liberal state have remained unchallenged in the political, economic and

---

9   National Bank of Serbia, *Banking Sector in Serbia: Second Quarter Report 2012*, September 2012, 3.

10   Vienna Institute for International Economic Studies, *wiiw Forecast for Central, East and Southeast Europe, 2012–2014*, 2012, 4.

social mainstream. However, in the wake of the global capitalist crisis, the first cracks in this narrative are now appearing. People are starting to question a future imagined by neoliberal EU technocrats and local elites and asking themselves whether these painful reforms dictated by the EU are worthwhile.

Over the last few years, a wave of protests and resistance from below has swept the Balkan states for the first time in more than twenty years. Citizens are reclaiming the public sphere, uniting against privatisation, austerity measures, the lowering of labour standards, the commodification of education, and government corruption, as well as against technocratic governments which undermine democracy. Some of these fights have been waged for a fairly long time, while some have emerged more recently. But they all point to a great sense of unease and discontent with the broken promises of transition. In the following sections, I provide an overview of examples of mobilisations, direct action and struggles in the former Yugoslavia. In doing so, I focus on workers' struggles and the process of deindustrialisation as well as student protests and direct democracy.

Workers' Struggles Against Deindustrialisation and Privatisations

Two different examples of workers' struggles in Serbia and Croatia are discussed in detail here. The first explores the tale of workers' shareholding and self-management of the Serbian pharmaceutical company Jugoremedija. The second investigates the anti-privatisation campaign of the workers of the Croatian petrochemical company Petrokemija, which resulted in a partnership between the state (as the main shareholder) and the workers as part of production and management.

Two decades of social and economic transformation in the former Yugoslavia have left behind a marginalised and impoverished industrial workforce in the former socially owned enterprises. The dominant neoliberal transformation consensus led to waves of corrupt privatisations, the destruction of social ownership and deindustrialisation that only benefited a small political and economic elite. As a response to these developments, workers' protests and resistance have intensified over the last few years and, for the first time since the breakdown of Yugoslavia, a new worker protest movement has established itself, reaching a peak when the global economic crisis hit the Balkans in 2008–9. Workers were dissatisfied with privatisation processes, which often meant that employees had not received their salaries or health and pension benefits for years, and led to the destruction of hundreds of thousands of workplaces.[11]

Serbia experienced a wave of strikes in 2009 that involved over 30,000 workers in forty to forty-five enterprises and included street blockades, city hall and police station takeovers, sleep-ins, 'boss-nappings', hunger strikes, self-mutilation and, in one case, a suicide. In order to connect the various protests and actions at factory level and extend solidarity between workers, the Freedom Fight collective (Pokret za Slobodu) helped to build a network between local Strike Committees. The idea was to support each other and fight against 'privatisation through bankruptcy'. As a reaction to neoliberal government policies and the feeling that the established trade unions were complicit with the government or even sabotaging the protests, the Strike Committees of the companies Šinvoz, Zastava Elektro, Srbolek and BEK established a joint, independent Workers' Protest Coordination Committee (WPCC) in August 2009. They were calling on all Strike Committees in Serbia 'to jointly find a way of preserving our jobs, for a way to survive'.[12] Given

11   In Croatia, industrial production in 2007 reached 90 per cent of the 1990 levels, in Serbia only 51 per cent of the 1990 levels in 2008. See J. Becker, 'Krisenmuster und Anti-Krisen-Politiken in Osteuropa (trans.)', *Wirtschaft und Gesellschaft*, vol. 36, 2010, 524. It is estimated that between October 2008 and April 2010 an additional 370,000 people lost their jobs. See M. Arandarenko and S. Avlijaš, 'Behind the Veil of Statistics: Bringing to Light Structural Weaknesses in Serbia', in V. Schmidt and D. Vaughan-Whitehead, eds, *The Impact of Crisis on Wages in South-East Europe*, Budapest: International Labour Organisation, 2011, 143.

12   Coordinating Committee for Workers' Protests in Serbia, *Declaration of the Coordinating Committee for Workers' Protests in Serbia*, 2009.

the seriousness of the problems faced by the working class, they called for coordinated actions and demanded systemic changes.

The struggle for self-management of the worker-shareholders of the pharmaceutical factory Jugoremedija in Zrenjanin has become the most famous and successful incident of all the recent workers' protests in Serbia and triggered similar actions in other formerly socially owned factories. The struggle dates back to early 2002 when the state sold its 42 per cent share to an indicted criminal, Jovica 'Nini' Stefanović, while 58 per cent remained in the hands of the workers and small shareholders. 'Nini's' aim was to gain control over the company, but his proposal to become the majority owner through recapitalisation was rejected by the small shareholders in 2003. As a consequence, he pushed the factory into debt, made illegal changes in the ownership structure and registered himself as a 62 per cent shareholder. At the same time he started persecuting trade union activists and the small shareholders' representatives. To express their protest and show their close ties to the factory, the workers Vladimir Pecikoza and Zdravko Deurić chained themselves to the factory gates in December 2003. Six more workers joined them and a few days later the largest trade union in the factory declared a strike. This meant the beginning of a series of workplace occupations, direct and legal actions and a long-lasting struggle. The struggle also exhibited a broader resentment against the ruling parties, which carried out privatisation in an often corrupt manner or refrained from acting to reinforce the rule of law, which implied that (criminal) investors could run down factories and engage in asset-stripping. In December 2006, after a nine-month factory occupation and a two-and-a-half-year strike, the Belgrade Higher Economic Court decided that the recapitalisation of Jugoremedija had been carried out illegally. In March 2007, Jugoremedija became the first factory to be run by worker-shareholders as a direct result of their struggle.

Despite this success and the ability of the workers to stabilise and expand production, the situation has remained fragile to this day. The difficult economic situation put heavy strains on the organisational model of Jugoremedija and the division between the worker-shareholders and the 'ordinary' workers became more visible. The latter were less willing to accept stagnating wages and working overtime for a factory which did not belong to them. Since no consensus could be established among the workers, a group of worker-shareholders decided in accordance with the management to build a new penicillin production plant (Penpharm) which was under their control. This was the time when rumours started to circulate about the abuse of company funds and the atmosphere became more hostile. Some worker-shareholders received threats and on 28 July 2012, an unknown person set fire to the vehicle of Jugoremedija's general manager Zdravko Deurić. In August 2012, Deurić and three other employees were arrested on suspicion of wrongly estimating Jugoremedija's investment and the abuse of company assets in regard to the new Penpharm factory. After the arrests there were protests by Jugoremedija workers and shareholders in front of Zrenjanin's police station and Zrenjanin City Hall was occupied. In this repressive atmosphere, Jugoremedija decided to take a step forward and filed a lawsuit against the Republic of Serbia for damages due to privatisation. They pressured the government to respect private property rights and the rule of law – the rights of the worker-shareholders of Jugoremedija had been violated – which finally resulted in talks with the new Serbian government in autumn 2012. The negotiations with Oliver Antić, adviser to the Serbian president Tomislav Nikolić, secured a promise from the government to conduct a thorough investigation into a number of illegal and contested privatisations. On 20 September 2012, Deurić was finally released after fifty days in prison, but the High Public Prosecutor expanded the investigation against him for alleged tax evasion. In the months to come there was no satisfactory response from the government following talks with the Serbian president. Thus, in April 2013 the workers decided to expand their struggle to the parliamentary field and register a new party under the working title Movement for Freedom and Social Justice (Pokret za slobodu i socijalnu pravdu (PSSP)).

In order to better understand these events and the legal attack on the worker-shareholders, we need to take a closer look at the dominant themes, aspirations and organisational model adopted by the movement. If we look at the issues, strategies and results of these protests, some tensions in relation to the goals and how to achieve them – ranging from desires for gradual improvement to more radical demands – become obvious. The movement is driven by both material grievances and the wish to run the companies effectively and thereby to save workplaces. This is embodied in the workers' understanding that they 'fought for their companies' and 'saved them'. Given the impoverished situation of many of the workers, the dominant theme was not first and foremost against 'capitalist exploitation' but for the 'right to work' and to protect and enlarge workplaces. Corrupt investors were blamed for 'bad management by the bosses', which in many cases had resulted in the factories coming to a standstill and large-scale dismissals of the workforce.

There are two important connections to be drawn in regard to the former Yugoslav system of self-management. First, research into industrial action in the 1950s and 1960s shows that strikes at the time were also often motivated by material grievances. They commonly ended with a quick victory for the workers and 'revealed a political bargain between the working class and the political elites which was peculiar to Yugoslavia' – a bargain that no longer exists in the age of neoliberalism.[13] Second, the construction of social ownership led to an increased identification of the workers with 'their' companies. This resulted in the willingness of the workers to make sacrifices for their companies but also to fight for them. Since the historical situation has changed dramatically and the grand coalition between workers and politicians has shifted in favour of private investors and capital, the recent workers' protests face different

---

13   M. Grdešić, 'Mapping the Paths of the Yugoslav Model: Labour Strength and Weakness in Slovenia, Croatia and Serbia', *European Journal of Industrial Relations*, vol. 14, 2008, 137.

challenges. Given the historical legacy of Yugoslav self-management, the workers found it difficult to make their claims heard in public. The historical 'failure' and breakdown of the Yugoslav system and the dominant, neoliberal discourse of 'liberation' from 'socialism' hindered more radical, full-scale anti-capitalist demands within the workers' movement. Hence, the situation of the working class and the possibility for alternative forms of organisation and decision making remains difficult and fragile. The crucial question is how the worker-shareholders conceptualise their relations internally and externally, and how they see themselves embedded in the capitalist system. An organisational model of self-management has the potential for a far-reaching socio-political transformation. Within a capitalist economy, the wish and decision of the workers to run the companies themselves, and to show that workers' self-management is viable or that they are performing the task even better, have more substantial implications in terms of emancipation and democratisation (of the workplace) than in the old days of Yugoslav self-management. The workers of Jugoremedija have been searching for an organisational model and strategic investments which they deem viable in a global market economy. As Branislav Markuš, Jugoremedija worker and member of the management board, puts it: 'Meanwhile, a large amount of money has been invested – approximately 10 million euros. Our aim is to produce drugs according to European Union production standards, which we will then be able to sell all around the world.'[14] Although the workers set up an organisational model which allowed the organisation of production by the workers, they did not abandon the old corporate business structure and the management board. The company was now run by worker-shareholders, but the formal right to participate in decision making was still based on (capital) ownership as opposed to employment or any other criteria.

---

14   Z. Bulatović et al., Interview with Branislav Markuš (member of the Coordinating Committee for Workers' Protests in Serbia), and Zoran Bulatović (representative of the Textile Workers Association of Novi Pazar, Sjenica and Tutin), 2009, at www.meta-don.org/newborder.

Despite their remarkable efforts, their unconditional solidarity with other workers on strike and their determination to fight for a better future, the whole process of finding an intellectual and geographical space for a new labour movement in Serbia in the twenty-first century exhibits certain tensions and contradictions that have yet to be overcome. The urgent problems of the Serbian workers will not be solved by a 'proper imposition' of private property rights. The time has come to conceptualise demands that go beyond the liberal notions of private property and the rule of law. Combined efforts need to seek system-wide changes and construct dense networks with other marginalised groups. Some steps are being taken in that direction with, for instance, the formation of the Coordination Committee of Workers' and Peasants' Organisations or the plans to register a political party, but they still represent small initiatives which are, unfortunately, marginalised and hardly noticed in mainstream society.

In Croatia, the situation of the working class has been similar to the Serbian case. Twenty years of an independent Croatia have been characterised by deindustrialisation, criminal activities in privatisation processes, high rates of unemployment, a deterioration of workers' rights, declining living standards, and the commercialisation of public services, as well as a deepening of social and economic inequalities. However, the workers' movement differed in the choice of methods, strategies and forms of organisation. While the workers of Jugoremedija fought for 'fair privatisation' and used the model of worker-shareholders to take control over production in order to preserve their jobs, their Croatian colleagues at Petrokemija created a different model of organised resistance: their 'headquarters for defence of companies' in order to prevent the privatisation of their factory. In 1998 workers of Petrokemija in the town of Kutina mobilised the local population to prevent the takeover of their company. The headquarters, which were non-institutional and had an informal character, consisted of two trade unions and an association of war veterans who worked in the company. Much as in Serbia, industrial action was organised outside traditional trade union structures. Moreover, the Croatian workers, like their Serbian colleagues, were strongly attached to the company emotionally, which also provided them with a great sense of belonging. As a result, their primary goal was to defend their jobs. When the Croatian state decided to privatise the company by offering shares to the public, the workers immediately recognised the danger. As the war veteran and head of staff association Željko Klaus puts it: 'This mode of privatisation was absolutely unacceptable for us because it would have definitely led to the extinction of production. It would have simply been an invitation to tycoons to make big money from a sell-off of assets, but we successfully resisted it.'[15]

The remarkable thing about this form of struggle is that the Petrokemija workers succeeded in mobilising a wider congregation of supporters, and entered into a coalition with other actors in society, as well as with the media. In public protests and mobilisations, they demanded that political institutions at the local and national level take responsibility and act in favour of the workers, the local community and the national interest. As Klaus explains further,

> all political parties and factions have unconditionally supported our actions and our struggle. And not just that, they have also participated actively. In 2002, at a temperature of minus 10 degrees Celsius, 5000 people took to the streets of Kutina, with the entire City Council physically present at the demonstration and the mayor at its head.[16]

The workers even took control of production for two months, ultimately preventing the privatisation of the company, with the state remaining a 51 per cent majority shareholder. This specific

---

15 Ž. Klaus and H. Bolldorf, 'Interview mit Željko Klaus zu den Arbeitskämpfen bei Petrokemija' [Interview with Željko Klaus Regarding the Workers' Struggles at Petrokemija], in M. Kraft, ed., *Soziale Kämpfe in Ex-Jugoslawien* [Social Struggles in Ex-Yugoslavia], Vienna: Mandelbaum, 2013.
16 Ibid.

form of resistance quickly spread to other companies, of which the most prominent examples are the Commercial Bank of Zagreb, the Croatia Bus transport firm, Jedinstvo Zagreb and the Tvornica Duhana Zagreb tobacco factory. The remarkable aspect of both the Petrokemija and Jugoremedija cases is that workers became active and took matters into their own hands. In their fight for social justice, they searched for new ways and modes of resistance outside the often corrupt trade union bureaucracy in order to preserve their jobs, production capacities and the industrial base of a once successfully industrialised country. Their struggle is a reminder also that one victory is not enough: the pressures continue to this day and require periodical mobilisations of workers.

Student Protests and Direct Democracy

Beyond the popular demands for democratic control in the field of production, another focus of recent protests has been attacks on the education system (the EU-directed 'Bologna Process') and a decrease in democratic decision making. With new student movements in Croatia, Serbia, Slovenia and Bosnia, the question of democracy, its meaning, and alternative models have all been placed back on the agenda across the Balkans. Since 2009, there have been several faculty occupations in these countries.

The fight against the commercialisation of higher education was most prominent in Croatia. It started in 2008 when students mobilised around an anti-NATO campaign, collecting an impressive 125,000 signatures for a referendum. Shortly after, they turned to the field of education. On 7 May 2008, they organised the first protest at the University of Zagreb with some 5,000 participants. Initially, the demands of the students were primarily directed against the introduction of tuition fees and the Bologna reforms. In the subsequent months, however, the struggle developed into a broader left-wing political movement. With their demand for 'free education' and a critique of neoliberalism and privatisation, the students were attacking the political mainstream. Even the process of EU accession was being discussed critically. For the first time in more than twenty years, the pillars of neoliberalism and capitalism were openly challenged and put into question. As a result, the student protests, practices and perspectives have opened up spaces far beyond the field of higher education.

In Zagreb, the occupation of the Faculty of Humanities and Social Sciences (Filozofski fakultet) in spring 2009 was self-organised, with direct democratic practices instituted at the heart of the movement. The students launched general assemblies (plenaries) and working groups outside the traditional systems of student representation. They refrained from electing leaders or spokespersons, refused to enter into negotiations with the government and developed an innovative media strategy. Another remarkable aspect of the occupation was that the students positioned universities amidst society as open spaces of debate and negotiation of social conflicts. When farmers started to protest against falling milk prices in December 2009, the students invited them to the occupied faculty and organised the first farmers' plenary in which they tackled the pressing problems. Such public discussions, plenaries and working group meetings were held on a regular basis and protesting workers from companies, such as the textile manufacturer Kamensko or Petrokemija, engaged in an open and critical discourse at the faculty in Zagreb. Another example of cooperation and alliances with workers was the initiative of university teachers. During the occupation and with the proposed neoliberal University Act in 2011, university staff also radicalised and ultimately founded the first teacher-student union based on the principles of direct democracy (called Academic Solidarity/ Akademska solidarnost) in Croatia.

The Croatian example also had a big influence on neighbouring Slovenia. In March 2011 student activists formed a loose network of smaller groups called 'We are the University' (MSU). In the same month the MSU held a plenary at the Faculty of Arts in Ljubljana, which was a great success: the activists rejected the new national higher education programme and research strategy and criticised the 'mini-jobs' bill.[17] They organised more plenaries in spring 2011, but it was not until the autumn that the movement gained new momentum. A working group of the local occupy movement 15o-Slovenia began to discuss the idea of occupying the Faculty of Arts in Ljubljana. After a plenary on 23 November 2011 activists occupied the faculty and subsequently organised a broad alternative programme of lectures, workshops and political discussions. The demands of the students included autonomous courses and spaces, the rejection of the 'Bologna Process', a reform of postgraduate studies and the expansion of social security and welfare for students and staff on short-term contracts alike. Despite their determination to fight for an alternative university, none of these demands were fulfilled. With only a few remaining activists present, the occupation ended on 26 January 2012.

Notwithstanding these temporary defeats, the student activists have successfully established a counter-model of education, participation and decision making in general. With their rejection of representative democracy and their implementation of directly democratic forms of organisation, they have opened up new practical and intellectual spaces that question the prevailing political discourse.

New Political Subjectivities in the Balkans and the Global Protest Cycle

The multiple crises of capitalism and an economic and political system that marginalises great swaths of society have fostered new forms of resistance and new political subjectivities in the Balkans. The relevance of the above-mentioned movements, although having links to the 'socialist' past, lies in the fact that they already exhibit certain specificities that relate them to the

---

17   In October 2010 the Slovenian government passed a law that extended temporary contracts previously reserved for student workers to unemployed or former temporary hires. Due to strong opposition from students and trade unions, a referendum was held in April 2011 in which more than 80 per cent voted against the legislative proposal. This meant a major victory for the students.

new global protest cycle. Even if each of them has its own specific characteristics, these 'new' movements have developed some common forms and practices. Thus, it makes sense to look at the protest movements in the Balkans that have emerged recently also from a global perspective.

One distinctive feature of these new movements is that they are searching for new political emancipation strategies which transcend the dichotomy between the market (individual responsibility) and the state (paternalistic care) in favour of new collective forms of social control and decision making. Both the student movement and the workers' struggles discussed above put collective and participatory decision making up front. The workers organised themselves outside traditional, hierarchical trade union structures and went well beyond classical forms of labour mobilisation. They were seeking broader alliances within society for their cause, which they articulated as a broader social issue. Trade unions can be part of such an alliance, but on their own they have no satisfactory answers to issues such as deindustrialisation, badly paid jobs in the service sector, unemployment, growing inequality, etc., which affect much wider parts of society than just those with union membership. In their long-running struggle the workers emancipated themselves from being the victims and losers of the transition process and gradually transformed themselves into conscious fighters for a better and more just future. In doing so, they adopted creative solutions and methods and showed that they are able to run the factories themselves. Hence, they made important references to alternative forms of economic organisation based on the principles of participatory decision making and self-management.

The student activists also went well beyond traditional models of representation and agency. They either wholly rejected the formal student representative system or subverted it with the electoral victories of their candidates. They pointed towards a broader phenomenon of diminishing democracy and accountability, as well as resisting technocratic solutions – and not only in the field of higher education. With their new organisational forms of direct democracy and their solidarity with other marginalised groups (workers, immigrants, farmers, etc.) they opened up new and fresh perspectives on the prevailing political, economic and social conditions. One could argue that the students have presented a practical example of an alternative organisation and new social ties and solidarity. During the university occupations the self-organised establishment of plenary assemblies and working groups on the principles of direct democracy constituted a method which was later implemented by the Occupy movement and the Spanish Indignados as well as some subsequent new movements in the Balkans (e.g. 150-Slovenia). The Facebook protests that began in 2011 in Zagreb, followed by the formation of a new left in Croatia and the first Balkan Forum in May 2012, showed that (international) networks are being established and that exchange, solidarity and discussions are taking place with international activists. Another significant aspect of these protests was the role of social media networks such as Facebook, Twitter, YouTube and weblogs as an important resource for popular mobilisation. The Croatian students set up a website called Slobodni Filozofski (the Free Faculty of Philosophy) as an alternative source of information and mobilisation. In order to spread the occupation model the students wrote an *Occupation Cookbook*, which describes the methods and foundations of direct democracy and which was quickly translated into German and English and published in a Serbian version as well.

Let us turn finally to one of the latest examples of new political emancipation strategies, the events occurring in late 2012 and early 2013 in Slovenia, the former star performer among the post-communist countries. The protests started rather unexpectedly in Maribor, Slovenia's second largest city, when on 2 November 2012 people took to the streets to protest against the corrupt mayor Franc Kangler. In autumn 2012 Kangler, who had been involved in a number of affairs and corruption scandals, signed a controversial public–private partnership for the implementation of a stationary traffic monitoring system. The cost of the installation of the system skyrocketed and the private company, which was to receive 92 per cent of all collected fines, was quick to record almost 25,000 traffic offences within the first few days. People started to question whether this was to ensure better road safety or simply to accrue private profits. As a result of the dissemination of the issue on social networks more and more people took to the streets (from fifty on 2 November to 10,000 on 14 December 2012), demanding the resignation of Kangler. Although he finally resigned in December 2012, he acknowledged no loss of credibility and portrayed himself as a victim of the left.

Before scrutinising the spread of the protests across the country let us briefly consider the context in which they took place. Already in 2009 the financial crisis had reached Slovenia: the economy plummeted, interest rates soared, the housing bubble burst and the country found itself in a severe economic recession. As elsewhere in Europe, the government's response was to impose austerity and cuts to social programmes, a strategy that only aggravated the severity of the fiscal crisis. As a result, in autumn 2011 the global Occupy movement reached Slovenia and on 15 October massive demonstrations against capitalism and austerity took place in Ljubljana. They became known as 15O-Slovenia (Occupy Slovenia). The protesters occupied a square in front of Ljubljana's stock exchange, setting up a tent camp. The idea was to remain visible to the public, to build a lasting movement based on new forms of political organisation and decision making and reconstruct society from below based on the ideals of direct democracy. 15O-Slovenia succeeded in uniting different social groups within the movement, such as migrants, social workers, unemployed, students, etc. Nevertheless, the Slovenian government ignored the message from the Occupy movement and passed another austerity package which included measures such as the liberalisation of employment law, cuts in unemployment benefits, the privatisation of state enterprises, drastic cuts in the social budget and plans to create a so-called bad bank to take non-performing loans away from state banks. These measures have driven the country towards the point of financial strangulation and social collapse.

The result of this situation was that the spontaneous protests in Maribor did not remain an isolated event, but triggered a wave of similar actions all over the country. There had already been a widespread feeling of discontent and unease, but it was not until November 2012 that tens of thousands of people from different social backgrounds – many of them formerly politically inactive – took to the streets and occupied central squares, forming a broad alliance against political elites and austerity policies. The single most important reason for the protests spreading across the country was a report of the national anti-corruption commission that accused both the prime minister, Janez Janša, and the leader of the largest opposition party, Zoran Janković, of corruption. On 21 December, the first so-called All-Slovenian Uprising took place in Ljubljana, assembling some 10,000 peaceful protesters. By March 2013 there had been three more, all of them prepared in a self-organised and decentralised way. Given these mass rallies and the report of the anti-corruption commission, most of the parties in the ruling coalition demanded that both Janša and Janković resign. Since Janša refused to step down, most of the parties left the ruling coalition and Janša lost the parliamentary majority. Finally, on 27 February 2013, he was ousted in a parliamentary vote of no confidence – partly due to mass mobilisations of a kind not seen since Slovenian independence in 1991. This meant a major victory for the new movement, but with another 'All-Slovenian Uprising' on 9 March 2013 the protesters were determined to keep up the pressure on the new provisional government of Alenka Bratušek.

Despite these successes we have to ask ourselves in what sense this outbreak of public rage constituted an emancipatory political act. The protests were a public outcry against the corrupt political and economic elites who have brought the country close to bankruptcy. Moving well beyond the issue of Maribor's corrupt mayor, the protesters demonstrated for social justice and equality, and against poverty, unemployment and austerity. However, the rejection of the political establishment and a profound discontent with representative democracy provided the most frequent theme in these protests, notably in the chants of

'It is over with them, they are done!' and 'Direct democracy now!' While the media and politicians were keen to reintegrate these events into the formal political processes which assign everyone a place in a given symbolic and material order, an order Rancière terms 'the partition of the sensible' (*le partage du sensible*), they have to be envisaged precisely as an act of contesting the existing order. The actions of socially diverse participants in and through space comprise elements of a novel form of political subjectivity and subjectification. These protesters are no longer organised along the lines of old political imaginaries. They are self-organised (over social networks) and comprise different groups of society, from war veterans, youth and pensioners to left activists and union members. Voicing slogans such as 'Neither left nor right, they all must go!', those who have no part in society make themselves count as speaking beings by staging the equality of a part in the sphere of appearance.[18] The importance of equality does not lie in the question as to whether we are all equal. The relevant factor is the statement that we are all equal and the ensuing consequences of that statement. This statement and its enactment is what political subjectification is about. The people who came together on the Slovenian streets in 2012 and 2013 were pointing precisely to the fact that our 'democratic' societies are all shaped by mechanisms of exclusion and oppression. They were reclaiming the political power of the people by appropriating the public sphere and spaces. In doing so, they constituted spaces of and for politics and ruptured the 'normal' distribution of positions and routinised sense-making practices. In seriously questioning the neoliberal combination of representative democracy and capital-demanded cuts and wage suppression there was a real political proposition in these protests – people of different social groups, political affiliations and generations were able to think not only for themselves, but for anybody. This opened up a political space far beyond the official political procedures.

---

18   J. Rancière, *Disagreement: Politics and Philosophy*, Minneapolis and London: University of Minnesota Press, 1995.

The concrete alternatives to party democracy and capitalism presented here may still sound immature or naive at times, and popular resentment and anger are still fairly vague. Thus, it is by no means clear how these heterogeneous movements will develop in the future or how they will succeed in working on a common political project. Nevertheless, in a country which was once called the 'Switzerland of the Balkans', these popular movements have triggered an important public debate about new ideas and visions beyond the status quo of liberal democracy and neoliberal capitalism.

To conclude, the examples of popular mobilisation discussed in this chapter point to the fact that after decades of neoliberal colonisation of the minds of the people with metaphors of the free market and self-responsibility as part of the narrative of transition, the consensus manufactured by political elites, big business and the media is now slowly exhibiting its first fractures in the Balkans. New social movements have ruptured the post-'socialist' consensus and the neoliberal foundations of free markets and liberal democracy. Disillusionment is gradually turning into action. If the widespread discomfort is directed into an emancipatory political force that is capable of uniting different groups of people, then we can 'learn the art of recognising, from an engaged subjective position, elements which are here, in our space, but whose time is the emancipated future'.[19] Therefore, the examples discussed above can be interpreted as a first step towards opening up epistemologies and practices on which future movements can draw. It is important that such new experiences and ideas of alternative forms of organisation and society are shared, thereby adding to an epistemology of resistance and facilitating important collective learning processes.

These movements are social laboratories that allow for other forms of social organisation and solidarity, as well as a new idea of community that is not mediated by market forces or financial interests. However, the isolated and often fragmented groups

---

19   S. Žižek, *The Year of Dreaming Dangerously*, London: Verso, 2012, 128.

need to work on a common narrative and an analysis of the crisis upon which they can base a future politics of social justice and deep democratisation. They need to establish strong links to their wider communities and other actors, spreading the word about their struggles, building up counter-hegemonic institutions and education, and drawing on the cultural and socio-political support of local communities. Such a change can only be achieved over a long period of time. Nevertheless, even while acknowledging the embryonic nature of these struggles, one thing is certain: given the recent economic collapse, Polanyi's message about the need to place the market under the control of society instead of mythologising about 'natural' and 'uncontrollable' market forces seems more relevant than ever. This can pave the way for building our vision of a society that can truly 'afford to be both just and free' and that expands democratic decision making into the economic sphere.[20]

---

20   K. Polanyi, *The Great Transformation: The Political and Economic Origins of Our Time*, Boston: Beacon Press, 1957, 256.

CHAPTER 11

'They had sex, drugs and rock 'n' roll; we'll have mini-jobs and loans to pay': Transition, Social Change and Student Movements in the Post-Yugoslav Region

Jana Baćević

In recent years there has been an almost unprecedented surge of student uprisings. Spreading through universities and secondary schools across the world, these movements have often addressed the same problem: the privatisation, commodification and marketisation of education. From Montreal to Santiago de Chile and from London to Athens, the banners 'One World – One Struggle' were a reminder that, despite local differences, the neoliberal restructuring of higher education had become a global issue.

The region formerly known as Yugoslavia has also seen its fair share of mobilisation around these issues. Besides the (probably most famous) student protests in Croatia in 2009, between 2006 and 2012 protests addressing different aspects of the transformation of higher education spread from Serbia to Slovenia. Although the dynamics, organisation and impact of these protests differ, not only between republics, but also between specific universities, collectively they have succeeded in 'shaking up' the academic – and not only the academic – spheres in the post-Yugoslav states.

How should we understand these protests? The history of student movements in the former Yugoslavia can be, at once, clarifying and obscuring. On the one hand, students are the traditional 'unruly subjects' and sources of opposition to the regime. From the protests between 1968 and 1971 that, despite their ideological heterogeneity ranging between radical left and ethno-nationalism, voiced a sharp critique of Yugoslavia's communist elites, to the famous 1996–7 protests in Serbia against Slobodan Milošević, student movements in the region have posed substantial challenges to the ruling class. Many commentators, especially on the left, have interpreted the recent student mobilisations as a sort of continuation of this 'historical mission'. They credit the students with having 'stunned the state-capitalist machinery and pushed it on the back foot',[1] committing an 'out-of-the-ordinary incursion and attack on the already normalised domestic Social Darwinist neoliberalism',[2] while occupied faculties have become 'islands of most vehement social criticism, welcoming anyone interested in radical social change'.[3] On the other hand, similar fears or expectations have probably inspired the criticism of these protests. In this context, student protests in the region have been labelled everything from 'inarticulate' and 'vague', to 'illegitimate' or 'terrorist'.

While different readings of these student movements can be almost as interesting as the movements themselves, here I want to resist the urge of over-interpretation. Instead of romanticising contemporary student protests as the 'new 1968', or, alternatively, criticising their lack of a coherent political ideology, I will focus on the meaning and significance of student protests *in their specific context*. This entails analysing the protests in relation to the social, political and economic dynamics of the post-socialist transformation of post-Yugoslavia, or, in other words, of the transition. Despite different manifestations, speed of implementation, or

1   T. Prug, 'University News: Student Control in Croatia', *Radical Philosophy*, vol. 161, May–June 2010, 65–6.

2   T. Kuljić, 'Studentski delatni otpor kapitalizmu' [Students' Active Resistance to Capitalism], *Novi Plamen*, vol. 17, 2012, 134–6.

3   L. Kovačević, 'A Five Weeks Introduction to Democracy', 2009, at http://slobodnifilozofski.org.

perceived success, this political framework – comprising primarily the combination of liberal democracy and market economy, but with numerous implications for other spheres of social life – certainly constitutes the most important common denominator in the post-Yugoslav states today. This chapter will thus offer an interpretation of the current student movements in the region within their broader historical and political context. I will begin with a brief account of the major events in the recent student protests. This by no means aspires to be an exhaustive review; rather, it should serve as the basis for an analysis of the meanings of the protests, which is the focus of the second part of the text. The concluding part will offer some thoughts on the possible implications of student mobilisations in the post-Yugoslav space and beyond.

Student Protests: From Serbia to Slovenia, from Repression to Accommodation

The earliest mass demonstrations against the current transformations of higher education took place in Serbia in the city of Niš, moving on to the universities of Belgrade and Novi Sad.[4] The protests began over a seemingly benign issue: the equivalence of degrees issued before and after the introduction of the Bologna Process. This aspect was, however, quickly overtaken by the broader critique of the commercialisation of education as such.[5] Banners with slogans such as 'Knowledge is not for sale', 'Down with tuition fees' and 'Free education for all' appeared. The students occupied a number of faculties in downtown Belgrade, asking for the fulfilment of demands that included both the recognition of pre-Bologna degrees and,

---

4   Kontrapukt, 'Studentski protesti 2006: nastavak' [Student Protests: Continuation], 2006, at http://protest.zbrka.net.

5   See V. Marković, 'A Re-examination of the Position of the Student Movement in Serbia', in R. Hudson and G. Bowman, eds, *After Yugoslavia: Identities and Politics Within the Successor States*, London: Palgrave Macmillan, 2012; T. Kurepa, ed., *Borba za znanje: studentski protest 2006* [Struggle for Knowledge: Student Protest, 2006], Belgrade: ATC, 2007.

interestingly, the *reduction* (not abolition) of tuition fees. The protest received a high degree of attention from the mainstream media, especially for its departure from the discourse and ideology of the student protests in 1996–7.[6] One of the most telling manifestations of the desire to make a clear distinction from the previous protests occurred when students booed Čedomir Jovanović and Čedomir Antić, two former student leaders who had meanwhile risen to influential political positions, and who visited the (occupied) Faculty of Philosophy in Belgrade to mark the anniversary of the 1996–7 protests. The students said they had no faith in political leaders and institutions, and did not want their protest to be 'politically abused'.

Early on, this protest exhibited dynamics that were in many ways similar to the future protests in the region. The contradiction between the demands for adaptation to what was presented as 'European' standards (in terms of the equivalence of Bachelors and Masters degrees), on the one hand, and the complete transformation of the trajectory of the reform (in terms of abolishing tuition fees) on the other, paved the way for the political elites to manipulate the protest. On the eve of the upcoming elections, the Parliament of the Republic of Serbia issued a ruling that formally equated the pre-2003 Bachelors degrees with Masters degrees. The students withdrew from the occupations, only later to realise that the faculties had taken to charging for certificates of equivalence.[7] However, although they were in a way 'tricked' by the political elites, the protesters highlighted the tension between the dominant political structures – including the traditional concepts and forms of student representation – and more horizontal, direct-democracy-based forms of organisation. The ultimate achievement of the protest was thus more radical: it was the earliest public demonstration to openly

---

6　'Spontanost, organizacija i pare' [Spontaneity, Organisation and Funding], *Vreme*, 30 November 2006, at http://vreme.com.

7　J. Baćević, 'Masters or Servants? Power and Discourse in Serbian Higher Education Reform', *Social Anthropology/Anthropologie Sociale*, Special Issue: Anthropologies of University Reform, vol. 18(1), 2010, 43–56.

diagnose the ongoing reforms as 'neoliberal'. In a society that had hitherto been complacent at the destruction of the commons, the student protest thus constituted the first comprehensive counter-narrative.

Arguably the most famous contemporary student movement in the region, in Croatia, took this agenda to an entirely new level. Student mobilisation in Croatia began with a protest in Zagreb in 2008, ostensibly triggered by the introduction of tuition fees. Not unlike the beginnings of the student movement in Serbia in 2006, the early phase was characterised by a vague and broad mishmash of requests.[8] The subsequent protest narrowed down the agenda, focusing on the abolition of tuition fees and the right to free education for all; in addition, the protest was held on the International Day against the Commercialisation of Education, thus symbolically positioning itself on the map of the struggles within the International Student Movement. Together, these events prepared the ground for the occupations that took place in spring 2009.

The occupations, which extended to twenty institutions in eight towns, put the Croatian student movement at the centre of public attention. Students moved into classrooms, visiting lectures and asking other students to join. They organised eating, sleeping and information sessions in the faculty buildings. Most notably, the occupations adopted plenums as the main method of deliberation and decision making. A plenum has no formal membership or leadership – instead, it gathers all interested students and distributes tasks on a voluntary basis, sometimes dividing them into working groups or sections.[9] Thus, the movement openly distanced itself from the traditional modes of student political organisation, emphasising the

---

8   M. Kapović, 'Two Years of the Struggle for Free Education and the Development of a New Student Movement in Croatia', 2011, at http://slobodni-filozofski.org.

9   Center for Anarchist Studies, *The Occupation Cookbook or the Model of the Occupation of the Faculty of Humanities and Social Sciences in Zagreb*, New York: Minor Compositions, 2009.

horizontal, consensus-based models founded on the principles of direct democracy.[10]

The political and academic elites in Croatia had a hard time adapting to these novel forms of student organising. At first, some members of the academic establishment, including the Rector of the University of Zagreb, expressed solidarity with the students, paying visits to the plenums and showing willingness to listen to the students' demands. The Academic Council of the Faculty of Philosophy, where the main occupation was taking place, even cancelled all lectures for a week, in solidarity with the students. Quickly, however, they encountered pressure from the Ministry of Science, Education and Sports, which demanded the restoration of 'order' at the universities. The students became increasingly isolated; although they had the support of the general public, they began losing ground at the faculties. A compromise solution was found: the universities committed to full funding for the first year of undergraduate studies, and the Plenum of the Faculty of Philosophy, the last remaining occupied faculty, voted to end the occupation in May 2009, thirty-five days after it began.

Another wave of occupations took place that autumn, but gathering fewer students from a smaller number of institutions.[11] Besides the demand for free education, the protests now addressed the proposed legislative changes in higher education. By this time, the student protests had morphed into a movement that, though without elected or appointed leaders or representatives, was increasingly becoming the main voice of the students. The

---

10   E. Eminagić, 'Direktno-demokratsko društvo: analiza novog vala studentskih protesta u zemljama bivše Jugoslavije' [Direct-Democratic Society: An Analysis of the New Wave of Student Protests in the Countries of Former Yugoslavia], *Novi Plamen*, vol. 17, 2012, 140–2; D. Petrović, 'Analiza političkih aspekata studentske blokade Filozofskoga fakulteta Univerziteta u Zagrebu: metoda i strategija studentske blockade' [The Analysis of the Political Aspects of the Student Blockade of the Faculty of Philosophy, University of Zagreb: Methods and Strategies], *Studia Ethnologica Croatica*, vol. 23, 2011, 327–47; S. Horvat and I. Štiks, *Pravo na pobunu: uvod u anatomiju građanskog otpora* [The Right to Rebellion: An Introduction to the Anatomy of Civic Resistance], Zaprešić: Faktura, 2010.

11   Kapović, 'Two Years of the Struggle for Free Education'.

plenums continued working after the end of occupations, organising public demonstrations and seeking to develop joint platforms with other social groups. One of the remarkable results of this process is the faculty-student initiative known as 'Academic Solidarity', launched in 2010, which has mobilised the broader academic community around the proposed changes to the governance and funding of higher education and research in Croatia. Furthermore, students are building links with workers and farmers, and have actively participated in 'The Right to the City' movement against the privatisations of urban space in Zagreb, thus creating the potential for the movement to transcend concerns related to higher education and develop a platform for broader social mobilisation.

The wide publicity gained by the 'successes' of the Croatian student struggle led to it becoming a sort of a 'blueprint' for similar initiatives in the region. In 2009, students at the University of Tuzla, in Bosnia-Herzegovina, organised a plenum and demanded the abolition of tuition fees. Students also started mobilising in Montenegro: the first and the most massive student protest to happen in the republic in the last two decades was held in November 2011, featuring requests for a decrease in tuition fees and for better living conditions. Students had also begun reaching out to workers and trade unions, but further mobilisation has been cut short due to alleged corruption in the Montenegrin student parliament.

In the autumn of 2011, students at the University of Belgrade, in Serbia, organised a series of protests that culminated in the occupations of the buildings of the Faculty of Philosophy and Faculty of Philology. Student plenums were organised. However, the agenda again became stuck between a seemingly 'technical' request – for the scrapping of tuition fees for students who had fulfilled the projected ECTS[12] load during

---

12   ECTS stands for the European Credit Transfer System, a system of credits that is equivalent to time invested in studying. Introduced as part of the Bologna Process, the system aims to simplify mobility and mutual recognition between study programmes and different institutions of higher education in Europe.

the preceding year – and a much more ambitious demand for full public funding of higher education. The reactions of the political and academic establishment, however, markedly differed from those in Croatia. Politicians and policy makers for the most part ignored the student demands, especially their more radical elements, or gave vague promises to 'resolve the issue' in the future, without committing to concrete forms of action. Perhaps surprisingly, it was in the faculties themselves that the student protests encountered the harshest response. With the exception of a couple of 'left-leaning' professors, the majority of the faculty remained silent. The administration refused to discuss the issues with 'non-elected' student representatives and threatened to summon the police. On a number of occasions, students were attacked by right-wing extremists. Finally, the administration proceeded to forcefully evict the students from the classrooms, bringing an end to the occupation. Although the protesters remain marginalised at their own faculties, they have kept up the plenum as a form of organisation, and are active in different grassroots and non-governmental initiatives.

Perhaps unsurprisingly for those acquainted with the post-Yugoslav space, Slovenia, although in a number of ways similar to other former Yugoslav republics, exhibits some peculiar characteristics. To begin with, it has an internationally recognised left-wing intellectual scene, as well as the Workers' and Punks' University (Delavsko-punkerska univerza, DPU) – an alternative education initiative that, at least in name, continues the tradition of workers' universities in socialist Yugoslavia, which aimed to provide venues for critical reflection and learning outside the 'traditional' universities. Since 1997, the DPU has functioned within the framework of the Peace Institute, which has made it sustainable and given it an institutional base. In the spring of 2010, thousands of Slovenian students protested against the proposed changes to the working conditions of students and academic workers that included limits to their working hours and income, sentencing them to 'mini-jobs', a casualised and precarious form of labour characteristic of transition economies.[13] The protests turned violent, as the students threw stones and eggs at the government building, and the riot police were called to intervene. Although at the time the protest did not challenge the structure of official student representation, it clearly demonstrated the differences between the old and new generation of political leaders. In a telling incident, the Speaker of the Slovenian Parliament expressed disapproval of the students' methods by invoking his own credentials as a former student activist: 'I've taken part in my fair share of protests since 1968 and I haven't seen anything like this. This is a clear rejection of dialogue in favour of violence.' The representative of the students responded: 'They [the politicians] had sex, drugs and rock 'n' roll; we'll have mini-jobs and loans to pay.'[14]

A more contained and at the same time broader protest started in the autumn of 2011. It began with the occupation of the Faculty of Philosophy at the University of Ljubljana. The occupation was organised by a movement known as 'We are the University' (Mi smo univerza, MSU). Although endorsing the struggle against neoliberalisation, the demands of the movement went beyond free higher education. In a letter sent to the Rector of the University of Ljubljana and to the Dean of the Faculty of Philosophy, the students demanded better working conditions for doctoral candidates, full employment for part-time academic workers, the right to continue using the occupied parts of the building, as well as the recognition of alternative educational programmes.[15] Although, not unlike Zagreb in 2009, the Rector publicly stated that he supported the demands of the students, in reality only a few were met: the students were 'given' a classroom in which to continue assembling, but that was the highest degree of recognition they received. On the

13   A. Fangman, 'Thousands of Slovenian Students Protest Attacks on Their Conditions', World Socialist Web Site, 22 May 2010, at www.wsws.org.

14   Republic of Slovenia, Government Communication Office, 'Angry Words, Stones Fly at Student Protest', 20 May 2010, at www.ukom.gov.si.

15   Mi smo univerza, 'Zahteve gibanja Mi smo univerza' [The Demands of the Movement We Are the University], 2011, at mismouniverza.org.

other hand, the support of the academic staff was stronger and more explicit than in Croatia or in Serbia: at the session of the Academic Council of the (at the time occupied) Faculty of Philosophy even the professors who did not support the students' methods thanked them for providing the academic staff with an incentive to take positions in relation to the changes in higher education, something they had previously been disinclined to do. Thus, like the 'Academic Solidarity' movement in Croatia, the student protests were conducive to the development of stronger links between academic staff and students. Although reduced to a single classroom, the movement at the University of Ljubljana continued organising alternative educational programmes together with the DPU, covering topics such as Marxist theory, European integration, and knowledge production.

The students also came to play a prominent role in the popular protests that took place across Slovenia at the end of 2012 and beginning of 2013. This time, the issues went beyond 'internal' university matters into the question of financing of higher education and research, threatened by the Slovene government's proposed austerity measures. This context propelled students, teachers and the university administration into joining forces with slogans such as 'We won't pay for your crisis', 'We won't give you our professors', and 'We're not selling public universities'.[16] Eventually, the protests forced the Slovenian government to resign. However, youth unemployment and the commodification of education remain salient issues that are likely to generate new protests in the future.

As can be deduced from this brief overview, since 2006, and especially in the period between 2009 and 2011, there were repeated expressions of student opposition to policies proposed and enacted by the governments in post-Yugoslav states. Despite their differences, all of the protests have challenged the 'accepted

16   N. Golič, 'Vzkliki pred DZ: "Ne bomo plačali vaše krize!"' [Shouts in Front of the Parliament: We Shall Not Pay for Your Crisis!], 6 December 2012, at www.dnevnik.si.

wisdom' of higher education transformation in the region, and drawn attention to the consequences of the commodification of knowledge. They cut across the borders of the post-Yugoslav states, connecting students from different institutions, different former Yugoslav republics, and even different generations. Seductive as it may be from both a political and an analytical perspective, however, this process should not be taken as a sign of the 'reunification' of the region. The affinities between student protests in the region are partly a function of global and regional networking; to a larger extent, however, they are the consequences of the specific dynamics of post-socialist transformation that are, though not without exceptions, shared across post-Yugoslav states. It is to these social and political dynamics that I will now turn, examining how they are related to the student movements in the region and, ultimately, to their effects.

Neoliberalism with a Post-socialist Twist: Student Protests in Context

When they first appeared, banners with the slogan 'Knowledge is not for sale' may have baffled the older generation in the post-Yugoslav states. Under socialism, as well as for a period of time in the 1990s, knowledge was, in a sense, free: the majority of students attended higher education without paying tuition fees, although some charges applied to part-time students. This, however, does not mean that the system was necessarily more equitable: secondary schools acted as a 'bottleneck' in transition to tertiary education, where advantaged social groups, such as bureaucratic or intellectual elites, were systematically overrepresented.[17] Education reforms introduced in the Socialist Federal Republic of Yugoslavia during the 1970s attempted to reverse this trend, but had rather limited success.

---

17   K. Miklavič, 'Definitions and Theories', in *Evolving Diversity: An Overview of Equitable Access to Higher Education in Europe*, Brussels: MENON Network, 2012, 7–16; Y. Shavit and H. Blossfeld, *Persistent Inequality: Changing Educational Attainment in Thirteen Countries*, Boulder, CO: Westview Press, 1993.

The dissolution of Yugoslavia left its successor states with relatively elitist and decentralised higher education systems, which were deemed inefficient and insufficient to support the transition to a capitalist economy. The solution was found in massification: the opening of higher education to larger proportions of the population, which was seen as instrumental for economic growth. Kogan writes: 'With the transition from socialism to capitalism and the accompanying liberalisation of educational policy, within a short period of time post-secondary education expanded and diversified in these countries to levels beyond those observed in . . . most Western European countries.'[18] This rapid massification, however, was not followed by a proportional increase in public spending. Instead, the path to reform was found in deregulation. In some cases, this entailed the expansion of private higher education, where the cost of studies is predominantly borne by students or their parents. Simultaneously, governments increasingly encouraged public higher education institutions to look for 'alternative' sources of funding. Most of them, not surprisingly, turned to students. Thus, in the past ten years, both the cost of studies and the proportion of students paying tuition fees continued growing, while governmental investment did not increase at the same rate.[19] The consequence of this imbalance was increased inequality in higher education.

The student protests were the first to draw the attention of the public to the implications of this trend, and to openly voice objections to it. In some cases, these objections took a rather conservative form, as in the case of demands for the reduction of the cost of tuition fees, or the alleviation of costs for specific cohorts of students. In others, it was more radical, calling for

---

18   I. Kogan, 'Tertiary Education Landscape and Labour Market Chances of the Highly Educated in Central and Eastern Europe', *European Sociological Review*, vol. 28(6), 2012, 701–3.

19   Overall, it is very difficult to give assessments of these trends in the post-Yugoslav states, given the differences in both the data collected and the methods of measurement. Some indicators can be found at www.herdata.org and www.Eurostudent.eu.

the abolition of tuition fees altogether and 'free' (i.e. fully publicly financed) education for 'all' (usually understood as eligible
secondary education graduates). The arguments against the
privatisation of education also ranged considerably. Sometimes
they were framed in nostalgic appeals for a 'return' to the traditional concept of the Humboldtian university; on other
occasions, they overlooked the possibility of challenging the
dominant economistic thinking that equated education with
economic growth. It was this variety of approaches that, to a
large extent, contributed to the characterisation of the students'
requests as 'vague' and 'inarticulate'. However, together they
opened the door to a much larger critique: that of neoliberalism
itself.

While routinely used in academic circles on the left to criticise the contemporary manifestations of liberal capitalism, as
a serious diagnostic category neoliberalism has been almost
completely absent from the post-Yugoslav public sphere. The
student movements were the first to make the connection
between this concept and the ongoing processes of transformation in the societies of the former Yugoslavia in public discourse.
Until then, most aspects of neoliberal transformation – the
leading role attributed to markets in determining the direction
of development, the privatisation of public services, and the
influence of transnational banks and financial institutions (IMF,
the World Bank) – were routinely framed as 'inescapable'
aspects of the post-socialist transition.[20] Higher education
reforms implemented in the post-Yugoslav states followed the
same logic. The marketisation and privatisation of education
systems were constructed as parts of the process of the
'Europeanisation' of higher education and research, thus using
the nostalgic narrative of the 'return' to Europe to justify policy
transformations. In the discourses of both the state and other
policy entrepreneurs, the Bologna Process was framed as an

20   S. Horvat and I. Štiks, 'Welcome to the Desert of Transition! Post-
Socialism, the European Union, and a New Left in the Balkans', *Monthly Review*,
vol. 63(10), 2012, 38–48.

externally driven programme that had to be implemented in order to attain a political goal, namely, the successful integration of national higher education systems into a European framework, making them internationally competitive as well as attractive to foreign students and networks. This led to the effective depoliticisation of the transformation of higher education and research. Removing these processes from the sphere of public deliberation – and thus, by definition, from the possibility of contestation – meant that responsibility for the reforms was reduced to mere 'translation' or implementation. In sum, political authority and agency were twice removed – first, from the students and citizens as (supposed) participants in democratic decision making; and second, from the local and national political elites, who 'abdicated' responsibility for the reforms.

This political framework is remarkably similar to what Shore and Chandler have termed, respectively, 'illiberal' or 'post-liberal' governance regimes.[21] Post-liberal governance is marked by the erosion of the democratic legitimacy of nation-states, and the increased role of international and transnational institutions which use economic and political conditionalities in order to 'push' for the implementation of (usually market-oriented) reforms. However, it would be misguided to see the reforms introduced under the shroud of post-liberal governance as *entirely* externally driven.[22] On the contrary, they require the joint endeavour of local and external actors, in a manner that Gramsci dubbed 'passive revolution'.[23] Passive revolutions denote processes of change in which local actors use externally legitimised reforms in order to pursue their own agendas. Local actors need external organisations to validate

21   C. Shore, 'Audit Culture and Illiberal Governance: Universities and the Politics of Accountability', *Anthropological Theory*, vol. 8, 2008, 278–98; D. Chandler, *International Statebuilding: The Rise of Post-Liberal Governance*, London: Routledge, 2010.

22   T. McCarthy, 'Why Did the EU Enlarge to the East? A Neo-Gramscian Critique of Schimmelfenig's Constructivist Approach', *e-International Relations*, 24 August 2011, at www.e-ir.info.

23   A. Gramsci, *Selection from Prison Notebooks*, ed. and trans. Q. Hoare and G. Nowell Smith, London: Elecbook, 1999 [1971].

their interpretations of these processes, but also to provide funding for structural transformation. External actors, on the other hand, need cooperative local actors in order to be able to claim the success of their reform agendas.

Using 'neoliberalism' as a diagnosis, the students thus did much more than just criticise the externally driven dimension of the Bologna Process and related policies. As a matter of fact, they pointed to the paramount role of the local elites in mediating, translating and thus, inevitably, *shaping* these processes. In other words, they framed the question of neoliberalism as, in effect, a practice of *state-building*. Wacquant has recently reminded us that neoliberalism is not an economic but a political project, which entails not the dismantling but the re-engineering of the state.[24] By pointing to the collusion between the neoliberal market transformations and local power relationships, the student protests in fact brought into question the hitherto unchallenged right of the political elites in the post-Yugoslav states to both interpret and implement different elements of the process of transition.

As in the other former communist countries, the political elites in the countries of the former Yugoslavia are predominantly composed of, on the one hand, the successors of the former *nomenklatura*, and, on the other, intellectuals and other white-collar professionals who earned their political credentials through opposition to the communist regimes – frequently, as in the case of the Speaker of the Slovenian Parliament, as student leaders. The source of the power of these elites, however, primarily rests not on economic capital – whose accumulation was anyway difficult during communism, and which, in the majority of former communist countries, continues to be considered somewhat 'suspicious' in the political domain – but on cultural capital: in other words, it is generated and reproduced through education. Their influence is predominantly based on the idea that they possess

---

24   L. Wacquant, 'Three Steps to a Historical Anthropology of Actually Existing Neoliberalism', *Social Anthropology/Anthropologie Sociale*, vol. 20, 2012, 166–79.

the technical 'expertise' – skills, knowledge and connections – needed to 'steer' their respective countries through the processes of transition.[25] At the same time, these 'transitional' elites see their work as fundamentally 'civilising': they are the enlightened interpreters of Modernity, whose role is to bring the fruits of its progress to the 'uncivilised' East.[26]

This perspective helps explain why universities became 'hotspots' for the contestation of neoliberal reforms. On the one hand, it is through higher education that students acquire the knowledge and skills to understand the social and political context and implications of these reforms. On the other hand, elites naturally tend to see universities as the traditional source of the reproduction of the ruling stratum, and thus, of themselves. Thus, they have trouble accepting that this 'sacred' breeding ground might actually become the source of initiatives that seek to challenge their own 'civilising' projects. The student protests have challenged this traditional elite-reproducing mission of higher education on at least three levels. Firstly, by their very composition: although the protests are still led by the social science and humanities faculties – the traditional sites of both dissent and the recruitment of future elites – the students are no longer privileged *héritiers* of the bureaucratic or academic oligarchs. They come from increasingly diverse backgrounds, holding different ideas and values than their predecessors. Secondly, through the physical occupation of the faculties, the students symbolically take control over the reproduction of social elites. Finally, they refuse to conform to the existing channels of political communication. Through the founding of plenums and the exercise of direct democracy, the student movements have rejected the very basis of the liberal political order that sustains the transitional elites in their social, political and economic positions.

---

25   L.P. King, and I. Szelenyi, *Theories of the New Class: Intellectuals and Power*, Minneapolis: University of Minnesota Press, 2004.

26   G. Eyal, I. Szelenyi and E. Townsley, *Taking Capitalism without Capitalists: Class Formation and Elite Struggles in Post-Communist Central Europe*, London: Verso, 1998.

The range of elite responses to the student protests in the region can in this sense be understood as the extension of different perceptions and strategies for addressing the challenges to existing power relationships. At the one end is ridicule: designating the protesters as 'kids', 'anarchists', 'terrorists' (or, in the words of the Croatian Minister of Internal Affairs, commenting on the general protests in 2011, 'Indians', supposedly meaning Native Americans caricatured in Westerns), seeking to exclude them from the realm of political subjects and thus deny them even the right to question the elites' monopoly on the interpretation of the transformation processes. In the centre are the calls for 'order', and invitations to the police to visit the campuses; they reflect the yearning for an 'ordo-liberal' resolution that would restore the elites' right to define the rules in higher education, while returning the students to the position of obedient subjects. Finally, the elite's appeals to their own student leader credentials, as well as meek pronouncements that 'the students are right', reflect their assumption that the students will eventually occupy elite positions themselves, and thus can be seen as attempts to 'pacify' them through incorporation into the existing political structure.

Conclusions: Student, the Transitional Subject

The contradictions between the transitional political elites in the post-Yugoslav states and the current student movements can be resolved in a number of ways in the future. On the one hand, student movements may remain on the margins of the political process, perhaps in time growing into a stronger extra-parliamentary opposition. On the other hand, they could develop unitary or plural forms of political opposition, in the wake of left-leaning political parties or coalitions like Syriza in Greece, which would aim to counterbalance the prevailing neo-liberal politics in the post-Yugoslav states. In some cases, depending on different external and internal factors, these opposition movements might come to occupy relatively important positions, and succeed in asserting a new hegemonic narrative. However, student movements have a much stronger transformational potential that stems less from what students do than from what they *represent*.

The process of transition and the process of education have a natural affinity. Like transition, student existence is temporally bounded: it is supposed to have an identifiable beginning and a (relatively) perceptible end. However, like transition, 'student-hood' is becoming indefinitely prolonged – through, for instance, the ideology of life-long learning, as well as the extension of the average years spent in schooling – and thus threatens to become the default, rather than an exceptional, state of affairs. 'Progress' in both transition and education is defined through the fulfilment of specific criteria (like openness of the markets and the rule of law, or taking exams and attendance in class) that are arbitrary (i.e. culturally and historically contingent) and reflect power ine-qualities. Furthermore, both transition and studenthood are predicated on their respective eschatologies, legitimised through the promise of the treasure that awaits at the end of the proverbial rainbow. In the case of transition, the goal is prosperity, economic and political stability, and a more democratic society; in the case of education, it is joining the labour force, getting a good job, and becoming a fully productive member of society. However, in both cases, these goals seem to be further and further away from reality. Transition, for many, has brought more economic hard-ship and less security; at the same time, the institutions of a democratic society are still largely dysfunctional or serve as an external legitimation for decision-making processes that, as in the case of the education reforms, exclude the majority of citi-zens. Equally, higher education is no longer a guarantee of a good job; in the countries of the former Yugoslavia, precariousness has become the norm.[27] Instead of prosperity, the majority of young educated people are now, indeed, looking towards a future of holding on to mini-jobs and paying off student loans.

---

27   T. Matković and I. Kogan, 'All or Nothing? The Consequences of Tertiary Education Non-Completion in Croatia and Serbia', *European Sociological Review*, vol. 28(6), 2012, 755–70.

The figure of the Student thus embodies perfectly the paradoxes of post-socialist transition. Decoupled from its historical claim to elite status, left at the mercy of the forces of the market mediated through an uneasy coalition of transnational institutions of post-liberal governance and the *realpolitik* of local transitional elites, the Student expects a future of incessant adaptations to an increasingly casualised labour market – the workings of which she can come to understand, but, by the virtue of her own position in the (semi-)periphery, cannot influence. Despite the language of historical precedence, transition, just like education, is almost completely scripted. To invert the slogan of Crimethinc: the future is already written. Student movements in the post-Yugoslav states are thus exceptional not because they go *against* this trend, but because they exist *in spite* of it. The student protests represent a rupture in the fabric of neoliberal post-socialist reality, a conscious choice to stop, question and criticise *even though* doing so is not 'useful' for one's own political or academic career. Rather than concrete blocks, the protests are 'grains of sand' thrown in the machinery of the 'rolling-out' of neoliberalism presented as historical inevitability.[28] Just like grains of sand, they cannot and probably will not stop the machine from functioning. But they are important acts of resistance in contexts previously dominated either by silent consensus or (predominantly ethno-nationalist) cleavage politics. The fact that the students have managed to raise a relatively coherent voice against neoliberalisation while participating in one of the most neoliberalised public services – higher education – is a useful reminder that political engagement need not only stem from the 'objective' categories of class and status, but can also seek to transcend them. That is a lesson they have given us all.

---

28   P. Bourdieu, *Firing Back: Against the Tyranny of the Market 2*, New York: The New Press, 2003.

CHAPTER 12

Women's Struggles and Political Economy: From Yugoslav Self-management to Neoliberal Austerity

Ankica Čakardić

This chapter aims to map women's struggles from the period of Yugoslav self-management to the current austerity regimes that dominate Balkan societies. Though there is scant literature on the Women's Anti-Fascist Front (AFŽ), the single most important women's organisation during the Second World War and the Yugoslav self-management period, it still serves as a basis on which to list the key elements for a historical-materialist analysis of women's position during this period. Similarly, very few works exist which offer a systematic review of feminist activism in the 1990s and later, during the 'transitional' period after the break-up of Yugoslavia. The dearth of such information can be accounted for, in the first case, by a phenomenon of 'collective amnesia' of a society that once lived under socialism, affirmed in parallel to the procedure of 'manufacturing consent', described by David Harvey as a necessary step in the establishment of a new regime. During the 1990s the ground was prepared for the further accumulation of capital and the privatisation of common/public goods. It was necessary to manufacture consent and legitimise the newly created classes (such as political leaders, corporate-media owners and the business elite) and to establish the capitalist relations of production. It is particularly interesting to consider the ideologies connected to feminist struggle after the demise of Yugoslavia. I will be paying special attention to the Croatian 'transition' as a paradigmatic case for all other post-Yugoslav states. Finally, in the last part, I consider feminist responses to the crisis in the time of austerity policies and their overall consequences. I argue that without serious historical-materialist analyses of the position of women in the post-Yugoslav region during the financialisation of capitalism, it is difficult to provide a basis for an anti-capitalist feminist struggle which would ally itself with contemporary leftist movements.

Women's Problems During Yugoslav Socialist Self-management

After 1945 Yugoslavia regularly introduced reforms to its economic system. The period can be roughly divided into the administrative-centralist phase (1945–50), which saw the introduction of workers' self-management that launched decentralisation, and the de-étatisation of the country (1950–60) that culminated, after the 1974 Constitution, in a system of socialist self-management.[1] To quote Edvard Kardelj, one of Josip Broz Tito's closest aides and the main conceptual creator of Yugoslav self-managing socialism:

> The basis of all freedoms and rights of working people and citizens in our socialist society is the right to self-manage. This is a new and directly democratic socialist right, which is possible solely in the conditions of the social ownership of the means of production and the working class at the ruling position in the society. This right is unquestionable and inalienable and as such belongs to all working people and citizens.[2]

---

1   V. Tomšič, *Žena u razvoju socijalističke samoupravne Jugoslavije* [Woman in the Development of Socialist Self-Managing Yugoslavia], Belgrade: Jugoslovenska stvarnost, 1981, 33.

2   E. Kardelj, *Pravci razvoja političkog sistema socijalističkog samoupravljanja* [The Directions of the Development of the Political System of Socialist Self-Management], Belgrade: IC 'Komunist', 1978, 132.

Taken as an ideal type and with regard to the emancipation of women, self-management advocated a restructuring of the private sphere with the aim of transforming it into a building component of a unified social organisation. However, despite the stated egalitarian demands of the self-managing system, in the wake of the first technocratic interventions two problems were to emerge: an insufficient affirmation of the working class within management, and a 'lag' in the progressive materialisation of the assumed equality of women.[3]

A study on the position of women in self-management and at work conducted in Bosnia-Herzegovina in the early 1970s offers an illustration. When asked 'What does social and self-managing engagement mean to women?', 35.7 per cent of respondents replied that it meant only numerous additional duties, for 16.4 per cent it meant nothing, 12.8 per cent expressed no opinion on the matter, while 32 per cent saw such engagement as a source of numerous benefits.[4]

In other words, over 50 per cent of respondents expressed a negative attitude towards self-management, primarily in connection with the burden of domestic and family obligations. What accounts for the 'source of numerous benefits' response is the fact that the sample included urban areas and a high percentage of women who were holding one type of office job or another. In this sense, the issue of women's engagement in social and self-managing practices was a class issue (cutting between women, as well as between women and men) based primarily around the problem of free time and the distribution of household and care work in the family. These were the responses to

---

3   In terms of women's participation in the work of socio-political organisations, they represented 23 per cent of the League of Communists, 34 per cent of the League of Trade Unions – which matched their portion in the total employed workforce – 30 per cent in the Veterans' Association, and 40 per cent in the League of Socialist Youth. Women were significantly under-represented in the governing and executive bodies of these organisations. Tomšič, *Žena u razvoju socijalističke samoupravne Jugoslavije*, 55.

4   F. Kožul, *Žena u samoupravljanju* [Woman in Self-Management], Sarajevo: Univerzitet u Sarajevu – Fakultet političkih nauka, 1973, 91.

the question 'Why do women insufficiently participate in self-managing decision making?':[5]

Self-management is insufficiently developed
   – 7.69 per cent
Traditional attitudes which hold that women's place is in the
   home, and not in political and self-managing activities
   – 20.17 per cent
Women's consciousness is insufficiently developed
   – 14 per cent
Women's burden of marriage and family work
   – 51.62 per cent
Self-management is not really 'women's business'
   – 4.78 per cent
No opinion
   – 1.36 per cent
No answer
   – 0.85 per cent

Without doubt, unpaid work in the family and at home, biological reproduction and care in general, are persistent problems which continuously reproduce women's subordination, even within a socio-political system dedicated to progressive democratisation. Such a historical-materialist argument significantly surpasses the framework of the gender-theoretical discourse, placing emphasis on the importance of gender positioning within the system of relations of production both in socialist self-management and in capitalism.

Nominally, the socialist strategists of economic development and the League of Communists of Yugoslavia emphasised the importance of studying the position of women in society and the family and encouraged the monitoring of global processes, part of which was the struggle for equal living and working conditions. At the same time, in the media sphere and in journals dedicated to women's issues, one could find statements such as

---

5   Ibid., 114.

the following: '[communists] should be more determined and effective in combating various deviations and resistances, and actively helping to more successfully surpass the regressive ideas on women, particularly various conservative and patriarchal conceptions, feminist and economic approaches, and the like'.[6]

When considering Yugoslav self-management, in addition to the problem of social reproduction and the meagre representation of women in self-managing and other bodies of political decision making, it is also important to mention a third factor relevant to the insufficient emancipation of women. The most important women's organisations created after the Second World War were quickly disbanded.[7] As Lidija Sklevicky notes, although the AFŽ was programmatically linked to the League of Communists, from the beginning it was working independently, and had an autonomous network of organisations and management.[8] By the end of 1942 the Croatian AFŽ had already gathered around 250,000 women, and was publishing its own journal *Žena u borbi* (Woman in Combat).[9] The AFŽ was dissolved in 1953 due to 'excessive engagement in political work' and because it was believed that issues directly affecting women were based not on gender but on class and conservative orientation.[10] In other words, only after issues of primary importance (workers – class issues) had been solved, were secondary phenomena – such as the oppression of women – to be dealt with. In the Resolution on Establishment of the League of

6   In *Žena*, Zagreb, vols 4–5, 1980.

7   More in N. Božinović, 'Ukidanje antifašističkog fronta žena i osnivanje saveza ženskih društava' [Abolishing the Anti-Fascist Women's Front and establishing the association of women's organisations], in N. Božinović, ed., *Žensko pitanje u Srbiji u XIX i XX veku* [Women's Question in Serbia in Nineteenth and Twentieth Centuries], Belgrade: Devedesetčetvrta and Žene u crnom, 1996.

8   L. Sklevicky, *Konji, žene, ratovi* [Women, Horses, Wars], Zagreb: Ženska infoteka, 1996.

9   More on AFŽ history in 'Žene u ratu – antifašistički front žena' [Women in war – Anti-Fascist Women's Front], in Božinović, *Žensko pitanje*; Yugoslav State Archive, Fund: CK KPJ; *Savez ženskih društava Jugoslavije* (trans.); *Konferencija za društvenu aktivnost žena* (trans.); *Socijalistički savez radnog naroda Jugoslavije* (trans.).

10   Tomšič, *Žena u razvoju socijalističke samoupravne Jugoslavije*, 85.

Yugoslav Women's Societies, the Congress elaborated its decision on dissolving the AFŽ largely with arguments presented in the introductory speech of an SSRN (Socialist Alliance of Working People of Yugoslavia) delegate, concluding that the existence of a separate women's organisation would 'overtly detach women from the common efforts in solving social problems and support a false idea of the women's position as some separate women's issue, and not an issue of our whole social community, of all fighters for socialism'.[11]

If we agree that Yugoslav self-management was able to identify the problems of the oppression of women with great precision, and 'encouraged' theoretical and practical engagement in this regard, we have to ask ourselves: how is it possible that, in spite of the strong feminist–anti-fascist tradition in Yugoslavia, the socialist development of strategies reappropriating domestic work, and a number of measures aimed at emancipating women, women still remained doubly oppressed by both social and political inequality?

The standard answers to this question usually repeat self-explanatory theses on patriarchy (the notoriety of which is also indicated by theses on contemporary re-patriarchalisation) which cannot explain the causes of the failure of women's emancipatory practices. Taking patriarchy for granted is what often characterises identity theories, which rarely move beyond the description of women's condition. They fail to offer any explanation other than a trans-historic interpretation of the male–female binary opposition, thus never coming up with a structural or class critique of the gender difference or an interpretation of patriarchy as a system of productive relations.[12]

---

11   Cited in Božinović, *Žensko pitanje*.
12   Here it is pertinent to mention a recent discussion between Tad Tietze and Richard Seymour, in the wake of the SWP crisis of January 2013 caused by leaked information on a rape case in its Central Committee, which prompted numerous discussions on the relations between feminism and the left, as well as the Trotskyist 'restrained' position with regard to feminist principles. See 'Debate on Patriarchy and Capitalist Mode of Production', *Left Flank*, 15 January 2013, at www.left-flank.org.

To say that an ideal position of women in the family and society was not achieved is not only a critique of the Titoist idea that women's issues were 'solved' in socialism but also a critique of feminism itself. Since the 1970s feminism has abandoned, in Yugoslavia and elsewhere, issues like the relations between productive and unproductive labour, strategies of feminist struggle and gender in a class perspective, focusing instead on contemporary global theoretical trends and placing itself within the often depoliticised field of academic feminism.

Because the socialist ideal of women's status still left women in the doubly oppressed position which was to be regenerated through neoliberal forms of labour inequality and exploitation, one can observe a certain consistency in the subordination of women in the *transition* from one model of political economy to another. In this sense, neoliberalism requires an active role for the post-socialist state in organising market oligopolies and commodifying the social sector, in spite of narratives of a 'minimal' or 'neutral' state.[13] The result was a fully regressive form of redistribution of domestic work that since the late 1990s has been rapidly transferred, together with other social and public sectors, to a privatising mode.

The Break-up of Yugoslavia, War and Transition

During the 1970s and 1980s, feminism in Yugoslavia was marked by new tendencies that were not significantly different from the global trends of the time.[14] By this I do not refer to a

---

13 See A. Čakardić, 'Minimalna država i neoliberalne strategije kapitalizma' [Minimal State and Neoliberal Strategies of Capitalism], in M. Jadžić, D. Maljković and A. Veselinović, eds, *Kriza, Odgovori, Levica: Prilozi za jedan kritički diskurs* [Crisis, Responses, the Left: Contributions Towards a Critical Discourse], Belgrade: Rosa Luxemburg Stiftung, 2012, 129–49.

14 Đ. Knežević, 'Kraj ili novi početak? Feminizam od šezdesetih do danas u Jugoslaviji/Hrvatskoj' [The End or a New Beginning? Feminism From the '60s to the Present in Yugoslavia/Croatia], in A. Feldman, ed., *Žene u Hrvatskoj. Ženska i kulturna povijest* [Women in Croatia: Women's and Cultural History], Zagreb: Institut Vlado Gotovac and Ženska infoteka, 2004, 247–60; S. Prlenda, 'Prema povijesti jugoslavenskih feminizama' [Towards a History of Yugoslav Feminisms],

specific theoretical current, activist practice or a 'new' social position of women, but to the second wave of feminism conceived as an 'epochal social phenomenon', as suggested by Nancy Fraser.[15] The focus moved away from the social and economic position of women towards the academic and depoliticising transformation of other social movements and subpolitical groups. Depoliticisation here refers to the sense of a break with the socio-materialistic feminist practice formed in Yugoslavia through the AFŽ and its heritage in favour of a focus on human rights, identity and juridical solutions. Since the early 1990s and in the context of extreme violence, post-Yugoslav feminist activists dealt with issues arising from war, such as physical and structural violence against women (mass rapes), the establishment of safe spaces for women, and peace or pacifist policies. At the same time, academic feminist discourse had at least two important consequences: feminism lost its progressive potential and its focus on the historical relations of gender and class, and, within a general pacifist practice, was reduced to a theoretical positioning towards dominant liberal feminism and polymorphous 'gender mainstreaming'.[16] There is no doubt that the anti-war and anti-nationalist agenda of feminist activists in the 1990s had a seminal role in establishing a relatively functioning civil society, as well as normalising public life after the war. However, the consequence was that feminism was transformed into a theory of representation and identity, which lacked socio-economic analyses.

It is important to stress that the so-called transition process varied across the former Yugoslav countries in the manner and pace of its implementation. The rhythm was most efficiently set by rapid privatisations and monopolisations, programmes of

---

in S. Prlenda, ed., *Kako je bilo . . . O Zagorki i ženskoj povijesti* [What It Was Like . . . on Zagorka and Women's History], Zagreb: Centar za ženske studije, 2011, 191–202.

15   N. Fraser, 'Feminism, Capitalism, and the Cunning of History', *New Left Review*, vol. 56, March–April 2009, 97–117.

16   V. Kesic et al., eds, *Women Recollecting Memories: The Center for Women War Victims Ten Years Later*, Zagreb: Center for Women War Victims, 2003.

structural adjustment and the pre-accession talks between Croatia and Slovenia on the one hand and the bureaucratic structures of the European Union on the other. A seminal point of entry for the liberalisation of the labour market is the 'creative destruction' of work contracts. In line with the theses of Nancy Fraser on the role of feminism in making neoliberalisation possible, or Silvia Federici's analysis of women's labour and the exploitation of women's bodies,[17] women's labour power (and the lack of feminist responses to crisis) played a key role in the primitive accumulation of capital in this region as well. It seems that it was precisely women in the global labour market who affirmed flexible employment contracts. For example, neoliberal changes to employment legislation in Croatia were launched within a rapid process of liberalisation and privatisation which started in the mid 1990s and was often hidden behind a pro-European Union discourse. This is the greatest paradox of the struggle for women's rights, with feminist groups unable to offer a response to recent changes in labour legislation or articulate emancipatory exit strategies. As trade unions and other subpolitical resistance movements equally failed, it seems necessary to consider feminism as an epochal social phenomenon which at a certain point in time became characterised by a pacification of social movements, in theory as well as in practice.

The Women's Problem and Austerity Measures

After the war, that is, since the mid 1990s, a 'period of transition' began in the post-Yugoslav countries, with passage to the capitalist mode of production which used trade union decentralisation and primitive accumulation (e.g. market monopolisation, liberalisation, privatisation and deindustrialisation) to implement a neoliberal ideological agenda in this corner of the periphery. This is why the past twenty years of

---

17   S. Federici, *Caliban and the Witch: Women, the Body, and Primitive Accumulation*, New York: Autonomedia, 2004.

'transition' have seen a frantic and rapid de-socialisation of public services and sectors and a forceful, controlled market integration of this part of the periphery into the global economy.

As in many other post-Yugoslav states, the two alternating governments of post-war Croatia (centre-right nationalist conservatives and social democrats) hardly strayed from a single economic course, equally introducing free market policies, dismantling the welfare state, and successfully preparing the ground for the commodification of public and common goods. To give an example, the crisis was marked by an attack on Croatian public education, with the introduction of entrepreneurial principles in educational policies and raising fees in higher education. The same happened even in the pre-school sector, with public kindergartens recently giving way to private services offered by licensed nannies.

The feminist responses to the commercialisation of education were not articulated as a specific form of struggle within the struggles exemplified by the 2009 student movement. Entry points into the discourse and analyses of the problems in educational and other policies connected with the attack on the state's social resources only began to appear in 2012, within informal feminist-Marxist study groups. The above-mentioned law on nannies was passed without ever being discussed by women's and feminist groups. Both examples point to a lack of systemic critique and engagement with political economy within feminist organisations. This can be seen as a result of the 'resignification' of the feminist foci that began in the 1980s, which meant that feminism relinquished the methodology of systemic materialist critique, mostly refocusing itself on identity theories, and which – except in the case of the already mentioned study groups – is still taking place today. The problem is doubled by the lack of historical-problematic research on the position of women in self-management, so important in identifying the passage to a liberal feminist orientation. This goes beyond an abstract, academic issue, as it points to a disappearance of topics connected to the position of women within the existing relations of production, and a lack of theoretical apparatus or a methodological framework reflecting women's material rights.

Unfortunately, it is difficult to find in current feminist discussions in the post-Yugoslav region a methodological/ theoretical framework suitable for an analysis of the current position of women in the labour market and in the household in post-socialism.[18] More precisely, there is no serious research on the impact of the current economic crisis on women or the family, either within orthodox economics or even in heterodox approaches and methodologies involving feminist epistemology. It is comparatively easy to find data on work and income, but what is lacking are feminist-materialist interpretations.[19] This is primarily a consequence of the already mentioned resignification process within post-war feminism, as well as the adoption of a new political-economic regime following the break-up of self-management and Yugoslavia.

In a leftist-feminist context, very roughly speaking, the attack on the public sector effects, among other things, the removal of the material rights gained by women's entrance to the labour market, a crisis of social and class reproduction, the

---

18   One extremely problematic and supposedly emancipatory practice is the phenomenon of 'women's business', represented as feminist as it pays attention to women and opens up new possibilities for them. A recent example is a 'women's project' of the Croatian Chamber of Commerce, aimed at: 'promoting women's business in South-Eastern Europe by combining efforts of public and private sector and promoting best practices in policies for women's business'. For more on the project 'Women Entrepreneurs – Creating New Workplaces in South-East Europe', see www.hgk.hr. This and similar 'feminist' projects present merely another elegant entry of flexisecure work into the capitalist mode of production, using the opportunity also to affirm an essentialist myth of the entrepreneurial specificity of women. What we have here is actually an oppression of women, a tool for reproducing exploitation, packaged as an emancipatory endeavour.

19   M. Stavropoulou and N. Jones, *Off the Balance Sheet: The Impact of the Economic Crisis on Girls and Young Women*, London: Plan, 2013, at http://plan-international.org. This report by the organisations Plan and ODI examines the impact of the economic crisis on girls and young women worldwide and offers data on long-term economic trends and the ways in which they affirm gender inequality, austerity measures which transfer the burden of crisis to women and their families, decreasing access to social services, etc., but it lacks a systematic feminist-materialist data analysis.

financial burdening of households, a change at the intimate level in (marital) partners' relationships, and a strengthening of patriarchy. Existentially speaking, the crisis delivered a hard blow to the lives of women, once again reducing their labour to the regressive work done within the household/family. On the one hand, 'the feminisation of labour' in the public and service sector indicates the gender segregation of work, and on the other it represents a devaluation of all labour. When the (cheaper) female labour force enters a sector of the labour market formerly dominated by men, the price of labour power is automatically lowered. The relations of labour and capital in global economic policy affect the two parallel processes. In developed countries economic restructuring is implemented through resource allocation, which hits male workers particularly hard (as industrial production is transferred to cheap labour countries, where physically dangerous and unfavourable work conditions are combined with a problematic treatment of foreigners and migrant workers), along with an expansion of the service sector which predominantly employs women. In the countries of the periphery, such as the post-Yugoslav states, the introduction of flexible labour legislation and precarisation has had particularly dire consequences for women workers, who are forced to accept part-time and flexible contracts.[20]

All the basic elements of the impact of austerity measures on the material position of women – from work, social reproduction and the role of households in the capitalist mode of production – apply to all post-Yugoslav countries. Regarding the feminist struggle, which is supposed to aim at abolishing

---

20 In Croatia, flexibilisation runs parallel to precarisation, both targeting a variety of groups, from researchers to temporary workers in agriculture. *Flexicurity* is supposed to particularly benefit women: according to the current labour and pensions minister, Mirando Mrsić, part-time work is perfect for women as they need to combine their family and work obligations. Seasonal contracts dominate in the service sector, which together with the introduction of temporary contracts into public education points to the links between the feminisation of labour and the introduction of flexicurity.

the double oppression of women, its leftist-feminist form should be focused on affirming the state's social resources as the primary instrument in activating the redistribution of care work. It should also prepare an exit strategy from the system of super-exploitation which hurts women even more than men. Even though Yugoslav socialism did not succeed in its idealistically proclaimed full emancipation of women, they were, however, provided with a considerable degree of financial independence and stability, which was to be lost soon after the break-up of Yugoslavia. Public schools, kindergartens and after schooling, together with free school meals, served to at least partially reduce the housework burden and enable women's emancipation outside the household. Although I have pointed out the aporias of the women's question and struggles in Yugoslav self-management, it is important to stress that the system was still much more emancipatory than the current state of the relations of production which produce a deeper double oppression and reproduce it by taking back a number of social and material rights. Since the late 1990s and especially after the onset of the crisis, such public services progressively disappeared, and women from low-income households were forced to choose unemployment as a cheaper option than hiring help for household tasks.

Since there is a lack of feminist struggle in the former Yugoslavia, and an absence of any methodological and theoretical articulation of a left-feminist agenda, it is necessary to engage in field work, studying the position of women in the labour market as well as their struggles within trade unions. During the past twenty years, the trade unions have been decentralised and lost their power to block changes in labour legislation and market deregulation, and women's union movements have disappeared completely. This also means that women workers are disconnected from feminist groups, although this is one of the key relations in the formation of new feminist struggles.

To illustrate the necessity of forming alliances between working-class women and feminist activists, I will present the example of the strike at the Kamensko textile factory in Zagreb in 2010, which united textile workers with feminist and student activists as well as parts of new social movements. The deindustrialisation and financialisation of the Croatian economy hit the working class especially hard, particularly women workers employed in a feminised industry such as the textile industry. In this context, the above general descriptions of austerity measures, market deregulation and privatisation as elements in reproducing the existing relations of production, which condition the material position of women, are fully applicable to the Croatian context. The case of the Kamensko factory is important for two reasons. Firstly, it is a good illustration of the privatisation model typical of Croatian transition, this time in a typically 'female' branch: corruption aimed at destroying production – successful until 2010 – with the gradual withdrawal of social and workers' rights, until the final closing of the factory which could not be stopped by the workers' protest. Secondly, the workers' protest was not the result of structured work by a women's trade union, but an example of women-workers' self-organisation. Their primary goal was to hold on to their jobs and return to their normal lives: there could hardly be any talk of class awareness, anti-capitalist struggle or the feminist disposition of the strike. Still, the example is indicative of the necessity to connect progressive feminist strategies with the struggles of working women (in both productive and unproductive spheres). It also demonstrates the necessity of rejecting the concepts of liberal gender dematerialisation, dedicated to a small group of 'middle-class' women, with its agenda reduced to breaking through the glass ceiling, quotas and women's entrepreneurship. The concrete aspects of new feminist struggles across the former Yugoslavia will surely be remodelled around the issues of women's work, social rights and the corrosive effects of market financialisation.

Concluding Remarks

It seems appropriate to conclude by emphasising the fundamental dilemma: should the position of women be changed to help them better adapt to the existing economic conditions, or should contemporary socio-economic relations and discourse be changed in order to function in line with feminist principles? The only adequate left-feminist political strategy for dealing with the 'women's issue' involves placing it in the context of the anti-capitalist struggle and historical materialism, with adoption of a heterodox economics framework as a necessity. In this sense, issues of precarisation, the privatisation of public and common goods, repayment and amortisation of debt, market financialisation and programmes of structural adjustment are just a few among many topics that position the discussion of gender and class inequality in the context of the critique of global capitalism from a feminist perspective. In order to situate the post-Yugoslav context in this epistemological field, it is best to study the history of feminist struggles in this part of the world, in order to fill the gaps in the collective memory of the Anti-Fascist Women's Front, socialist self-management, and the shift in the position of women in the neoliberal transition and the current austerity-based economic model.

Hence this chapter has endeavoured to offer a brief historical-materialist sketch of the women's question, from Yugoslav self-management to transition and austerity, with a focus on the relations between social reproduction and capitalism. The intention was also to offer a critique of a reductionist approach to the problem of women's oppression which does not consider it as an integral component of capitalism. Dual-system theories are important here precisely for pointing out the two regimes in operation: one governing social reproduction and the other governing productive work. At the same time, the difficulties in establishing an explanatory relation between these two regimes should be noted, as they are similar to the problems that arise in analysing patriarchy alongside capitalism, which frequently results in transhistorical conclusions.[21] Both the dual-system approach and the study of capitalism in relation to patriarchy's effects on women are too often based on describing the transhistorical structure of male domination. This risks subsuming all the mechanisms and relations in which the subordination of women has historically been secured under a single logic. It is empirically unsustainable.

What would it mean, in a concrete sense, to form a new feminist movement in the post-Yugoslav region? At one level it concerns the epistemological register discussed above, directed towards a critique of liberal and cultural-identity feminist agendas. At another it involves a reaffirmation of the historic legacy of socialism, which insisted on redistributing family-household work and introduced socio-economic structures favourable to women's emancipation – even though the concrete outcomes significantly varied and were not devoid of contradictions. It is now time to actualise them in the context of neoliberal capitalism. This already points to a third level: the simultaneous struggle for activating the social resources of the state and resisting their commodification. Moreover, the feminist issues present in the Balkans and the wider European periphery intersect with those in the centre in many important ways, regarding the emancipation of women as well as the working class in general. Demands are identical not only at the level of the geopolitical context, but also when the wider subpolitical context of anti-neoliberal struggles is considered. These struggles should not be focused only on demarcated gender issues, because, very quickly, their other dimensions such as those of race, class and sexuality start to unravel. Alliances between feminist anti-capitalist struggles and left movements, such as student, union and workers' movements, and struggles for the commons, are necessary to link diverse and occasionally antagonistic subject-positions. All are responding to the experience of

---

21   J. Brenner and M. Ramas, 'Rethinking Women's Oppression', *New Left Review*, vol. 144, March–April 1984, 33–71.

post-socialist primitive accumulation and the further loss of material rights within austerity policies. It is time for all these actors to develop progressive emancipatory strategies appropriate for their time and the geographical region in which their struggles take place.

The Future of Radical Politics in the Balkans – Protests, Plenums, Parties

Igor Štiks and Srećko Horvat

The year 2015 brings two significant anniversaries: the seventieth anniversary of the establishment of socialist Yugoslavia, and the twenty-fifth anniversary of the introduction of liberal democracy and a free market economy (which signalled not only the end of the socialist project but also, soon after, the end of Yugoslavia itself). These anniversaries offer the chance to reflect on both legacies, their successes and failures, and to consider the ideology and practice of both socialist and liberal-democratic regimes. On the one hand, the critical reflections in this volume provide us with an ample amount of material for a much-needed confrontation with the twentieth century, with our current predicament, and with the future social, economic and political development of both the Balkans and Europe in general. On the other hand, this volume testifies to the definitive return of radical, left and progressive politics in the Balkans via protest movements, experiments with horizontal democracy, and other mostly non-institutional ways of political organising and action. A clear proof of this return came during the preparation of the volume itself.

After the submission of the manuscript, probably the most important social upheaval in the post-socialist Balkans erupted in Bosnia-Herzegovina in February 2014. Only eight months after the 2013 protests that for the first time significantly transcended imposed ethnic divisions, on 5 February 2014 workers from several factories that had been privatised or destroyed united on the streets of Tuzla to demand their unpaid salaries and pensions. They were soon joined by students and other citizens from all walks of life. Clashes with police resulted in the burning of government buildings in Tuzla, which was then replicated in other cities such as Mostar, Zenica and Sarajevo. And while the media and political class were denouncing 'hooliganism' and 'vandalism', the protesters were busy establishing 'plenums', self-governed citizens' assemblies that spread throughout the country, from Tuzla itself where the first plenum was formed, to the capital Sarajevo, regional centres such as Mostar and Zenica, and smaller cities such as Bugojno, Bihać, Brčko, Travnik and others. Most canton governments resigned and the canton assemblies mostly accepted the main demands of the plenums – although their implementation remains another issue. After long deliberations open to all citizens, almost uniformly, although with some regional variety, they demanded the revision of privatisations, an end to politicians' excessive benefits, and the formation of new state-level and local governments made up of people with proven expertise and no record of corruption.

In our view, the plenums in Bosnia represent the most radical experiment in non-institutional politics that can be found across the Balkans since the collapse of Yugoslavia. Their form is clearly radical, although the participants themselves are of various political stripes and cannot be easily identified as left-leaning or belonging to the left. Enraged citizens simply rebelled against the degrading conditions of social and political life and spontaneously adopted citizens' assemblies and horizontal forms of democracy as a way to articulate their demands and organise themselves autonomously. The plenum movement shook the foundations of post-war Bosnia and the wider post-Yugoslav region, surprising both the ethno-nationalist political elites and the international community, and opening up new spaces for social and political action. The plenums were operational for three months, with varying success depending on the local situation. In various forms, via working groups, many plenums are still active. Engaged citizens now understand that plenums represent a precious instrument that can be easily reactivated. To sum up, a growing social movement in Bosnia-Herzegovina came out of the protests and the plenums, redefining the public sphere and imposing a new political agenda, this time centred on the question of social justice and equality coupled with a profound critique of the disastrous capitalist economy implemented in this post-conflict country.

Nevertheless, what the current protests in Bosnia-Herzegovina, and elsewhere in the Balkans, clearly show is that protest energy can soon dissipate and give way to an even greater despair, or what Walter Benjamin called the 'melancholy of the Left'. But if the protests can be developed into some sort of institutionalised politics – be it self-created parallel institutions such as citizen-led assemblies and/or new political parties that are ready to face electoral struggles – then the progressive movements' potential for a wider social and political impact can remain strong. Without the protests, the plenums would lose their capacity to apply pressure, and without the plenums, the protests would lose their legitimacy and articulation. In turn, any future attempt at party or representative politics will have to be based on, inspired and guided by social movements. In other words, in order to transcend its 'current impotence', what the left must rethink is the complex dialectics between the three Ps: protests, plenums, parties. Instead of being overwhelmed by 'new spring(s)', what we need more than ever is long-term political and social work that will combine a variety of organisational forms and remain open to changing local and global circumstances. Hopefully this volume will serve as a modest contribution to this ongoing task.

List of Contributors

Jana Baćević is a Marie Curie postdoctoral researcher at the Faculty of Education in Copenhagen, Denmark. Her book *From Class to Identity: Politics of Education Reforms in Former Yugoslavia* (2013) deals with the socio-political dynamics of transformations of regimes of knowledge production during and after socialism.

Boris Buden is a writer, philosopher and cultural critic based in Berlin. In the 1990s he worked as editor of the magazine *Arkzin* in Zagreb. Among his recent books is *Zone of Transition: On the End of Post-communism* (2009).

Ankica Čakardić works as Assistant Professor and holds the chair of Social Philosophy at the Department of Philosophy at the University of Zagreb. She is a coordinator of the educational programme at the Centre for Women's Studies and has edited two books on feminist theory.

Marko Grdešić is a PhD student at the Department of Sociology, University of Wisconsin Madison. He studied at the University of Zagreb and the Central European University in Budapest. His interests include trade unions, social movements and political sociology. His dissertation deals with protests in communist Yugoslavia in the late 1980s.

Agon Hamza is completing his PhD in philosophy, on Hegel and Althusser. He is a co-founder and member of the Dialectical Materialism Collective in Pristina, Kosovo. His latest publication is a book co-authored with Slavoj Žižek, entitled *From Myth to Symptom: The Case of Kosovo* (2013).

Srećko Horvat is a philosopher based in Zagreb, Croatia. His latest books include *After the End of History: From the Arab Spring to the Occupy Movement* (2013) and, together with Slavoj Žižek, *What Does Europe Want?* (2014).

Michael G. Kraft is a lecturer on social movements at the Johannes Kepler University Linz, Austria. He obtained his PhD in the history of economic thought from the Vienna University of Business in 2004 with the dissertation *Economics Between Science and Ethics: An inquiry into the history of economic thought from Léon Walras to Milton Friedman*. He edited the volume *Social Struggles in Ex-Yugoslavia* (2013).

Andrej Nikolaidis is a writer based in Montenegro. He has published eleven works of fiction, and was the winner of the European Union prize for literature in 2011. His novels have been translated into a dozen languages. His novels *The Coming* and *The Son* are published in the UK by Istros. He has also published a cultural theory book entitled *Homo Sucker: The Poetics of Apocalypse*.

Tanja Petrović is a linguist and anthropologist. She is a senior research associate at the Scientific Research Centre of the Slovenian Academy of Sciences and Arts in Ljubljana. Her research interests lie at the interface of linguistic, social and cultural phenomena in the former Yugoslav societies, with an emphasis on ideology and remembering.

Igor Štiks is a senior research fellow at the University of Edinburgh. Together with Jo Shaw he edited the collections *Citizenship after Yugoslavia* (2012) and *Citizenship Rights* (2013). He is the author of two novels, *A Castle in Romagna* and *Elijah's Chair*, which have won numerous awards and been translated into a dozen European languages.

Maria Todorova is Professor of History at the University of Illinois at Urbana-Champaign. Her publications include the widely-praised *Balkan Identities: Nation and Memory* (2004) and *Imagining the Balkans* (1997), as well as a volume edited together with Zsuzsa Gille, *Post-communist Nostalgia* (2010).

Vladimir Unkovski-Korica is Assistant Professor of History, National Research University - Higher School of Economics, Moscow. His doctorate has been published with I.B. Tauris as *The Economic Struggle for Power in Tito's Yugoslavia: From World War II to Non-Alignment*. He is also co-editor of the socialist webzine *Marks21*, based in Serbia.

Mitja Velikonja is a Professor for Cultural Studies and head of the Center for Cultural and Religious Studies at University of Ljubljana, Slovenia. His recent monographs are *Titostalgia: A Study of Nostalgia for Josip Broz* (2008), *Eurosis: A Critique of the New Eurocentrism* (2005), and *Religious Separation and Political Intolerance in Bosnia-Herzegovina* (2003).

Andreja Živković is a sociologist and editor of the Serbian left webzine *Marks21*. He is co-author of *The Balkan Socialist Tradition and the Balkan Federation* (2003) and co-editor of *Revolution in the Making of the Modern World* (2007).

Index

Wacquant, Loïc, 237
wages, 73, 76
  income sharing in Yugoslavia,
    28–29
walls of Europe, 112–17
  Schengen Area, 9, 105, 117, 151,
    161n13
war, 5, 67, 145
  and European Union, 147, 153
  and IMF, 146–47
  in Kosovo, 87
  and transition, 147–48
  and unions, 71
  in Yugoslavia, 146–47, 149, 154–56
Warsaw Pact, 85–86, 94
wealth concentration, 56–57, 137, 147
West, and Yugoslavia, 149–50, 161
Western aid, 47
Western Balkans *See* Balkans, Western
Western Europe, 91, 94, 100–101, 107,
  117
  Balkan task for, 101
  obsessed with Eastern Europe, 100
Whitehead, Laurence, 126
WikiLeaks, 146, 154
Woman in Combat (journal), 247
women:
  and crisis, 253–55
  home and family work of, 245–46,
    254–55, 258
  at Kamensko factory, 256
  League of Yugoslav Women's
    Societies, 247–48
  and media, 246–47
  scholarship on, 253
  and self-management, 245–48, 255
  and socialism, 255, 258
  and transition, 249–58
  and workers, 254–56
  See also feminism
Women's Anti-Fascist Front (AFZ),
  243, 247–48, 250, 257
workers:
  benefits, 70
  and civil society, 79–81
  company takeovers, 72–73
  demonisation of, 71
  ideology of, 65, 77

  militancy of, 67, 72
  and neoliberalism, 67
  protest privatisation, 71–72, 74,
    205–8, 212, 256, 262
  and self management, 66
  and self-management, 66, 77
  transformation of, 65
  and women, 254–56
  See also jobs; self management;
    strikes; unemployment; unions;
    wages; workers' struggles
Workers' and Punks' University, 80, 230
Workers' Protest Coordination
  Committee (WPCC), 206
workers' struggles, 14–15, 67, 69,
  71–74, 205–13
  and nostalgia, 76
  Workers' and Punks' University, 80,
    230
  See also strikes; unions; workers

Youth Day, 176, 179, 184
YouTube, 217
Yugonostalgia, 98, 173–74, 176–77,
  187, 193–94
  and age, 176
Yugoslavia, 2, 9–10
  austerity in, 39, 43
  BAOLS in, 37
  constitution of 1974, 34, 37–38, 49,
    244
  debt economy of, 48–51, 55–56
  debt of, 34–36, 39, 41, 43
  disintegration of, 182
  economic decline of, 35
  economic growth of, 27–28
  education reforms in, 233–34
  elected to UN Security Council,
    25
  and Europe metaphors, 113
  export orientation of, 47–49
  financial crisis, 49
  and IMF, 39, 41, 43, 49–51, 53,
    146
  informal economy in, 40
  League of Communists of (LCY),
    26, 29, 31, 33, 37–41, 246–47
  market reform, 33–34